Nuclear deterrence theory

Nuclear deterrence theory
The search for credibility

ROBERT POWELL

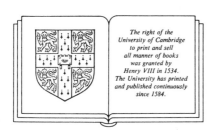

The right of the
University of Cambridge
to print and sell
all manner of books
was granted by
Henry VIII in 1534.
The University has printed
and published continuously
since 1584.

CAMBRIDGE UNIVERSITY PRESS

Cambridge
New York   Port Chester   Melbourne   Sydney

Published by the Press Syndicate of the University of Cambridge
The Pitt Building, Trumpington Street, Cambridge CB2 1RP
40 West 20th Street, New York, NY 10011, USA
10 Stamford Road, Oakleigh, Melbourne 3166, Australia

First published 1990

Printed in the United States of America

Library of Congress Cataloging-in-Publication Data
Powell, Robert.
Nuclear deterrence theory : the search for credibility / Robert
Powell.
p. cm.
ISBN 0-521-37527-4
1. Deterrence (Strategy). 2. Nuclear warfare. I. Title.
U162.6.P69 1990
355.02'17 – dc20   89–17462
                                                                  CIP

British Library Cataloguing in Publication Data
Powell, Robert
Nuclear deterrence theory : the search for credibility.
1. Nuclear power. Political aspects.
I. Title
333.79'24
ISBN 0-521-37527-4

Contents

Preface

The first atomic attack, on August 6, 1945, killed more than seventy thousand people. In *Hiroshima*, John Hersey described some of the horror of that day: the terrible burns; the soldiers who apparently had been looking up when the bomb exploded, "their faces were wholly burned, their eyesockets hollow, the fluid from their melted eyes had run down their cheeks"; the haunting silhouettes of people etched in stone by the nuclear flash. That was one bomb on one city. A general nuclear war today would be unimaginably worse.

This book is about the relation between force and states' efforts to further their ends in the nuclear age. It uses abstractions and mathematical models to try to understand this relation better. These tools may help to bring the essence of this relation into sharper focus, but these clean abstractions may also make it easier to forget what they represent. Should the event that, it may seem, is too casually referred to in the coming chapters as "disaster" actually occur, hundreds of millions will be dead. Thinking about these issues requires a certain amount of detachment, but we must guard against becoming too detached.

In 1780, John Adams wrote to his wife, Abigail, "I must study politics and war that my sons may have liberty to study mathematics and philosophy. My sons ought to study mathematics and philosophy, geography, natural history, naval architecture, navigation, commerce, and agriculture, in order to give their children a right to study painting, poetry, music, architecture, statuary, tapestry, and porcelain." Written more than two centuries after Adams's letter, this book is about war and politics and is a sad measure of how far short of the mark we have fallen.

I have incurred many debts in writing this book that I cannot possibly repay. The best I can do is to acknowledge them and offer my thanks. Many read and commented on the separate essays from which this book draws, and I appreciate all of those comments. Vinod Aggarwal, James Fearon, Albert Fishlow, Chaim Kaufmann, Robert Keohane, Barry O'Neill, Thomas Schelling, Leo Simon, Marc Trachtenberg, Harrison Wagner, and Steven Weber read the manuscript in draft. I have benefited greatly from their comments and criticisms. I am especially grateful to James Alt for having the courage to look at more than one draft and to James Morrow for reading the manuscript and for many discussions about international politics and modeling. In a more general way, I am deeply indebted to Kenneth Waltz, who as my teacher showed me how to begin to think about international politics.

I have also enjoyed the generous support of several institutions. A Fulbright Scholarship permitted me to spend a year at Cambridge University, where I first began to try to explain nuclear deterrence theory to myself. A Social Science Research Council–MacArthur Post-Doctoral Fellowship in International Peace and Security, a grant from the National Science Foundation, and a John M. Olin Research Associateship freed me from teaching and administrative responsibilities for an inordinate amount of time so that I could write. The MacArthur Interdisciplinary Group in Strategic Studies and the Institute of International Studies at the University of California, Berkeley, gave me an opportunity to present my work at their seminar and offered a stimulating place to revise the manuscript. Finally, Samuel Huntington and the Center for International Affairs at Harvard University under his directorship have provided a challenging and intellectually exciting place to work. I am pleased that this book appears under the auspices of the Center for International Affairs.

CHAPTER 1

Introduction

Even after the advent of secure second-strike capabilities marked the nuclear revolution by rendering defense impossible, force remained the final arbiter of disputes among states in the anarchy of international politics. A state could still try to use force or threaten to use it if that seemed to be in its best interest. Of course, one state might do this in an effort to prevent another state from resorting to violence. But that only underscores the point that states could use force if such use seemed to them to further their ends. The nuclear revolution did, however, undercut the relation that had previously existed between the use or threatened use of force and states' attempts to secure their interests, for this relation implicitly depended on defense. How has the nuclear revolution changed the relation between force or the threat of it and states' political objectives? Explaining this change is the central problem for nuclear deterrence theory.

This book examines the ways in which nuclear deterrence theory has tried to solve this problem. The book aims at two ends. The first is to extend the existing formal analyses of some aspects of deterrence theory's attempted solutions. These include the strategy that leaves something to chance, crisis stability, and the strategy of limited retaliation. Formalization often comes at a high price, and that is certainly the case with the models developed here. Much must be sacrificed in the name of simplification and tractability. But these sacrifices bring compensating advantages. They bring the essence of these issues into sharper focus and in this way make it possible to see connections among them that were formerly obscure. The second, more important end of this work is to try to describe a general and unifying analytic perspective that will draw out and clarify the relations among these issues. This perspective should provide a context in which questions about nuclear deterrence may be asked more precisely and related more carefully and clearly to other questions and issues. Ironically, the closer this work comes to meeting this second end of elaborating this perspective, the less important the first end will become, for one of the uses of this perspective will be to point the way toward richer, better, and more useful models that will demand fewer sacrifices than do the models examined here.

This unifying perspective emerges when nuclear deterrence theory is seen

1

as a search for credibility. Once both the United States and the Soviet Union acquired secure second-strike capabilities, each state could destroy the other even after absorbing a first strike. Mutually assured destruction had become the technological state of affairs. In this condition, each state's ability to impose costs on the other sufficient to outweigh the potential gains from altering the status quo was no longer at issue. But could a state use this capability to protect its interests? Could a state make the threat to use this capability credible when the state was vulnerable to its adversary's retaliatory second strike? This was the credibility problem facing nuclear deterrence, and it has motivated and guided the conceptual evolution of nuclear deterrence theory's attempts to explain the relation between the use or threatened use of force and states' efforts to further their interests after the nuclear revolution.

The method used to elaborate this general perspective is to begin with simple formulations and then expand their scope in order to bring out the underlying connections linking the issues. This is done in three steps. The first is to describe a stylization of the environment in which states must act. This kind of stylization is ideally a historically or experientially informed simplification. History and experience do not enter into a stylization in the more rigorous and systematic ways that come into play when claims based on stylizations are evaluated empirically. Rather, history and experience enter a stylization in a less formal, more intuitive way. They suggest what the essence of a situation is. Then, by abstracting away from the overwhelming complexities of the actual situation, a stylization tries to bring this essence into sharper focus. Stylizations anchor models. They constrain the set of potential models by defining some idealized conditions to which an acceptable model must conform.

The second step is to examine models that conform to the stylizations in nuclear deterrence theory. For example, the nuclear revolution will be stylized as having made defense impossible. The brinkmanship and limited-retaliation models that are subsequently used to examine the relation between force and political objectives after the nuclear revolution will then have to be consistent with the assumption that defense is impossible.

A good model clarifies how certain conclusions follow from the model's specific assumptions and the stylization's more general assumptions. But this poses a question: How would changing the assumptions affect the conclusions? The third step in tracing the search for credibility is to show how the assumptions underlying one model and set of issues raise questions that are then examined with models and stylizations based on a related but different set of assumptions and how these assumptions in turn raise still other questions.

The next chapter describes the classical logic of war; the way that the nuclear revolution undercut that logic; the two approaches nuclear deterrence theory has taken toward explaining the relation between force and states' political ends after the revolution; and, finally, how these two approaches, although appearing to be quite different, are fundamentally alike. The classical logic of war was based on two assumptions. First, a state's ability to defend itself and its ability to threaten an adversary were conflated in the same military forces. The army used to repel an invasion could also be used to launch one. Second, should a profound conflict of interests divide adversaries, then a state in this extreme could still hope to defend itself by destroying its enemy's military forces. The nuclear revolution made these assumptions problematic. In a condition of mutually assured destruction, defense is impossible. Given this new and seemingly more appropriate assumption, nuclear deterrence theory has generally linked force or the threat of it to states' attempts to further their ends in one of two ways. The first appeals to what Thomas Schelling (1960, 1966) called a "threat that leaves something to chance." States in the strategy based on this type of threat bring coercive pressure to bear by taking steps that raise the risk that the crisis will go out of control and end in a general nuclear exchange. Deterrence in this approach ultimately appeals to the fear of suffering the unlimited sanction of a general nuclear attack. The second approach to the credibility problem does not rest on an unlimited sanction, but on limited sanctions. In the strategy of limited retaliation, a state brings coercive pressure to bear on an adversary by carrying out limited attacks in order to make the threat of future attacks more credible. These two approaches seem quite different, but at a more general level they are essentially alike. Each tries to solve the credibility problem and relate force to states' political interests in the same way. Each approach uses limited options to bridge the gap between doing too much in response to limited aggression or too little, that is, between retaliating with a massive nuclear attack or simply acquiescing to an adversary.

Although these two approaches are equivalent at a high level of generality, different issues and concerns motivate these approaches at a somewhat lower level of generality. Chapters 3 through 7 use several game-theoretic models to illuminate these issues and the connections among them. Many of the basic models have appeared elsewhere in separate essays.[1] The following chapters extend the formal analysis of these models and in this way contribute to meeting the first end of this work. But, more important, bringing these models together in a single place makes it possible to discuss the relations between them, to show how one model

---

[1] Chapter 2 draws on Powell (1985), Chapter 3 on Powell (1987, 1988), Chapter 4 on Powell (1989c), Chapter 5 on Powell (1989a), and Chapter 7 on Powell (1989b).

addresses questions posed by previous models and then poses new questions for subsequent models. It is this broader discussion of the models, the stylizations underlying them, and the relations among them that further the second end of this work.

Chapters 3 and 4 examine more closely the strategy that leaves something to chance. Schelling (1960, pp. 199–201; 1962b; 1966, pp. 92–125) offered brinkmanship as a useful analogy for understanding the dynamics of crises in which states use this strategy to exert coercive pressure. These chapters formalize this analogy by modeling it as a game of sequential bargaining with incomplete information. The game is sufficiently simple that its equilibria may be characterized explicitly and then used to study the roles of resolve, misperception, the value of the status quo, and uncertainty in crisis bargaining.

The defining concern of the strategy that leaves something to chance is to explain how a state can exert coercive pressure with a sanction that it would never impose deliberately on an adversary. Accordingly, the brinkmanship analogy and the game-theoretic models of it also assume that there is no situation in which a state would deliberately launch a massive, society-destroying nuclear first strike. That, in turn, means that there is no advantage to striking first rather than second, for if there were a first-strike advantage, then there would be at least one situation in which a state would deliberately impose the sanction of a general nuclear attack. Preemption would become the best of a terrible set of alternatives if there were an advantage to striking first and a state became sufficiently confident that its adversary was about to attack. Chapters 5 and 6 explore the consequences of relaxing the assumption that there is no advantage to striking first. These chapters, in effect, reconsider the problem of crisis stability and first-strike advantages. This reexamination shows that deterrence theory's analysis of this problem previously has focused too narrowly on the size of the advantage to striking first. Stability results from a more subtle interaction of several factors.

The strategy that leaves something to chance and the problem of crisis stability center on the unlimited sanction of a massive nuclear attack. This leads naturally to a question about the effects of broadening the scope to include limited sanctions. What happens if the sanction is no longer unlimited? Chapter 7 takes up this question. It examines the strategy of limited retaliation and the problems surrounding the use of limited sanctions. One of these problems is the effect of having smaller, less destructive limited options. Do these options make war more likely because, being less destructive, they are more likely to be used? Or do these options make war less likely because a potential aggressor, appreciating that aggression is more likely to be resisted, is less likely to challenge the status quo? Different views on the answers to these questions have played important roles in the debate about American nuclear doctrine at least since the Kennedy administration began to move toward the doctrine of flexible response in the early 1960s. The analysis in Chapter 7 of the dynamics of crisis bargaining, in which states use the strategy of limited retaliation, sheds some light on these questions.

Chapter 8 offers a concluding appraisal. It summarizes some of the specific results derived from the models examined here and discusses some of the strengths, weaknesses, and limits of the models and, more generally, of nuclear deterrence theory.

A game-theoretic Appendix follows Chapter 8. It introduces the game-theoretic vocabulary and concepts used here to study nuclear deterrence theory. The mathematical formulations in the following chapters are for the most part quite simple, generally requiring nothing more than algebra. Unfortunately, the derivations tend to be long and tedious. That and the fact that they employ some special game-theoretic terms and concepts may make them and their discussion difficult to follow. The Appendix describes these concepts in order to make these discussions easier to follow.

CHAPTER 2

The nuclear revolution and the problem of credibility

This chapter elaborates a framework within which to place the more detailed and narrowly focused analyses of the subsequent chapters. That framework encompasses the broader themes that will connect the more specific issues examined in later chapters. This chapter develops the framework in three steps. The first step summarizes what will be called the classical logic of war: the stylized relation that existed between the use or threatened use of force and states' attempts to further their interests before the nuclear revolution. The nuclear revolution undercut the classical logic and made the problem of credibility the paramount theoretical concern. The second step then reviews the two apparently quite different ways in which nuclear deterrence theory has tried to solve this problem by explaining how the use or threatened use of force is related to states' political objectives after the nuclear revolution. The first is based on Schelling's "threats that leave something to chance" (1960, 1966). In this approach to the credibility problem, states take steps during a crisis that raise the risk that the crisis will go out of control and escalate to a general nuclear war. The second approach is not based on the risk of losing control. Instead, a state deliberately imposes severe but nevertheless limited sanctions on an adversary in order to make the threat of future punishment sufficiently credible that the adversary will come to terms. After outlining these two approaches, the third step is to show that despite their apparent differences, the two approaches are fundamentally alike. Each attempts to solve the credibility problem in essentially the same way. Each uses an array of limited options to bridge the gap between doing too much by launching a massive nuclear attack and doing too little by acquiescing to an adversary. The idea behind these limited options is that a state may be able to make the threat to use them more credible than the threat to launch a massive nuclear attack and in this way avoid having to submit to its adversary.

The classical logic of war

What is the nuclear revolution, and what are its consequences? How has it changed the logic of war? How, that is, has the nuclear revolution changed the relation between the use or threatened use of force and states' attempts to secure their political ends? To address these questions, one must first have some notion of what the logic of war was before the nuclear revolution.[1]

Carl von Clausewitz, writing in the aftermath of the Napoleonic Wars, described the logic of war that existed before the nuclear revolution: "If the enemy is to be coerced you must put him in a situation that is even more unpleasant that the sacrifice you call on him to make" (Clausewitz 1976, p. 77). As it stands, this formulation of coercion is timeless. If an adversary is to make the political sacrifices demanded of it, then the cost of refusing to make them must appear to be still greater. What bounds this formulation and gives it meaning is the way that force or the threat of it can be used to make an adversary's situation unpleasant. Indeed, what will distinguish the relations between the use and threatened use of force and states' attempts to further their interests before and after the nuclear revolution are the different ways that force can be used to bring coercive pressure to bear.

Deterrence and the distinction between punitive and defensive capabilities are crucial to describing the different ways that coercive pressure may be exerted. Deterrence is a form of coercion. A state deters an adversary from doing something like attacking by convincing it that the cost of doing so would be greater than the potential gain.[2] A state's defensive capability is the state's physical ability to limit the costs an adversary can impose on it (Snyder 1961, p. 3). The greater a state's defensive capability, the less an adversary can hurt it. In addition to being able to limit the costs an adversary can impose on it, a state may be able to inflict costs on an adversary. These costs may include the invasion and occupation of some of its territory, the destruction of its military forces, the devastation of some of its industrial capability, or, more simply and gruesomely, the killing of some of its people. A state's punitive capability is its ability to inflict costs on an adversary. The greater a state's punitive capability, the more punishment it can impose.

The adjective "physical" in the definition of defensive capability is important. If a state deters an adversary from invading it by threatening to

---

[1] This discussion of the logic of war and the nature of the nuclear revolution draws heavily on the important contributions of Brodie (1959), Snyder (1961, pp. 3–51), and Schelling (1966, pp. 1–34).

[2] In some contexts it may be useful to distinguish between *deterring* an adversary from doing something and *compelling* an adversary to do something; see Schelling (1966, pp. 69–91) for a discussion of the difference between deterrence and compellence. This distinction is, however, conceptually elusive. The difference between deterring an adversary from attacking and compelling it not to attack is unclear. At a more general level, deterrence and compellence are alike: In each, a state is trying to coerce its adversary into acting in certain ways and not in others by shaping the adversary's estimates of the costs and benefits. No distinction will be made here between deterrence and compellence.

impose grave punishment, then the state will have succeeded in limiting its costs. But this does not imply that the state has a strong defense, for the state might have been physically unable to limit the cost of being invaded had its adversary actually decided to invade. Instead, the state, although physically unable to repel an invasion had it occurred, was able to coerce its adversary into not attacking by making the prospect of unacceptable punishment sufficiently likely that the adversary did not invade because the expected cost of doing so seemed greater than the expected gain.

Three aspects of the distinction between punitive and defensive capabilities should be emphasized. First, as just suggested, both capabilities may contribute to deterrence. Whether a state is trying to deter an adversary from invading or convince an adversary not to mount further resistance after it has been invaded, both capabilities are related to a state's ability to influence its adversary's actions. To make the cost of failing to comply greater than the cost of doing so, a state must have, or at least appear to have, the ability actually to impose sufficiently high costs on an adversary. This is the role of a state's punitive capabilities. But deterrence requires more than the ability to impose costs. An adversary must be sufficiently convinced that the state will use its punitive capabilities. This judgment would seem to be affected by the state's ability to limit the costs that an adversary can impose on it in retaliation. The greater a state's defensive capability, the less its adversary can hurt it, and the more likely it may be to use its punitive capabilities on its adversary. Accordingly, the ability to place an adversary in a situation the continuation of which will be more costly than the sacrifice it is being asked to make is related to both punitive and defensive capabilities.[3]

---

[3]   Snyder (1961, pp. 14–16) and others, such as Schelling (1966) and Jervis (1984), point out that both capabilities may contribute to deterrence. However, trying to identify a separate form of deterrence with each type of capability, as Snyder does with his distinction between deterrence by denial and deterrence by punishment, is quite problematic.

In Snyder's formulation, a state deters an adversary from invading by denial by being physically able to "deny territorial gains to the enemy" (Snyder 1961, p. 14), or at least to make a successful invasion less likely. More generally, a state deters by denial by being physically able to deny an adversary its goal or, as Snyder puts it, by affecting "the probability of gaining his [the adversary's] objective" (1961, p. 15). Deterrence by punishment is different. Here, a state deters an adversary from invading not by being physically able to stop an invasion but by credibly threatening to impose enough punishment so that the costs of invading will seem greater than the potential gains. In this formulation, an army that would fight the invaders primarily contributes to deterrence by denial. A strategic nuclear force only capable of inflicting punishment by destroying an adversary's cities contributes mostly to deterrence by punishment.

The difficulty with this formulation is that it is more natural to think of a potential invader's objective not as simply to invade and occupy some territory but to do so at some acceptable cost. But then, as soon as a state's strategic nuclear arsenal can impose still

The second point is that a state's punitive capability is related to its adversary's defensive capability. The greater a state's punitive capabilities, the higher the costs it can impose on an adversary, and thus the less physically able an adversary is to limit the costs that can be imposed on it. There is an inverse relation between a state's punitive capability and its adversary's defensive capability.

Finally, it is important to emphasize that although these two capabilities are conceptually separate, actual military forces may combine both of these capabilities. An army capable of repelling an invasion and thereby limiting the costs an adversary can impose may also be used to launch an invasion and inflict costs on an adversary by taking some of its territory. By helping to limit costs, the army contributes to the state's defensive capabilities. By being able to take what an adversary values, the army contributes to a state's punitive capabilities.

Much turns on whether or not punitive and defensive capabilities are generally conflated in the same forces. Indeed, this crucially affects the relation between the use and threatened use of force and states' attempts to secure their ends. The classical logic of war assumed that these capabilities were conflated. As will be seen, the separation of these capabilities and the development of states' punitive capabilities undercut the classical logic and marked the nuclear revolution (Snyder 1961, pp. 8–9; Schelling 1966, pp. 1–34; Jervis 1984, p. 26).

When these two capabilities were conflated, the same forces that limited the costs an adversary could impose also increased a state's ability to impose costs on its adversary, especially by taking its territory. Two consequences follow from the conflation of these two capabilities in the same forces. First, being militarily stronger could enhance deterrence by raising the expected cost an adversary would have to bear if it attacked. The state's greater punitive capability would mean that the adversary would have to pay a higher price if the state actually used its capability. Second, this state, because it would be less vulnerable to its adversary, might be more willing to use its capability. To the extent that raising the expected

---

higher costs, the state becomes physically able to deny its adversary its objective. Thus, what is perhaps the clearest example of a punitive capability (i.e., a state's strategic nuclear force capable only of destroying an adversary's cities) appears now to be deterring by denial, because this force is physically able to deny an adversary its broader political objective of occupying some of this state's territory at some acceptable cost. Identifying types of deterrence with types of capabilities is problematic. Snyder may be closer to the mark when he suggests that the difference between deterrence by denial and deterrence by punishment may have less to do with a formal distinction between the means of deterring and more to do with beliefs (which are perhaps based on historical experience) about the types of reactions that various actions, such as invasions, are likely to provoke (Snyder 1961, pp. 14–16).

cost of attacking for the adversary enhanced deterrence by reducing the chances of an attack, military strength was the key to security in the classical logic of war.[4]

The conflation of punitive and defensive capabilities also defined a reasonably clear relation between the use or threatened use of force and states' political ends, at least in the case in which a profound conflict of interest divided the states. If a supremely important political objective required an adversary to give up something of great value, then in this extreme a state might want to try to put its adversary in the worst of all possible positions. For Clausewitz, "the worst of all conditions in which a belligerent can find himself is to be utterly defenseless. Consequently, if you are to force the enemy, by making war on him, to do your bidding, you must either make him literally defenseless or at least put him in a position that makes this danger probable" (1976, p. 77).

Because punitive and defensive capabilities were conflated, rendering an adversary defenseless would also destroy its punitive capabilities. The destruction of both of these capabilities would give a state political control over its adversary. But that control would not be absolute. Even after becoming defenseless, a state still could refuse to do the victor's bidding. But in doing so, this state would have to suffer whatever punishment the victor decided to inflict and would be unable to retaliate against the victor in any meaningful way.[5] Before the nuclear revolution, "military victory was the price of admission," to use Schelling's apt description (Schelling 1966, p. 17). That is, the victor, after having already destroyed its adversary's military forces, might have to inflict still more punishment on the defeated state in order to convince it to do the victor's bidding. Its defeat did not assure that the adversary would do this automatically. But because the defenseless adversary could no longer pose a significant threat to hurt the victor in retaliation, the cost to the victor of carrying out its threats to hurt its adversary if the adversary refused to do the victor's bidding was as low as possible. In this way, the victor's being able to protect itself from

---

[4] Strengthening the state may make an adversary less likely to attack, but it may not. By becoming stronger, a state may raise the expected cost of attacking for an adversary. But because the strengthened state will have greater punitive capabilities, its adversary will be more vulnerable and, fearing still greater vulnerability, may find that the expected cost of not attacking is also rising. On balance, this may leave the adversary more likely to attack. This is the essence of the security dilemma, in which one state's effort to increase its own security by reducing its vulnerability reduces another state's security by increasing its vulnerability. For a discussion of this, see Jervis (1978).

[5] The assumed conflation of punitive and defensive capabilities is, of course, a simplification and a stylization. Even after losing its military forces, an adversary may still retain some punitive capabilities in the form of guerrilla resistance, for example. The assumption here is that any residual punitive capabilities are insignificant.

any retaliation made its threats to punish its adversary as believable as possible.

In the stylization of the classical logic of war, a great war fought over a profound conflict of interest could be thought of as a two-stage process. The first was a contest of relative military strength. During this stage each state still tried to coerce the other by making the cost of resistance seem greater than the cost of compliance. But these costs were primarily affected by course of the military struggle. Once the military struggle had been decided, then if the threat inherent in having been defeated had not already done so, the victor could use the "power to hurt" (Schelling 1966, p. 3) to raise the expected cost of further resistance to such a level that it would exceed the expected cost of coming to terms (Snyder 1961, p. 11; Schelling 1966, pp. 12–18; Jervis 1984, p. 27).

The assumption that the punitive and defensive capabilities were conflated in the same forces was crucial to the stylized relation between the use and threatened use of force and states' aims that existed before the nuclear revolution. This assumption meant that a state that had rendered its adversary defenseless would be able to defend itself. If, therefore, the victor chose to try to coerce a defeated yet defiant adversary into doing its bidding by punishing it, the victor could be confident of defending itself from any attempted retaliation. This is critical, for if the victor were unable to protect itself, it would not have control. "So long as I have not overthrown my opponent [i.e., rendered him defenseless] I am bound to fear that he may overthrow me. Thus I am not in control: he dictates to me as much as I dictate to him" (Clausewitz 1976, p. 77). The essence of the classical logic of war was that defense, at least for the victor, was possible (Brodie 1959, pp. 147–222; Schelling 1966, pp. 1–34). That defined the aim of warfare, at least in the extreme in which a profound conflict of interest divided two states. By rendering an adversary defenseless, a state, because it still could protect itself, would have put its adversary in the worst of all possible positions (Clausewitz 1976, p. 77).

The rise of strategic air power, the development of intercontinental ballistic missiles, and the advent of atomic and then thermonuclear weapons separated the ability to punish from the ability to limit the punishment one might have to suffer.[6] This growing separation cast doubt

---

[6] These two capabilities had in reality always been separate in varying degrees. The English forces used to carry out the *chevauchées* during the Hundred Years War, the British naval forces used to blockade Germany during World War I, the German submarines that attempted to blockade Great Britain, and the strategic air forces employed during World War II were more effective in punishing an adversary than in limiting the costs an adversary could impose. The classical logic of war and the assumption that punitive and defensive capabilities are conflated are at best useful stylizations and simplifications.

on the classical logic.[7] The nuclear revolution, that is, the advent of a technological condition of mutually assured destruction, completely undercut this logic. Rendering an adversary defenseless no longer meant that a state could also effectively limit the cost that its adversary could impose on it. Once two superpowers acquired secure second-strike capabilities, each state in effect had already rendered its adversary defenseless. Neither had the physical ability to limit the damage that the other could impose on it should the other decide to do so. But because the ability to punish was no longer conflated with the physical ability to limit punishment to oneself, rendering an adversary defenseless no longer brought political control. How did deterrence work when punitive and defensive capabilities were no longer reinforcing each other?

Coercion still required a state to be able to put its adversary in a situation the continuation of which would seem more costly than would complying with the state's demands. That, in turn, depended, first, on a state's being able to inflict a sufficient amount of punishment on an adversary and, second, on a state's being able to make the threat to use that capability sufficiently credible. In a condition of mutually assured destruction in which each state could destroy the other even after absorbing a first strike, the first condition certainly seemed to be satisfied. But what of the second? What of the credibility problem? Could a state convince its adversary that it would use its capability to punish when it was vulnerable to its adversary's retaliation? Could the threat to use these capabilities be credible? Once the rise of air power and then ballistic missiles had separated punitive and defensive capabilities, and once the nuclear revolution had made defense impossible, what was the relation between the use and threatened use of force and states' attempts to secure their interests?

The arrays of risk and punishment

The debate over the doctrine of massive retaliation brought the problem of credibility to the fore. In January 1954, Secretary of State Dulles, in a major speech on American foreign policy, reemphasized some of the themes of President Eisenhower's state-of-the-union address. Dulles's speech was ambiguous, but when seen in the context of the administration's efforts to limit military spending and its emphasis on nuclear weapons, the speech was interpreted by some to imply that the United States had adopted a strategy of massive retaliation: "in the event of another proxy or brushfire war in Korea, Indochina, Iran or anywhere else, the United States might retaliate instantly with atomic weapons against the U.S.S.R. or Red China"

---

[7] For discussions of the effects of the rise of air power and the advent of nuclear weapons, see Brodie (1959, pp. 3–222), Quester (1966), and Freedman (1989, pp. 3–44).

(Reston 1954). That is, the United States would rely on the threat of massive nuclear retaliation to protect the entire spectrum of American interests, ranging from the most peripheral to the most vital.[8]

Almost immediately the doctrine of massive retaliation was harshly criticized as being incredible and therefore ineffective.[9] This, however, was a debate about how best to protect less important American interests. As long as the United States was relatively invulnerable to a Soviet nuclear attack, massive retaliation seemed to be a credible means of protecting vital American interests like Western Europe (Brodie 1966, pp. 27–8). But once the United States became vulnerable to a devastating Soviet attack, the credibility of an American threat to launch a massive nuclear attack even in an attempt to protect vital interests became problematic.[10] How could a state credibly threaten to launch a massive nuclear attack when carrying out the threat would bring its own destruction? The policy debate focused on the problem of extended deterrence. How, that is, could the United States extend its ability to deter the Soviet Union from attacking the United States to deterring the Soviet Union from attacking Western Europe?[11] The more general issue was to understand how a state might credibly threaten to do what seemed to be inherently incredible.[12]

As technical and political circumstances and conditions changed after the demise of the doctrine of massive retaliation, many nuclear strategies and policies were devised. The 1960s saw Secretary of Defence McNamara propose the "no cities" doctrine, in which American strategic nuclear forces would not be aimed at Soviet cities but at Soviet military capabilities. The

---

[8] For a more detailed discussion of massive retaliation, see Gaddis (1981) and, especially, Wells (1981). Rosenberg (1983) offers an illuminating discussion of the Eisenhower administration's attitudes toward nuclear weapons and attempts to control them.

[9] Kaufmann (1956) has provided the classical criticism.

[10] Betts (1987, pp. 144–72) has traced the evolution of American assessments of American vulnerability to a Soviet nuclear attack.

[11] The problem of extending deterrence to cover vital American interests such as Western Europe has greatly influenced the evolution of American nuclear strategy. Freedman (1989) has provided a summary of this work and an extensive bibliography.

[12] There is an important implicit assumption here that should be made explicit. The credibility problem arises because it is assumed that the chances that a state will see any political objective as being worth the cost of bringing about its own destruction by launching a massive nuclear attack against an adversary are too small to deter this adversary. This assumption implies that the threat to order this attack and thereby bring a devastating counterattack in return is incredible, because sacrificing the political objective is less costly than launching a massive nuclear attack. This makes carrying out the threat inherent in the doctrine of massive retaliation irrational. If, however, some political objectives are worth certain destruction, then implementing the threat may be rational, and the doctrine of massive retaliation may be credible. In order to focus on the credibility problem, it will be assumed that no political objective is worth certain destruction.

United States would, in effect, try to hold Soviet cities hostage in order to give the Soviet Union the "strongest imaginable incentive to refrain from striking our own [i.e., American] cities" (McNamara 1962, p. 62). That strategy was quickly forsaken for the doctrine of assured destruction, which emphasized being able to destroy 20 to 25 percent of the Soviet population and 50 percent of its industrial capacity after absorbing a first strike (Enthoven and Smith 1971, p. 175). The North Atlantic Treaty Organization (NATO) debated and then in 1967 adopted the doctrine of flexible response, which, at least from the American perspective, was designed to enhance deterrence by raising the nuclear threshold by reducing NATO's dependence on the early use of nuclear weapons. The call for greater flexibility continued in the early 1970s with the Schlesinger doctrine, which tried to find implementable limited nuclear options that might be used to strike Soviet military targets or to demonstrate resolve. At the same time, President Nixon spoke of the strategy of "sufficiency," which meant "the maintenance of forces adequate to prevent us and our allies from being coerced" (Nixon 1971, p. 170). Later in the decade and into the early 1980s, nuclear policy centered on the countervailing strategy and the importance of having escalation dominance. In 1983, strategic defenses returned to center stage.[13]

The connections linking these policies and strategies to nuclear deterrence theory often were loose and rather tenuous. There were at least two reasons for this. First, nuclear policies and strategies have been the outcomes of bureaucratic and political processes that have reflected more than national security concerns.[14] A second and perhaps more important reason has to do with the weakness of deterrence theory itself. A powerful theory of nuclear deterrence would specify in more or less detail the likely consequences of various strategies and policies. If there were such a powerful theory, a state might then be expected to take it into account in formulating its nuclear strategies and policies. There would be a close connection between theory and policy. But when the theory is weak and often provides little insight into the detailed and pressing problems of policy, there is little reason to expect a state's strategies and policies to be anything more than vaguely related to nuclear deterrence theory's account of the relation between the use of force or the threat of it and states' attempts to further their ends.

Although there have been many nuclear policies and strategies, nuclear

---

[13] For discussions of these policies and strategies, see Enthoven and Smith (1971), Kahan (1975), Ball (1980), Freedman (1989), Schilling (1981), Slocombe (1981), Jervis (1984), and Sagan (1989b).

[14] Steinbruner (1974), Ball (1980), and Rosenberg (1983) have described examples of these processes.

deterrence theory has generally approached the credibility problem from one of two perspectives. Both approaches try to link the possible use of force to states' political objectives in what would seem to be the most difficult and demanding case. This is the stylization in which the condition of mutually assured destruction is interpreted in its strictest sense. In this stylization, there is no advantage to launching an unlimited nuclear attack first rather than second. In the event of a general exchange, it makes no difference if a state strikes first or is struck first. This is the strictest interpretation, because if there is no advantage to striking first, then as long as a state believes that there is the slightest chance that early warnings are erroneous and an adversary has not attacked, this state will not launch a general attack. It is always better to do something else. In this strictest interpretation, there is no situation in which it is rational for a state deliberately to launch an unlimited nuclear attack first.

The first approach to understanding the credibility problem is a direct conceptual descendant of the doctrine of massive retaliation, in that both appeal to the same sanction. In this approach, a state would still try to secure its interests by relying on the sanction of a massive nuclear attack. Schelling (1960, 1962b, 1966) provided the insight that explains how, at least in principle, this sanction might be linked to states' attempts to secure their ends after the nuclear revolution. Although in the strictest interpretation of mutually assured destruction the threat to launch a first strike deliberately would never be credible, deterrence could still be based on the fear of "things getting out of hand," on the fear that the crisis would go out of control and escalate to a general nuclear exchange (Schelling 1960, 1962b, 1966). It was unnecessary to rely on an incredible threat to launch a massive nuclear attack deliberately. Rather, a state could threaten to take steps that would increase the likelihood of uncontrolled escalation to an unlimited nuclear exchange. A state could make "threats that leave something to chance" (Schelling 1960). Credibility, then, was to be found in having a set of limited options, each of which, if exercised, would raise the risk of the crisis going out of control. Because exercising an option was not certain to trigger a general nuclear war, but only created the risk of it, the expected cost of exercising an option would be less than the expected cost of deliberately imposing the sanction of launching an unlimited attack. If, moreover, a state's stake in the crisis were high, the expected cost of escalating by exercising a limited option might be less than the expected cost of giving in to an adversary's demands. In that case, the threat to escalate would be credible. As Schelling put it, "a response that carries some risk of war can be plausible, even reasonable at a time when a final, ultimate decision to have a general war would be implausible or unreasonable" (1966, p. 98).

The set of limited options links the sanction of a massive nuclear attack to states' attempts to secure their interests. By being able to vary the risk of the crisis going out of control, the strategy that leaves something to chance offers a state a means of exerting coercive pressure on its adversary even in a condition of mutually assured destruction. Whether a state exercises a limited option in order to raise the risk or despite the greater risk, raising the risk of a general nuclear exchange increases the expected cost to its adversary of continuing the crisis. If this cost is greater than the cost of submitting, an adversary will quit the crisis. Of course, both states might take steps that would raise the risk. In the strategy that leaves something to chance, the crisis continues until one of the states finds the risk intolerable or until the crisis goes out of control and there is a general nuclear exchange.[15]

In this approach, limited options manipulate the risk of the crisis going out of control and escalating to an unlimited nuclear exchange. Accordingly, these options are not to be judged primarily in terms of their effects on the battlefield of a limited war. Relative military strength and superiority would seem to be unimportant. What matters would seem to be the ability and willingness to create risks. Limited options are to be judged by their effects on the risk of uncontrolled escalation to a general nuclear war (Schelling 1960, 1962b, 1966; Jervis 1979–80, 1984). In this way, the set of limited options, each of which carries a different risk of escalation, constitutes an array of risk.

The array of risk and a strategy based on threats that leave something to chance offered one means of coping with a situation in which mutually assured destruction was the technological state of affairs. Even if there were no advantage to striking first and no situation in which a state could

---

[15] There are really two variants of this approach. In the first, states exercise a limited option in order to raise the risk of disaster. A crisis becomes a "competition in risk-taking" (Schelling 1966, p. 166) in which each state tries to demonstrate that its resolve, i.e., its willingness to run the risk that the crisis will go out of control, is greater than its adversary's resolve. In the second variant, the effect of exercising a limited option is to raise the risk, and it is this greater risk that actually exerts the coercive pressure, but the state exercises the option because it appears to further its ends in some other way. The greater risk is seen as an undesirable but unavoidable consequence of acting.

Historical evidence generally does not support the first variant. Leaders do not seem to take steps because they raise the risk of war (Snyder and Diesing 1977, p. 242; Trachtenberg 1985, p. 146). The second variant seems more viable: States do not act in order to increase the risk of war, but act in ways that do raise the risk, and this risk is the source of coercive pressure. This formulation, however, begs an important question: If states are not exercising limited options in order to raise the risk but because they appear to further their ends in some other way, what are these other ways, and what is the evidence for concluding that it is the greater risk and not these other ways that may coerce an adversary into submitting?

rationally and deliberately launch what it knew to be an unlimited first strike, a state might still be able to use the sanction of a massive nuclear attack coercively to protect its interests by manipulating the risk that a crisis would go out of control and escalate to a general nuclear exchange. This is one of the ways that deterrence theory has addressed the problem of credibility.

There is also a second approach, in which deterrence is not based on an unlimited attack but on limited attacks or limited retaliation.[16] A state would no longer threaten the complete destruction of its adversary through a massive nuclear attack. Rather, a state would attempt to deter its adversary by threatening to extract a toll in pain and destruction that, although sufficiently large to outweigh any potential gains, would still be limited. Should this threat initially prove insufficiently credible to dissuade an adversary, then a state might try to make it more credible by actually carrying out a limited option and inflicting some punishment.

If limited options were to be used in this way, they had to satisfy two criteria. First, a state at least had to appear to be able to impose high enough costs on an adversary that it would rather back down than endure the punishment that could be inflicted. But, second, the options had to be sufficiently limited that even if they had been exercised, the adversary still would be left with something more to lose. That was the key to the credibility problem. If a state had been completely destroyed by an unlimited attack, so that it had nothing left to lose, it would have no incentive to limit its retaliation. If, however, a state had suffered a limited attack and was left with something more to lose, that state might be deterred from retaliating in order not to lose what was left. A state might, for example, threaten to destroy one of its adversary's cities in order to coerce that adversary into backing down during a severe confrontation in which vital national interests were at stake. If, during the course of that confrontation, that threat were carried out, then, despite the horrendous loss of a city, the adversary still would have much left that could be lost. Moreover, the fact that it had already lost one city might make the threat that it was about to lose another very credible. That, in turn, might convince it not to retaliate and to back down.

Clearly, whatever coercive pressure the exercise of a limited option creates in this approach arises only by increasing the credibility of the threat of future destruction. Coming to terms after a city has been destroyed does not rebuild the city or bring the dead back to life or alleviate the survivors' suffering. At most, it preserves what remains. "The hurting

---

[16] For early studies of the strategy of limited retaliation, see Snyder (1961), Kaplan (1962), Kahn (1962), Knorr (1962), Schelling (1962a, 1965, 1966), and Halperin (1963).

does no good directly; it can only work indirectly. Coercion depends more on the threat of what is yet to come than on the damage already done" (Schelling 1966, p. 172). In sum, by exercising a limited option, a state attempts to demonstrate that its resolve is greater than that of its adversary, in the sense that it is more willing than is its adversary to inflict and endure future punishment in order to secure its ends.

In the strategy based on threats that leave something to chance, limited options raised the risk of the crisis going out of control and escalating to an unlimited nuclear exchange. The set of limited options thus constituted an array of risk. In the second approach to deterrence, limited options inflict limited amounts of punishment to make the threat of future punishment more credible. These options now form an array of punishment.[17]

Uncertainty and the struggle to control events play crucial roles in escalation and crisis bargaining. "The essence of the crisis is its unpredictability. The 'crisis' that involves no risk of things getting out of hand is no crisis. . . . It is the essence of a crisis that the participants are not fully in control of events" (Schelling 1966, p. 97). But "not [being] fully in control of events" has two interpretations, and the distinction between them is crucial to understanding the relations between the use or threatened use of force and states' attempts to secure their political objectives that underlie the strategies of leaving something to chance and of limited retaliation.

The first interpretation of the participants not being fully in control of events is that the participants do not have complete collective control. Even if the participants agree on a certain outcome and jointly act to effect this outcome, they cannot guarantee that this particular outcome will be realized. There is, to use Snyder and Diesing's phrase (1977, p. 210), some "autonomous risk" that some other outcome will eventuate.

Schelling (1966, pp. 99–105) offered a modified game of chess as an analogy for the strategy that leaves something to chance. This analogy also helps to clarify the first interpretation of events not being fully under control. To the three possible outcomes of the standard game of chess, win, lose, or draw, Schelling added a fourth, disaster, which is the analogue of a general nuclear exchange. If the game ends in disaster, each side will be worse off than if it had simply lost. The game may end in disaster in only one way: If a knight and queen of opposite colors cross the center line, then "the

---

[17] In an earlier essay (Powell 1985), these arrays were called the "spectrum of risk" and the "spectrum of violence." The word "spectrum" was a poor choice, for it connotes a continuum of limited options. That connotation was unintended and is inappropriate, for nuclear weapons may be very blunt, and there may be few limited options. For this reason, "array" is a better description of the set of limited options.

referee rolls a die. If an ace comes up the game is over and both sides are scored with a disaster, but if any other number comes up play goes on. If after the next move the queen and knight are still across the center line the [die is] rolled again, and so on" (Schelling 1966, p. 102). The addition of the referee and the die means that black and white are not in complete collective control of the game. Once a knight and queen of opposite colors cross the center line, the players can no longer guarantee that the game will not end in disaster. Although neither player would ever deliberately end the game in disaster, there is some chance of its ending that way. In moving a knight and queen across the center line, the players lose collective control of the outcome of the game. Their fate passes to the autonomous risk involved in the referee's throw of the die.

In the second interpretation of events not being fully under control, the participants are in complete collective control. If they agree on a particular outcome, the participants can effect any agreed outcome. Control is not something that can be lost. Events, however, are not fully under control, in the sense that no participant can control the actions and reactions of another.

The standard game of chess offers a good example of events not being fully under control in this second sense. If the players agree to a particular series of moves, then as long as this series is consistent with the rules of chess, the players, who collectively control all of the pieces, can effect this series of moves. If the players agree to a series of moves ending in white being checkmated, then the players can follow this series. But, of course, white does not want to be checkmated. White has no interest in following this series of moves and, not being under black's control, need not. This is the essence of the second interpretation of events not being fully under control.[18]

Failing to distinguish between these two interpretations can lead to apparently paradoxical conclusions about escalation in both nuclear and nonnuclear contexts. For example, concerning the crisis preceding World War I, the historian F. H. Hinsley wrote that if historians had gone as far as the evidence was trying to take them,

> they would have recognised that the dice had been set rolling for all the Powers before Russia mobilised – and not by any of the Powers but by a Balkan assassination. They would have seen that what makes some governments appear more responsible than others, or some governments more responsible at some stages and other governments more responsible at others, is not the fact that some governments were more instrumental than others in affecting the course of events. It is the fact that the positions

[18] The second interpretation of events not being fully under control is the permissive cause of war underlying Waltz's third image of international relations (Waltz 1959, p. 232).

of the different governments varied with the course of events over which they had lost control. They would have recognised that, although it is theoretically possible to say that war would have been avoided if this or that government had acted otherwise, it was not possible for them to have acted otherwise. All the evidence goes to show that the beginning of the crisis which has been studied so largely with a view to discovering and distributing human responsibility, was one of those moments in history when events passed beyond men's control. [1963, p. 296]

According to Hinsley, people lost control of events after Sarajevo, and that resulted in war. But of the causes of World War II Hinsley said that "a war is always an alternative to some other course and is known to be so" (1963, p. 331). Juxtaposed, these comments seem paradoxical. How is it possible for one not to have control over war and peace and at the same time claim that war is always an alternative to some other course of action? If this other course is to have any meaning, it must be possible to follow it and thereby avoid war. But if one can avoid war by following another course, then one has control over war and peace.

The difficulty here is that the two interpretations of events not being fully under control have been conflated. The Balkan assassination that set the dice rolling was an example of the first interpretation. The shooting of the archduke was akin to the referee's throw of the die in Schelling's modified game of chess. It was an event beyond the collective control of the Great Powers. In that sense, the Great Powers lost control. But this did not lead directly to war. States acted and reacted to the actions of other states. The war, in Hinsley's account, was the result of the interaction of these reactions. The Great Powers did not lose collective control over whether or not there would be a world war. Had all of them agreed on a resolution of the crisis and acted jointly, they could have effected it. The war resulted from events not being fully under control in the second sense: No state could control the reactions of the other states.[19]

Distinguishing between these two interpretations resolves the apparent paradox. If a state can avoid war by submitting to its adversary, war is an alternative to some other course of action. But if a state does not believe that pursuing that course is in its best interest, given what is at stake in the confrontation, then because no state can control the actions of another, there will be war.

The distinction between the two interpretations of events not being fully under control is crucial to understanding the strategy of leaving something

---

[19]   For nuclear deterrence theory, the July 1914 crisis is the archetypal crisis that goes out of control. See Trachtenberg (1989) for an historical reexamination of this thesis that casts doubt on this interpretation of the crisis.

to chance and the strategy of limited retaliation. If events are not fully under control only in the sense that no state can control the actions and reactions of other states, there is still risk and uncertainty. An adversary may escalate when it was expected to submit. But unless events are not fully under control in the first sense, the logic of the strategy that leaves something to chance will generally not be coherent. This dependence follows from the strategy's reliance on a sanction that would be so costly to impose that it would never be imposed deliberately. If the fear of suffering a sanction is to exert any coercive pressure, there must be some possibility of suffering it. If, therefore, no state would deliberately impose the sanction, there must be some other way for it to happen. Indeed, the something that is left to chance in the strategy of leaving something to chance is precisely that the sanction can arise in one of these other ways. Consequently, the states cannot be in complete collective control. There must be some autonomous risk underlying the strategy that leaves something to chance. The risk "must come from somewhere outside of the threatener's control" (Schelling 1960, p. 188). If the states always were in control in the first sense, there would be nothing to be left to chance. There would be no risk that could be manipulated in order to exert coercive pressure. There would no longer be an array of risk.

Two aspects of this dependence should be emphasized. First, the assumption that there is an autonomous risk is at once more and less demanding than it may initially seem. It may not appear to be very demanding at first because there are always events that are beyond collective control. There is always some autonomous risk of something. Some events are never fully under control in the first sense. But that is not sufficient for the strategy that leaves something to chance. A very specific event, the imposition of the sanction, must be imposed autonomously, and that is more demanding. At the height of the Cuban missile crisis, an American U-2 strayed into Soviet airspace. Soviet fighters were launched, and American interceptors, which because of the crisis and nuclear alert were armed with nuclear air-to-air missiles, were also scrambled. The interceptors did not make contact, and the U-2 found its way back to Alaska. Even so, President Kennedy was reported to have been concerned that Khrushchev might have thought that the U-2 was on a last-minute reconnaissance mission before an American nuclear attack (Sagan 1989a; 1989b, pp. 147–8). And the situation might have been much worse had one of the American fighters used a nuclear weapon.

The existence of an autonomous risk for events of this kind, serious and frightening as they may be, is not enough to ensure coherence for the logic of the strategy that leaves something to chance. The U-2 incident was akin to the Balkan assassination in Hinsley's account of the July 1914 crisis: It might have set the dice rolling. But just as the assassination did not lead directly to war, but did so only indirectly through a series of actions and reactions, the U-2 incident could have led to the sanction's imposition only indirectly. It would have had to have been followed by a series of interacting decisions. But if, as is assumed in the strategy that leaves something to chance, the sanction would not have been imposed deliberately, the decision to launch a general nuclear war would not have been made, and the incident would not in the end have led to a general nuclear attack unless there had subsequently been a loss of collective control that had imposed the sanction directly. Describing the strategy of leaving something to chance as manipulating the risk that the crisis will go out of control obscures the fact that a very specific type of accident is required if there is to be a chance of losing control. The logic of this strategy generally depends on the autonomous risk of an event that will lead directly to the sanction without the participants having to make a series of decisions that ultimately will end in a deliberate decision to impose the sanction. The failure of, say, a computer chip would be required to launch a general nuclear attack directly. If there is no autonomous risk that the sanction will be imposed directly, there is nothing for the strategy that leaves something to chance to leave to chance.[20]

The fact that the sanction must be imposed directly makes the dependence on autonomous risks more demanding than it may initially appear. But another aspect of this dependence makes this requirement less demanding. Although it will be convenient to refer to the participants in a crisis as states, it is more reasonable to conceive of the participants as the leader of each state and the group of advisors who will be trying to deal with the crisis. This distinction is important because the source of the autonomous risk must lie beyond the participants' control; therefore, which sources are beyond the participants' collective control clearly depends on how one defines the participants. When, for example, the participants are taken to be a small group of advisors, risks that lie within the collective control of the state and its institutions and organizations, but beyond the control of the national command authorities, are still autonomous. For example, the risk that an order to carry out a limited option will result in a general nuclear attack because of organizational

---

[20] There is an exception to this strategy's general dependence on events not being fully under control in the first sense. That is, there is a way in which the sanction might be imposed without the states losing collective control. Suppose a state launches a limited attack deliberately, but because of poor attack assessment the adversary is absolutely convinced that it suffered an unlimited attack and then retaliates in kind. In retaliating, the adversary, believing itself to be launching an unlimited second strike, deliberately attacks and thereby intentionally launches what is actually a first strike. The problems of false alarms and their effects on escalation are examined in more detail in Chapters 5 and 6.

rigidities and routines is an autonomous risk.[21] Thus, this narrower description of the participants expands the scope of possible sources of autonomous risk, and that makes the logical dependence of the strategy that leaves something to chance on this risk empirically less demanding.

The second aspect of this strategy's dependence on autonomous risk that should be emphasized has to do with rationality. The credibility problem in the strategy that leaves something to chance arises because this strategy relies on a sanction that no rational actor would knowingly be the first to impose. As long as rationality is assumed, the logic of this strategy generally requires that it be physically possible for the states to lose collective control (e.g., because of technical failure). But if the rationality assumption is relaxed, there is another way in which the states may "lose" collective control: If there is some chance that under the stress of a crisis a state might act irrationally by imposing the sanction, then this possibility may exert coercive pressure during the confrontation. Recognizing this, a state might, at least in principle, pursue what has been called the strategy of the rationality of the irrational (Snyder 1961, pp. 24–7; Kahn 1965, pp. 57–8; Maxwell 1968) by trying to convince its adversary that it might act irrationally. In any case, allowing for irrationality does not fundamentally change the understanding of the credibility problem in the approach based on the strategy that leaves something to chance. If the stakes are high enough, then taking a step that leaves something to chance, when that something includes the possibility of an adversary acting irrationally, may still be rational, and so the threat to take the step may be credible. Indeed, models based on the assumption that a state believes that its adversary may act irrationally will be used in subsequent chapters to study the dynamics of strategies based on manipulation of risk and on limited retaliation.

The general dependence of the strategy of leaving something to chance on there being an autonomous risk of the sanction being imposed offers one means of assessing the empirical significance of this approach. Suppose that there is negligible risk from the narrow range of accidental or irrational acts that would impose the sanction directly. Then, although the array of risk might link the use or threatened use of force to states' political ends in principle, it would not seem to do so in practice. Although logically consistent, this approach would not seem adequate to account for the dynamics of escalation.[22]

---

[21] Sagan (1985, 1989a, 1989b) has described some of the accidents and problems of control that the United States has actually experienced during nuclear crises and alerts.

[22] Although not motivated by this issue, studies of the command and control systems of nuclear forces (Ball 1981, 1985–6; Bracken 1983; Blair 1985; Carter 1987), studies of previous accidents (Sagan 1985, 1989a, 1989b), and psychologically oriented studies of crises (Jervis 1977; Lebow 1981; Jervis et al. 1985) may shed some light on the size of this autonomous risk and, potentially, on the suitability of this description.

In sum, nuclear deterrence theory has approached the problem of credibility in two ways. It has generally linked force or the threat of it to states' political objectives after the nuclear revolution through arrays of risk and punishment. By raising the risk of unlimited destruction to an intolerably high level through the array of risk, or by posing too great a danger of limited but nevertheless terrible damage through the array of punishment, a state might be able to coerce its adversary into coming to terms and in that way be able to secure its interests. This, of course, is not to say that a state will exert coercive pressure in these ways. A state may not believe that doing so is in its best interest. The chance that an adversary will actually submit may seem too remote, and therefore the cost of pursuing these strategies may seem greater than the benefits. But whether or not a state actually uses or threatens to use force, these two approaches are solutions to the credibility problem facing nuclear deterrence theory, for they describe, at least in principle, the relation between the use or threatened use of force and states' attempts to achieve their ends within a stylized environment in which defense is impossible.

By limiting its focus to these two approaches, nuclear deterrence theory may seem much too narrow and entirely unrelated to many of the debates about counterforce strategies that have shaped American nuclear policy.[23] A more careful examination of the implicit assumptions that seem to underlie these strategies will show, however, that these approaches are more relevant than they may at first seem. Indeed, a better understanding of these approaches would seem to be a prerequisite to understanding these strategies.

In the counterforce strategy based on having escalation dominance,[24] for example, a state uses its counterforce capability and escalation dominance to force its adversary to bear the onus of escalation. Thus, it would seem that the closer a state can come to achieving escalation dominance at all levels, the more an adversary will have to bear the burden of escalation and the less likely it will be to escalate or to provoke a confrontation in the first place. Believing that to be the relation between force and states' political objectives after the nuclear revolution, a state may attempt to further its ends by trying to attain escalation dominance at as many levels as it can.

But if, because of relatively invulnerable strategic forces, a state has the ability to destroy its adversary, then even when faced with a military defeat

---

[23] For an overview of these debates, see Freedman (1989).

[24] A state has escalation dominance at a certain level of conflict because of its superior counterforce capabilities if that state's military capabilities are such that it can force its adversary to choose between accepting defeat at that level or escalating to another level of violence (Kahn 1965, p. 290).

at a given level of violence, that state does not have to accept defeat or escalate to a higher level of military conflict. The state may try to exert coercive pressure on its adversary through the arrays of risk and punishment. Exerting pressure in these ways does not, moreover, require significant counterforce capabilities. Accordingly, the assumption that escalation dominance will significantly enhance deterrence implicitly discounts the possibility that a state will turn to these other means of bringing coercive pressure to bear. That is, when facing defeat at a given level, a state will accept defeat and be deterred from turning to the arrays of risk and punishment. But is this implicit assumption well founded? What factors affect a state's decision whether or not to try to coerce an adversary in these ways? A better understanding of the two approaches to deterrence based on the arrays of risk and punishment and, especially, of the conditions in which a state will or will not turn to these coercive means will shed some light on these questions. In this way, a better appreciation of these two strategies will provide a deeper understanding of counterforce strategies.[25]

Limited options and the problem of credibility

Nuclear deterrence theory has linked force and states' political ends in two ways. The strategy that leaves something to chance works through an array of risk and ultimately appeals to the sanction of an unlimited nuclear attack or, more generally, to a sanction that no state would ever deliberately be the first to impose. The strategy of limited retaliation, however, never appeals to the possibility of an unlimited attack. The array of punishment is used to impose limited sanctions in order to make the threat of future destruction sufficiently credible that an adversary will be coerced into coming to terms. Although these two approaches seem quite different, they are at a general level fundamentally alike. Each attempts to solve the credibility problem in the same way. Each uses an array of limited options to bridge the gap between doing too much by launching an unlimited nuclear attack, as in the doctrine of massive retaliation, and doing too little by acquiescing. Because these options are limited, a state may be able to make the threat to use them more credible. The remainder of this chapter is devoted to bringing out the essential similarities underlying these approaches.

---

[25] Schelling (1965; 1966, pp. 190–204) has made a similar point. A counterforce contest as envisioned in McNamara's "no cities" doctrine, for example, would eventually confront the losing state with a choice between continuing to lose the counterforce struggle or turning to a strategy of limited retaliation. Accordingly, a better appreciation of this strategy and, especially, of the circumstances in which a state is likely to adopt it would also seem to be relevant to a deeper understanding of this counterforce doctrine.

A useful way to begin is to formalize the doctrine of massive retaliation and the criticisms made of it. The formalization furthers two ends. First, redescribing the doctrine of massive retaliation and its criticisms in different and more formal terms makes the fundamental similarities of the two approaches to the credibility problem easier to see. The second end is to build confidence in the formal tools that will be used in subsequent chapters to examine these two approaches in more detail. The doctrine of massive retaliation and its weaknesses are relatively straightforward. Formal analytic tools are not needed for adequate explication of the issues. If, however, the formal analysis corresponds well with a nonformal analysis of a given situation, like massive retaliation, in which one can be relatively confident of the nonformal analysis, then one may place more confidence in applying the formal analysis to more complicated situations in which, because of the greater complexity, a nonformal analysis would be much more problematic.

In its simplest form, the doctrine of massive retaliation relies on a threat to launch a massive nuclear attack in response to any challenge to any American interest, ranging from the most peripheral to the most vital. Recall further that the credibility and therefore the efficacy of this doctrine were initially criticized only when this doctrine was used as a means of protecting less important interests. As long as the United States was perceived to be relatively invulnerable to a Soviet nuclear attack, the threat to launch a massive nuclear attack in order to protect vital American interests like Western Europe seemed credible. But once the United States became vulnerable to a devastating Soviet retaliatory attack, the credibility of this threat, even if made only in the context of attempting to protect vital American interests, became problematic.

The game in Figure 2.1 illustrates the doctrine of massive retaliation. The game tree shows what the sequence of play is and what alternatives each state has when it must decide what to do. The Soviet Union begins the game by deciding whether or not to exploit a situation by challenging the status quo. These alternatives are denoted by E and $\sim E$, respectively. If the Soviet Union accepts the status quo by playing $\sim E$, the game ends. If the Soviet Union exploits an opportunity to challenge the status quo, then the United States must choose between two options.[26] It can launch a massive nuclear attack, A, or it can quit the confrontation, Q, by acquiescing to the Soviet challenge.

To complete the specification of the game, the payoffs must be defined. There are three different sets of payoffs, each corresponding to a different

---

[26] Although this simple version of the doctrine of massive retaliation may seem to be a caricature of what this doctrine actually was, it is the version of the doctrine that the critics seemed to have in mind. See, for example, Kaufmann (1956).

Figure 2.1. The credibility of massive retaliation.

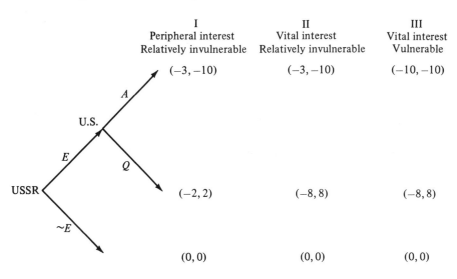

	I Peripheral interest Relatively invulnerable	II Vital interest Relatively invulnerable	III Vital interest Vulnerable
A	(-3, -10)	(-3, -10)	(-10, -10)
Q	(-2, 2)	(-8, 8)	(-8, 8)
~E	(0, 0)	(0, 0)	(0, 0)

situation in which the United States might try to rely on the doctrine of massive retaliation. Column I illustrates the situation in which the United States is relatively invulnerable and a peripheral American interest is involved. The United States is still assumed to be invulnerable in column II, but now a vital American interest is at issue. Finally, in column III, the United States is vulnerable to a Soviet nuclear counterattack, and a vital American interest is at stake.

To specify the payoffs in column I, where the United States is vulnerable and a peripheral interest is at risk, normalize the status quo payoffs to be (0, 0), where the first number is the American payoff and the second is the Soviet payoff. If the Soviet Union challenges the status quo in this situation and the United States replies with a massive nuclear attack, the Soviet Union will be completely destroyed. The United States will also suffer, but less so, because the United States is assumed to be relatively invulnerable. Let the payoffs to this outcome be, say, (-3, -10).[27] If the Soviet Union challenges the status quo and the United States acquiesces, the Soviet Union improves its position compared with the status quo. The United States loses, but not much, for only a peripheral interest is assumed to be at stake. The payoffs corresponding to this outcome will be taken to be (-2, 2).

Now consider the situation in which the United States remains relatively

[27] The specific numerical values of these payoffs are, of course, rather arbitrary. They are intended only to illustrate the differences between the three situations in a very simple way.

invulnerable, but a vital American interest is at risk. The status quo payoffs in column II are still $(0, 0)$. The payoffs if there is a war are also the same: If the Soviet Union challenges the status quo and the United States attacks, they receive $(-3, -10)$. The only payoffs that change from column I to II are those that obtain if the Soviet Union disputes the status quo and then the United States acquiesces. This change reflects the assumption that a vital American interest is at stake in column II. If the United States does not act in this situation and thereby lets the Soviet Union have its way, the United States will pay a high price. The payoffs depicting this condition are taken to be $(-8, 8)$.

Finally, if a vital American interest is at stake and the United States is vulnerable to a devastating Soviet retaliatory attack, then the only difference between the payoffs in columns II and III is that the payoffs corresponding to a Soviet challenge followed by an American first strike now reflect the greater American vulnerability. As long as the United States was relatively invulnerable, its payoff to attacking and then having to endure Soviet retaliation was -3. Being more vulnerable, Soviet retaliation will impose higher costs and leave the United States with -10.

With the game thus defined, its equilibria may now be described. The doctrine of massive retaliation turns out to be a Nash equilibrium.[28] To see this, the states' strategies must be formally specified. The American strategy in the doctrine of massive retaliation is to attack the Soviet Union only if the Soviet Union challenges the status quo (i.e., the United States plays A in the game in Figure 2.1). The Soviet strategy is not to challenge the status quo. To show that this combination of strategies constitutes a Nash equilibrium, it need only be shown that no state has an incentive to deviate from its strategy given its adversary's strategy. Consider the situation in column I, in which the United States is relatively invulnerable, and only a peripheral American interest is at risk. Clearly, the Soviet Union has no incentive to alter its strategy of not disputing the status quo. Given the American strategy of responding to a challenge with an unlimited nuclear attack, if the Soviet Union deviates from its strategy by challenging the status quo its payoff will be -10, whereas following the strategy of accepting the status quo will assure the Soviet Union of 0. The United States also has no incentive to deviate from the doctrine of massive retaliation. Given that the Soviet Union is not challenging the status quo, the American payoff is always 0 regardless of what it would do if challenged. Because neither state has any incentive to deviate from its strategy given the strategy of the other state, the doctrine of massive

---

[28] See the Appendix following Chapter 8 for an introduction to the game-theoretic concepts, such as Nash equilibria, that are used in this and subsequent chapters.

retaliation in the game represented by the payoffs in column I is a Nash equilibrium. Similar arguments show that this doctrine is also a Nash equilibrium in the situations illustrated by columns II and III.

Although the doctrine of massive retaliation is a Nash equilibrium, there is a troubling feature about this equilibrium, and this goes to the heart of the criticisms of this doctrine. Suppose that the Soviet Union does, for some reason, challenge the status quo. The United States will then have to decide between launching a massive nuclear attack, which will bring a payoff of -3, or acquiescing, which, with only a peripheral interest involved, will yield -2. Assuming that states act in ways that they believe to be in their best interest, the United States will choose -2 when confronted with a choice between -2 and -3. The United States will not launch a massive nuclear attack, for the cost of carrying out its threat would be greater than the cost of not doing so. The Soviet Union, understanding this, will find the doctrine of massive retaliation incredible and will not be deterred by it. That is, in effect, the criticism William Kaufmann made in 1956: that even if the United States were relatively invulnerable, the doctrine of massive retaliation could not protect less important American interests.

This criticism can be stated more formally, and doing so helps to build confidence in the ability of formal methods to contribute to the analysis of more complicated situations. Although the doctrine of massive retaliation is a Nash equilibrium, it is not a sequential equilibrium.[29] In a sequential equilibrium, agents are required to act in their best interest everywhere in the game tree given their beliefs and the strategies of the other agents. Thus, when confronted with a choice between -2 and -3, the United States must choose the former. When the United States is relatively invulnerable, but only a peripheral interest at stake, there is a unique sequential equilibrium. In it, the Soviet Union challenges the status quo, and the United States acquiesces.[30] The doctrine of massive retaliation founders on the credibility problem in the sense that it is not a sequential equilibrium.

Viewing the credibility problem from the perspective of sequential equilibria also accounts for the other criticisms of the doctrine of massive

---

[29] It would suffice at this point to look only to the more appealing and less demanding notion of subgame perfection in order to eliminate this Nash equilibrium. Subgame perfection, however, will be insufficient in subsequent chapters, where incomplete-information games will be studied. For a discussion of the relation between subgame perfection and sequential equilibria, see Kreps and Wilson (1982b) or the Appendix following Chapter 8.

[30] Neither the Soviet Union nor the United States has any incentive to deviate from its strategy given the other's strategy. Challenging the status quo brings the Soviet Union 3, whereas forgoing a challenge yields 0. Similarly, the United States will lower its payoff from -2 to -3 if it deviates from acquiescing by attacking. This combination of strategies thus forms a Nash equilibrium. Moreover, no state has any incentive to deviate from its strategy anywhere in the game tree given its beliefs.

retaliation. That doctrine seemed to be credible as long as the United States was relatively invulnerable and a vital American interest was at risk. That situation corresponds to the payoffs in column II. With these payoffs, the game also has a unique sequential equilibrium. But this time, the United States will attack if challenged, for this brings -3, whereas surrendering a vital interest leaves the United States with -8. Given this American strategy, the Soviet Union's best response is not to dispute the status quo. When the cost of acquiescing is so high, the threat to retaliate massively rather than submit is credible, and the doctrine of massive retaliation is effective in protecting vital interests. But, of course, once the United States became vulnerable to a devastating Soviet retaliatory attack, this doctrine seemed incredible even with vital interests at stake. Again, insisting that equilibria be not only Nash but also sequential accounts for this. With the payoffs of column III, the Soviet Union challenges the status quo, and the United States acquiesces, preferring to suffer the large but limited loss rather than the still larger loss that a Soviet retaliation would cause.

All of this indicates that focusing on sequential equilibria in games modeling not only massive retaliation but also crises based on the arrays of risk and punishment will do much to provide an understanding of the credibility problem. Strategies that are part of a sequential equilibrium cannot rely on threats that are inherently incredible, because carrying them out would be more costly than not doing so. The close correspondence

Figure 2.2. The array of limited options.

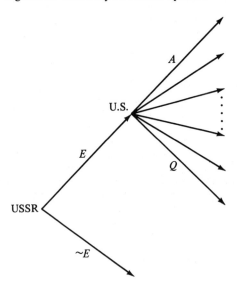

between the formal and less formal critiques of the doctrine of massive retaliation suggests that these more formal tools will be useful in analyzing the more complicated approaches to the credibility problem based on the arrays of risk and punishment.

In addition to building confidence in the game-theoretic analysis of the credibility problem, the game in Figure 2.1 may be used to bring out the fundamental similarities underlying deterrence theory's two approaches to this problem. Intuitively, this problem arises because the two options in Figure 2.1 of launching a massive nuclear attack and of quitting are too far apart. One option does too much, the other too little. Credibility, then, would seem to require the creation of an array of limited options in which the distance between any two adjacent options in this array is less than the distance between the option of launching a massive attack and that of doing nothing. This array, in effect, bridges the gap between doing too much and too little. Figure 2.2 illustrates this array by filling the gap between these two extremes with a number of limited options. There are, however, two different ways to measure the distance between adjacent options, and each of these ways corresponds to one of the approaches deterrence theory has taken to the credibility problem.

The first way of measuring the distance is in terms of the probability that the crisis will end in an unlimited exchange. Measured in this way, the distance between launching an unlimited attack, which would end the crisis in a general nuclear exchange with probability 1, and quitting, which would ensure that there would be no exchange, is 1. No two options could be farther apart. The array of limited options fills this gap by making it possible to create intermediate levels of risk. Associated with each limited option is the level of risk that the exercise of this option will generate. Indeed, what distinguishes any option from any other is that they generate different levels of risk. In this way the set of limited options constitutes the array of risk that underlies the strategy that leaves something to chance.

Damage is the second way of measuring the distance between the extremes of launching a massive nuclear attack and submitting. The former inflicts complete destruction, and the latter inflicts none. Again, these options are very far apart, and, as before, limited options are used to bridge this gap. But in this case what defines and distinguishes one limited option from another is the amount of punishment it will impose if exercised. When measured in terms of damage, the set of limited options now forms an array of punishment.

So, when viewed from this more general perspective, the two seemingly disparate approaches to linking force or the threat of it to states' political ends appear to be fundamentally alike. Each addresses the credibility problem in essentially the same way, by creating an array of limited options to bridge the gap between doing too much and too little. This is not to say that many options can be created such that there will be fine gradations in the levels of risk or damage separating these options. Nuclear weapons may be very blunt. It is only to say that what distinguishes these approaches is not the general role or relative importance of limited options but the particular way that this gap is measured.

The rise of strategic air power and the development of intercontinental ballistic missiles and atomic and then thermonuclear weapons separated the ability to defend from the ability to punish. These developments culminated in the nuclear revolution, in which mutually assured destruction became the technological state of affairs. The separation of these capabilities and the impossibility of defense undercut the classical logic of war.

After the nuclear revolution, a state's ability to impose costs that would exceed an adversary's gains was no longer at issue. But given that defense was impossible, could a state make the threat to use its punitive capabilities sufficiently credible? What was the relation between force or the threat of it and states' efforts to secure their ends after the nuclear revolution? That was the credibility problem.

Nuclear deterrence theory has generally approached this problem in two ways. Force or the threat of it is linked to states' political objectives through either an array of risk or an array of punishment. Although these two approaches initially appear quite different, they are, at a more general level, essentially alike. Each tries to solve the credibility problem in the same way.

But how far does this fundamental similarity extend? The following chapters examine this in two ways. The first is a more detailed study of the dynamics of crisis bargaining and escalation when force is related to political ends through the arrays of risk and punishment. The second is to elaborate the relation between these two approaches. Although both approaches are, at a high level of generality, attempts to solve the credibility problem, they are primarily concerned with different issues at somewhat lower levels of generalization. But these lower-level issues are connected. An analysis of the strategy that leaves something to chance leads naturally to questions about crisis stability and first-strike advantages, and these in turn raise questions about the role of limited sanctions and the strategy of limited retaliation. The following chapters trace these connections and in this way further clarify the relation between these two approaches to the credibility problem.

CHAPTER 3

The dynamics of nuclear brinkmanship

The strategy that leaves something to chance and the array of risk link the use or threatened use of force to states' attempts to further their interests. Even in a condition of mutually assured destruction, a state still might be able to use the sanction of launching a massive nuclear attack coercively. A state would no longer threaten to impose this sanction deliberately, but rather to take steps that would raise the risk that the crisis would go out of control and end in disaster. Because no state ever threatens to bring this disaster about deliberately, but only to create some risk of it, then, depending on the stakes involved in the crisis, the threat to take these steps and generate these risks may be quite credible. Crises in this stylization become contests of resolve in which the states compete by taking risks. During a crisis, each state exerts coercive pressure on its adversary by acting in ways that vary the risk of disaster. Eventually, one of the states finds the risk too high and withdraws.

The preceding chapter discussed the general role the array of risk plays in the approach to deterrence based on the strategy that leaves something to chance. That approach attempted to link force or the threat of it to states' efforts to further their ends with a set of limited options that were differentiated on the basis of the autonomous risk that exercising them would generate. Those options filled the gap between doing too much by launching a general nuclear attack and doing too little by acquiescing to a challenge to the status quo. But what are the dynamics of a confrontation in which the states are pursuing this strategy? Is a more resolute state more or less likely to escalate, and does that make the crisis more or less likely to end disastrously? Is a state more or less likely to escalate the greater the resolve of its adversary? What are the effects of misperception on the dynamics of escalation and on crisis stability? Does a state's having a greater stake in the status quo make it more or less likely to challenge the status quo? Suppose that the grain of the array of risk is finer, in the sense that there are smaller, more limited options that permit a state to raise the risk of losing control in smaller steps. How does that affect the escalatory process and the probability that the crisis will end in a general nuclear exchange? This chapter and the next examine these questions.

The analysis to follow indicates that many arguments about the dynamics of escalation that at first seem quite compelling turn out to be problematic. It may, for example, seem that a state would not escalate if it were certain that its adversary's resolve were greater than its own. Escalation in that case would be dangerous and apparently pointless. Or it might seem that the greater an adversary's resolve, the more likely it would be to stand firm in a crisis, and consequently the less likely a state would be to resist that adversary by escalating. Similarly, it may appear that the greater an adversary's resolve, the more likely it would be to prevail in a crisis. In the model to be presented, none of these arguments holds: A state may escalate even though it is certain that its adversary's resolve is greater than its own. The greater an adversary's resolve, the more likely a state may be to escalate. And the greater an adversary's resolve, the less likely it may be to prevail. The model also helps to explain why these arguments do not hold by showing that they generally fail to take into account important interactions between the states' strategies and their beliefs about their adversaries.

The brinkmanship analogy and the game of chicken

The essence of the strategy that leaves something to chance is manipulation of an autonomous risk of disaster. Schelling (1960, pp. 199–201; 1966, pp. 92–125) offered the analogy of brinkmanship as an aid to understanding the dynamics of crisis bargaining in which the states pursue this strategy. The models that will be developed later will formalize this analogy. In the analogy, two adversaries are tied together with a rope and are standing near a brink. The rope binds their fates: If one goes over the brink, the other will be dragged over too, and both will perish. The brinkmanship analogy thus describes a situation in which imposing the sanction would always be more costly to oneself than not imposing it. Deliberately pushing that linked adversary into the abyss would be the analogue of launching a deliberate first strike, and neither party can credibly threaten to do that.

Because neither would ever deliberately impose the sanction of pushing its adversary over the brink, there is no danger of going over as long as the adversaries have complete collective control. If, for example, the brink is a sharp edge that can be approached without any risk of falling off unintentionally, the fear of going over cannot exert any coercive pressure, because there is no fear (Schelling 1966, p. 99). But suppose that the brink is not a sharp edge that one can approach safely and then decide whether or not to jump. The brink is, rather, "a curved slope that one can stand on with some risk of slipping, the slope gets steeper and the risk of slipping greater as one moves toward the chasm" (Schelling 1960, p. 199). Describing the brink in this way means that the parties are no longer in complete collective control of whether or not they will fall into the abyss. One could go over the brink despite both adversaries' unwillingness to take any action that would be certain to force them into the abyss. With gusty winds overhead and loose gravel underfoot, the parties would not be fully in control of events. Accordingly, each could exert coercive pressure on the other by approaching the chasm. In the analogy, each step toward the brink corresponds to the exercise of one of the limited options in the array of risk. Each step raises the risk that despite one's desire not to slip, one might do so accidentally. Assuming that neither does slip, then, as both near the brink, one of them will sooner or later find the risk intolerable and will submit. In this way, the confrontation at the brink becomes a competition in taking risks.

The game of "chicken" has been used to model brinkmanship and deterrence (Kahn 1965; Schelling 1966; Snyder 1971; Jervis 1972, 1976, 1979; Snyder and Diesing 1977; Brams 1985; Brams and Kilgour 1985, 1987, 1988; Zagare 1985, 1987; O'Neill 1987). The simplest game of chicken, which is a 2 × 2 game, as illustrated in Figure 3.1, has often provided a point of departure for these analyses, and it will do so here. A brief review of this game will suggest that, at least in this simplest form, it can shed very little light on the dynamics of escalation in brinkmanship crises.

There are two players in the game, *I* and *II*, and they are usually taken to be states. Each state must choose between standing firm or submitting to its adversary. If both stand firm, the crisis ends in the disaster of a general nuclear exchange. If one stands firm and the other submits, the former prevails. The latter, although perhaps sacrificing an important national interest by submitting, escapes the complete destruction that would have been wrought had both stood firm. If both submit, the crisis ends in

Figure 3.1. The game of chicken.

| | | *II* | |
		Stand firm	Submit
I	Stand firm	d_I, d_{II}	w_I, s_{II}
	Submit	s_I, w_{II}	c_I, c_{II}

compromise. Letting w, c, s, and d denote the payoffs to prevailing, compromise, submitting, and disaster, respectively, the payoffs satisfy the relations $w_I > c_I > s_I > d_I$ and $w_{II} > c_{II} > s_{II} > d_{II}$. These relations are intended to formalize the stylization of the nuclear era as one in which no state would deliberately launch a first strike. Prevailing is better than submitting; $w > s$. Before the development of secure second-strike capabilities, standing firm might have been preferred to submitting, even if one's adversary also stood firm. That would have implied that $d > s$. But in a condition of mutually assured destruction, standing firm is no longer preferred to submitting if one's adversary also stands firm, for if a state believes that its adversary is going to stand firm, then its decision to stand firm is equivalent to initiating a general nuclear exchange deliberately. Avoiding this outcome, albeit at the cost of submitting, is preferable (i.e., $s > d$).

The game has two equilibria in pure strategies. In the first, I stands firm and II submits. That is, given that I is standing firm, II can attain s_{II} by submitting and d_{II} by standing firm. II, therefore, can do no better than to submit; submitting is II's best reply to I's standing firm. And given that II is submitting, I's best reply is to stand firm. Each state's strategy is a best response to the other's strategy, and thus this combination of strategies forms an equilibrium. In the second equilibrium, II stands firm and I submits. There is also one equilibrium in mixed strategies in which I stands firm with probability $\phi_I = (w_{II} - c_{II})/[(w_{II} - c_{II}) + (s_{II} - d_{II})]$, and II stands firm with probability $\phi_{II} = (w_I - c_I)/[(w_I - c_I) + (s_I - d_I)]$.[1]

Two related characteristics of this model suggest that it will have little to say about the dynamics of nuclear brinkmanship. First, the two pure-strategy equilibria are unaffected by changes in the payoffs as long as $w_I > c_I > s_I > d_I$ and $w_{II} > c_{II} > s_{II} > d_{II}$. For example, the situation in which one state stands firm and the other submits remains an equilibrium whenever these relations hold, even if the payoff to the "cooperative" outcome of mutual compromise is only slightly worse than the payoff to prevailing. As long as $w > c$, an increase in the payoff to compromising does not make a compromise more likely in these equilibria.

The insensitivity of these equilibria to changes in the payoffs is troubling. Intuitively, it would seem that the level of a state's resolve[2] in a crisis should be affected by these payoffs and that changes in a state's resolve would be reflected in the outcome of the contest of resolve. Yet, if these pure-strategy equilibria are taken to represent the potential outcomes of the crisis, then

---

[1]   See the Appendix following Chapter 8 for the derivation of these probabilities, as well as a discussion of mixed-strategy equilibria and some of the properties of the mixed-strategy equilibrium of chicken.

[2]   This term will be defined formally later.

resolve has no role. The balance of resolve plays no part in affecting the outcome of a crisis. Worse, there is no way to decide which equilibrium ought to be taken to represent the outcome of the crisis.[3] There is no way to determine if *I* or *II* will submit. These equilibria do nothing to illuminate the process through which a state convinces its adversary that it will be the one to stand firm.

Unlike the pure-strategy equilibria, the mixed equilibrium is sensitive to changes in the payoffs. The probability that the crisis will end in compromise is the product of the probabilities that each state will compromise; that is, $(1 - \phi_I)(1 - \phi_{II})$. Moreover, the probability of compromise varies with the payoffs as one would expect intuitively. Compromise is more likely the greater the payoff to compromising, the greater the cost of disaster, and the smaller the payoff to prevailing.[4]

But even if attention is restricted to the mixed equilibrium because of its intuitively appealing sensitivity to changes in the payoffs, a second characteristic of this model severely limits its usefulness in studying the dynamics of brinkmanship. There simply are no real dynamics in the model. Each state makes a single decision: It decides whether or not to stand firm. There is no sequence of play, no series of interacting decisions, no process in the model. There is no way that a state can take its adversary's past actions into account in assessing the likelihood that the adversary will stand firm, for in the model there are no past actions. Whatever bargaining process may have led to the point at which the states have to decide whether or not to stand firm has been left out of the model.

The brinkmanship analogy is dynamic, but lacks formalization. In trying to assess how much nearer the brink an adversary may be willing to go, for example, a state can base its judgment on how many steps toward the brink its adversary has already been willing to take. Conversely, the simplest game of chicken is formally well defined, but lacks any dynamic process. The model of nuclear brinkmanship developed next attempts to formalize the bargaining process by explicitly modeling a series of interacting decisions.

A model of nuclear brinkmanship

In many models there is a tension inherent in incorporating as many important aspects of a problem as possible without making the model intractable. If everything cannot be included, a model implicity reflects a

---

[3] See Harsanyi and Selten (1988) for an analysis of the problem of selecting a single equilibrium if more than one exists.

[4] This follows by taking the partial derivatives of $(1 - \phi_I)(1 - \phi_{II})$ with respect to the payoffs c, d, and w.

judgment about what the essence of the problem is. Three elements seem essential to brinkmanship. First, there is a series of decisions. Second, the states involved in the crisis create risks that they will lose collective control and that the crisis will end in disaster. Third, each state lacks complete information, perhaps concerning its adversary's payoffs or level of resolve.[5] The difficulty with the 2×2 game of chicken is that it leaves out too much of the essence of brinkmanship. Each state makes only one decision and does so in ignorance of what the other is doing in the simple game of chicken. There is no series of decisions. Moreover, each state knows its adversary's payoffs and level of resolve; there is complete information.

The model of brinkmanship developed here tries to formalize these three elements in a more satisfying way. The series of decisions will be modeled by letting one state, the potential challenger, decide whether or not it wants to dispute the status quo. If it does, then the other state, the defender, decides whether or not it will take a step toward the brink. If it takes a step, then the challenger must choose between submitting or taking a step closer to the abyss. These decisions alternate back and forth until one state submits or until the states accidentally slip into the chasm. The model also explicitly represents the way the states manipulate the autonomous risk of their losing collective control. The closer a state is to the brink, the larger the risk the next step entails. In the next section, incomplete information will be added to the model. Each state will be uncertain of the payoffs and therefore the level of resolve of its adversary. A state will be unsure whether its adversary is resolute and willing to run high risks or irresolute and willing to run only small risks.

Turning now to a more formal description of the model, the confrontation at the brink, which is depicted in Figure 3.2, begins with the potential challenger, C, having to accept the status quo, challenge it, or launch a massive nuclear attack. These alternatives are labeled $\sim E$, E, and A, respectively. If C launches a massive attack, the game ends with payoffs (d_C, d_D). If C accepts the status quo by playing $\sim E$, the game ends with payoffs (q_C, q_D). If C disputes the status quo, then the onus of escalation shifts to the defender, D.

D has three options. It can quit the crisis by playing Q. That leaves C with the payoff to prevailing, w_C, and gives D the payoff to submitting, s_D. D may also decide to launch a massive nuclear attack. That is assumed to bring a devastating nuclear reply from C, and the game ends in disaster, with

---

[5] In the models in this volume, the states' strategies are obtained by solving complicated optimization problems. The states in this sense have unbounded rationality. Another important element of brinkmanship and crisis bargaining more generally may be that actors have bounded rationality. This issue lies beyond the scope of the models presented here. See Langlois (1988) for a discussion of brinkmanship and bounded rationality.

payoffs (d_C, d_D). Finally, D may escalate by taking a step toward the brink. That generates an autonomous risk of disaster δ. That is, the probability that the states will lose collective control at that point and that the crisis will end in a general nuclear exchange is δ.

D's step toward the brink is modeled by letting Nature, N, move immediately after D if D decides to escalate. Nature then plays disaster with probability δ and continues with probability $1 - \delta$. If there is a disaster, the game ends, and the payoffs are (d_C, d_D). If the game continues, then D's escalation has not triggered a disaster, and the onus of escalation shifts back to C.

Now the challenger faces the same three options that just confronted D. Submission ends the game with (s_C, w_D). Attacking, as always, brings an attack in retaliation and ends the game with (d_C, d_D). C may also escalate by taking a step toward the brink. But to do so, C must generate a larger risk of disaster than D created when it escalated. Specifically, C must increase the risk in an increment of δ. That is, if C escalates, it must do so by generating a risk of 2δ. If the game does not now end in disaster, the onus of escalation shifts back to D. The game continues in this way, with the onus of escalation shifting back and forth until one of the states quits or until there is a disaster.

The game can end with one of four pairs of payoffs: (q_C, q_D), (w_C, s_D), (s_C, w_D), and (d_C, d_D). Because prevailing is better than submitting, and submitting is better than having to endure a nuclear attack, $w_C > s_C > d_C$ and $w_D > s_D > d_D$. Because the status quo is better than submitting, $q_C > s_C$ and $q_D > s_D$. For C, it must also be that prevailing is better than the status quo: $w_C > q_C$. Otherwise, C could obtain its highest payoff at its first move by not exploiting the situation, and there would be no crisis. Hence, $w_C > q_C > s_C > d_C$. The relation between w_D and q_D is ambiguous, but also inconsequential, because by the time D has to make its first decision, q_D is already in the past and no longer relevant to D's decision.

The risks that escalation creates in the crisis follow the pattern $\delta, 2\delta$, $3\delta, \ldots, K\delta$, where $K\delta = 1$. (For convenience, $1/\delta$ is assumed to be an integer.) When the defender escalates for the mth time, it does so by generating a risk

Figure 3.2. Brinkmanship with complete information.

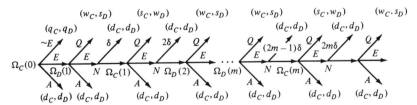

of $(2m-1)\delta$, and the pattern of risks it creates is $\delta, 3\delta, 5\delta, \ldots$. The challenger creates a risk of $2m\delta$ if it escalates for the mth time, and the pattern of risks it generates is $2\delta, 4\delta, 6\delta, \ldots$. If K is even, C has the last move in the game, because to escalate for the $(K/2)$th time, it must generate a probability of disaster equal to 1. If K is odd, D's $[(K+1)/2]$th move is the last possible move. Some analyses (Schelling 1966; Snyder and Diesing 1977; Wagner 1982) have suggested that a significant bargaining disadvantage accrues to the side with the last possible chance to avoid disaster. But, as will be seen, who actually has the last physical move in the game tree generally has no effect on the solution to this game. Accordingly, K will merely be assumed to be even, and therefore C has the last move.

It will prove convenient to adopt the following notation for the states' information sets and behavioral strategies. Let $\Omega_D(m)$ be the information set at which D must decide whether or not to escalate for the mth time, where $1 \le m \le K/2$. Thus, $\Omega_D(m)$ presents D with the choice of submitting, attacking, or escalating by creating an autonomous risk of $(2m-1)\delta$. For C, take $\Omega_C(m)$, for $1 \le m \le K/2$, to be the information set at which C must decide to submit, attack, or escalate with probability $2m\delta$. $\Omega_C(0)$ is the information set at which C has to choose among attacking, exploiting the situation, or not exploiting it. At each of its information sets, a state has to choose from among three alternatives. Accordingly, a behavioral strategy for any state at any information set is defined by two probabilities. At, say, $\Omega_D(m)$, D's strategy may be described by the probability of attacking at that set, $a_D(m)$, and the probability of escalating, $e_D(m)$. The probability of submission is given by $1 - a_D(m) - e_D(m)$.

The notion of a *crisis equilibrium* will play an important role in the analysis of both brinkmanship and, later, the strategy of limited retaliation. For Snyder and Diesing, "there is no crisis unless one state challenges another and this challenge is resisted" (1977, p. 13). Formalizing this, a crisis equilibrium in the game will be taken to be an equilibrium in which there is some positive probability that the challenger will exploit the situation and the defender will escalate or attack. The positive probability that C will exploit the situation [i.e., that $e_C(0) > 0$] means there is some chance that C will challenge D. Similarly, the positive probability that D will resist by escalating or attacking [i.e., that $e_D(1) > 0$ or $a_D(1) > 0$] implies that there is some chance that the challenge will be resisted. Crisis equilibria are also the only equilibria in the game in which there is a positive probability that a challenge will lead to disaster. This is in keeping with the work of Schelling (1966, pp. 92–105) and Snyder and Diesing (1977, pp. 6–21), for whom there must be some risk of war for there to be a crisis.

As in the previous discussion of the credibility of massive retaliation, the notion of a sequential equilibrium also plays an essential role in the analysis of brinkmanship. This notion provides the formal key to solving the credibility problem. In a sequential equilibrium, a state's equilibrium strategy starting from any place in the game tree is an optimal strategy for the rest of the game, given that state's information and beliefs at that stage of the game and given the other state's strategy. In a sequential equilibrium, no state can improve its payoff by deviating from its equilibrium strategy regardless of where it is in the game. Consequently, a state cannot rely on a threat to impose a sanction when it believes that actually imposing the sanction would be more costly than not doing so. In the previous context of the model of massive retaliation, focusing on sequential equilibria eliminated other equilibria that depended on inherently incredible threats. Analyzing the brinkmanship model in terms of its sequential equilibria will do the same.[6]

The analysis of the extensive game in Figure 3.2 begins by recalling that the 2×2 game of chicken discussed earlier had two equilibria in pure strategies in which one state or the other stood firm while its adversary submitted. Those equilibria were insensitive to changes in the payoffs, and that seemed to leave no role for resolve to play. In the extensive game, there is an obvious parallel to the strategy of standing firm in the simple game of chicken: the strategy of always escalating. That is, a state escalates at every information set regardless of what its adversary does. Similarly, the parallel to the strategy of submitting in the simple game of chicken is always to submit in the extensive game of brinkmanship.

Given these definitions, the combination of strategies in which one state stands firm and the other submits forms a Nash equilibrium. But, as will be seen, these equilibria are not sequential, for like the doctrine of massive retaliation, they rely on inherently incredible threats. If C stands firm by always escalating [i.e., $e_C(m) = 1$ for all $0 \leq m \leq K/2$], D can never prevail. The best it can do is to avoid running any risk of disaster by submitting and obtaining s_D. Submitting is D's best reply to C's strategy of standing firm. Similarly, if D always submits, then standing firm is C's best reply. Neither state can gain by deviating from its strategy given its adversary's strategy, and the strategies constitute a Nash equilibrium. A similar argument shows that C's submission and D's standing firm also compose a Nash equilibrium.

These two equilibria, like their analogues in the simple game of chicken, are insensitive to changes in the states' payoffs. As long as $w_C > q_C > s_C > d_C$ and $w_D > s_D > d_D$, the situation of one state standing firm and the other submitting remains an equilibrium regardless of the size of the difference

---

[6] See the Appendix following Chapter 8 for an introduction to sequential equilibria, and see Kreps and Wilson (1982b) and Kreps and Ramey (1987) for further discussion.

between winning and losing. Whether $w_C - s_C$ is large or small, the states follow the same strategies. The balance of resolve does not affect these two equilibria. So far, then, resolve plays no part in this model.

But these equilibria are not sequential. To see this, consider, for example, the equilibrium in which C stands firm by always escalating, and D always submits. The last move in the game belongs to C. At this point, C must generate a risk of disaster of 1 if it decides to escalate. C, in effect, is relying on the strategy of massive retaliation here. If C finds itself in this position, it will take a step that is certain to lead to a massive nuclear attack. The doctrine of massive retaliation is, however, inherently incredible in a technological condition of mutually assured destruction, and because C is implicitly appealing to this doctrine in its strategy of always standing firm, this strategy should also be incredible. More formally, at the point in the game where C must generate a certainty of disaster if it escalates, escalation will bring a payoff of d_C, whereas submission, as always, will bring s_C. If, therefore, the game somehow reaches this stage, escalating will not be in C's own interest. Thus, implicit in C's strategy of always escalating is a threat that is formally incredible, for if C ever finds itself in a position in which it must decide whether or not to carry it out, implementing the threat will not be in C's own interest. This means that in at least one place in the tree, namely, at the last decision node, C has an incentive to deviate from its strategy of standing firm given D's strategy. Accordingly, the combination of strategies in which C stands firm and D submits is not a sequential equilibrium.[7]

When the game is solved for its sequential equilibria, the states cannot rely on inherently incredible threats. Moreover, resolve begins to play a role. Indeed, when, as has been assumed so far, information is complete, so that each state knows its adversary's level of resolve as well as its own, the state with the greatest effective resolve prevails. To demonstrate this, *resolve* must be defined formally. Critical-risk models of crisis bargaining often define a state's resolve to be the greatest risk of disaster that the state is willing to run in a crisis in order to achieve its ends (Snyder and Diesing 1977, p. 190). In keeping with this, a state's resolve will be taken to be the probability of disaster that leaves this state indifferent between the payoffs of quitting and of escalating, given that if this state escalates, its adversary will then quit at its next opportunity. This implies that if a state must accept a risk greater than its resolve in order to escalate, then the cost of escalating will certainly be higher than the cost of submitting, and the state will quit. To find an expression for the challenger's resolve, R_C, note that if the

---

[7] Technically, the combination of strategies in which D stands firm and C submits may be a sequential equilibrium if D prefers running the large risk of disaster of $1 - \delta$ to submitting and thereby obtaining s_D. For small δ, this technicality may be disregarded.

probability of disaster is R_C, then the expected payoff to escalating is the probability of disaster times the payoff to disaster, $R_C d_C$, plus the probability that there will not be a disaster, $1 - R_C$, times the payoff to this. By assumption, the challenger's adversary (i.e., the defender) is certain to quit if it has an opportunity to do so, and it will have an opportunity if there is not a disaster. This means that the challenger's payoff if there is no disaster after it escalates will be w_C. Thus, the expected payoff to escalating is $R_C d_C + (1 - R_C)w_C$. Quitting will bring s_C; so indifference implies $R_C d_C + (1 - R_C)w_C = s_C$. Resolve is given by $R_C = (w_C - s_C)/(w_C - d_C)$. Similarly, the defender's resolve is given by $R_D = (w_D - s_D)/(w_D - d_D)$. Note that a state's resolve is actually only an upper bound on the risk that a state is willing to run at any particular stage in the crisis, because a state generally will be unsure whether or not its adversary will quit at its next opportunity. If there is some chance that its adversary will not quit immediately, then that reduces the expected payoff to the state of escalating, which in turn reduces the level of risk required to make the state indifferent between escalating and submitting.

A state's resolve may be used to determine the last information set at which a state might be willing to escalate. In terms of the brinkmanship analogy, this information set is the last spot on the curved slope leading to the abyss at which the inherent risk of taking another step is still less than the state's resolve. This, therefore, is the last point at which the state would be willing to take another step toward the chasm even if it were sure that if it stepped forward and there was not a disaster, then its adversary would submit immediately. This place, this information set, turns out to be crucial to finding the game's sequential equilibria. By definition, a state clearly will not escalate if to do so it must create a risk of disaster greater than its resolve. Letting M_C denote the greatest integer m that satisfies $2m\delta < R_C$, then $\Omega_C(M_C)$ is the last information set at which C could rationally decide to escalate.[8] If $m > M_C$, then escalating at $\Omega_C(m)$ would generate too great a risk, and C prefers to submit. Similarly, let M_D be the largest m satisfying $(2m - 1)\delta < R_D$. Then $\Omega_D(M_D)$ is the last information set at which D might escalate.

Now define the state with the greatest *effective resolve* to be the state that can be closer to the brink before the inherent risk of taking another step

---

[8] This statement is not strictly correct. In the special circumstances in which $2m\delta < R_C$ but $2(m + 1)\delta = R_C$, then $\Omega_C(m + 1)$, not $\Omega_C(m)$, is the last information set at which C might escalate. This possibility will be disregarded because this work will focus throughout on generic properties, and the statement that the largest m satisfying $2m\delta < R_C$ makes $\Omega_C(m)$ the last information set at which C might escalate is generically true. Informally, a proposition is generically true if it holds except in a small set of circumstances. More formally, a statement is generically true if the closure of the set of payoffs at which the statement is false has measure zero (Kreps and Wilson 1982b, p. 877).

forward is too high. So C has the greatest effective resolve if $M_C \geq M_D$, and D has the greatest effective resolve if $M_D > M_C$. Given these definitions, the state with the greatest effective resolve prevails in the unique sequential equilibrium. More formally:

> **Proposition 3.1:** *The extensive game with complete information has a unique sequential equilibrium. If $M_C \geq M_D$, C prevails in this equilibrium, and if $M_D > M_C$, D prevails in the sense that C does not challenge the status quo.*[9]

Proof: Given the simple information structure of the game (i.e., that all of the information sets are singletons, so that there is perfect information), finding the sequential equilibrium amounts to finding a strategy for each state at each of its information sets, that is, specifying $a_C(m)$ and $e_C(m)$ for $0 \leq m \leq K/2$ and $a_D(m)$ and $e_D(m)$ for $1 \leq m < K/2$ such that at no place in the game tree can a state gain by deviating from its strategy given its adversary's strategy. The sequential equilibrium is found through backward programming. Assume $M_C \geq M_D$. (The proof is identical if $M_D > M_C$.) By definition, $\Omega_C(M_C)$ is the last information set at which C would escalate if it were certain that D would then submit. Accordingly, C will quit at all information sets coming after $\Omega_C(M_C)$. C's unique best response at any of these information sets is to submit. The risk of escalation is simply too high; so $a_C^*(m) = 0$ and $e_C^*(m) = 0$ for $M_C < m \leq K/2$. (An asterisk denotes an equilibrium strategy.) Similarly, D's best response at $\Omega_D(m)$ for $M_D < m \leq K/2$ is submission: $a_D^*(m) = 0$ and $e_D^*(m) = 0$. C again has a unique best reply at $\Omega_C(m)$ for $M_D \leq m \leq M_C$. The risk of escalating given that D will quit immediately thereafter is now acceptable: $a_C^*(m) = 0$ and $e_C^*(m) = 1$. Given C's strategy of escalating at $\Omega_C(m)$ for $M_D \leq m \leq M_C$, D's only best response at $\Omega_D(M_D)$ is to submit. Given that the defender is submitting at $\Omega_D(M_D)$, C again has a unique best reply. At $\Omega_C(M_D - 1)$, C escalates: $e_C^*(M_D - 1) = 1$. Given that C escalates at $\Omega_C(m)$ for $M_D - 1 \leq m \leq M_C$, D's best response at $\Omega_D(M_D - 1)$ is to quit. This process eventually yields a combination of equilibrium strategies in which C escalates with probability 1 for $0 \leq m \leq M_C$ and submits with probability 1 for $M_C < m \leq K/2$

---

[9] The definition of effective resolve finesses a small point. Although the state with the greatest effective resolve prevails, it is not quite the case that the state with the greatest resolve prevails. To see this, recall that M_C and M_D must satisfy $2M_C\delta < R_C < 2(M_C + 1)\delta$ and $(2M_D - 1)\delta < R_D < (2M_D + 1)\delta$. Hence, $[2(M_D - M_C) - 3]\delta < R_D - R_C < [2(M_D - M_C) + 1]\delta$. Now, if $M_D - M_C$ equals 1 or 0, then both small positive and negative values of $R_D - R_C$ can satisfy these inequalities. Thus, because of the discrete bidding structure, if M_C and M_D are sufficiently close together, it may be that D will prevail even though C's resolve is greater. This occurs if, for example, $M_D - M_C = 1$, so that $M_D > M_C$, and if $R_D - R_C < 0$, so that $R_C > R_D$.

and in which D quits with probability 1 for all m. Because all of the best replies are unique and there is only one set of consistent beliefs, this equilibrium is also the unique sequential equilibrium.   ■

Thus, modeling the autonomous risk of disaster generated by escalation explicitly as Nature's move and requiring equilibria to be sequential in a well-defined game will yield some of the conclusions suggested by previous analyses of brinkmanship and deterrence. No state attaches any positive probability to launching a massive nuclear attack: $a_C^*(m) = 0$ and $a_D^*(m) = 0$ for all m. No state ever launches a first strike deliberately. Moreover, the sequential equilibrium depends on the states' payoffs. Indeed, the game is a contest of resolve in which the state with the greatest effective resolve prevails.

But note that there are no sequential crisis equilibria. That is, there are no sequential equilibria that are also crisis equilibria. If the balance of effective resolve favors the potential challenger, it will challenge the defender, and the defender will quit. There will be no resisted challenge and no crisis. If, conversely, the balance favors the defender, there is no challenge and still no crisis. On reflection, the fact that with complete information there are no crises is hardly surprising. If bargaining is costly, as it is when a state must bargain by generating risks of disaster, and if because of complete information one can foresee the outcome of the bargaining process, then it would seem that one should immediately agree to this outcome and thereby at least avoid the costs of bargaining.[10] Incomplete information is an essential aspect of crises.

Nuclear brinkmanship with incomplete information

The model just described formalizes two of the essential aspects of brinkmanship. There is a series of decisions, and the role of autonomous risk is represented explicitly. The third aspect of brinkmanship to be modeled is that each state has incomplete information about what type of adversary it is facing. In particular, each state is uncertain about the level of resolve of its adversary. To simplify matters still further, there are only two possible types of adversaries. The defender is unsure whether it is facing a resolute challenger, which will be denoted by C', or an irresolute challenger, C. The resolve of the resolute challenger is sufficiently high that it would be willing to take at least two steps toward the brink if that would ensure that

---

[10] This is a familiar result from game-theoretic models of bargaining. See, for example, Rubinstein (1982).

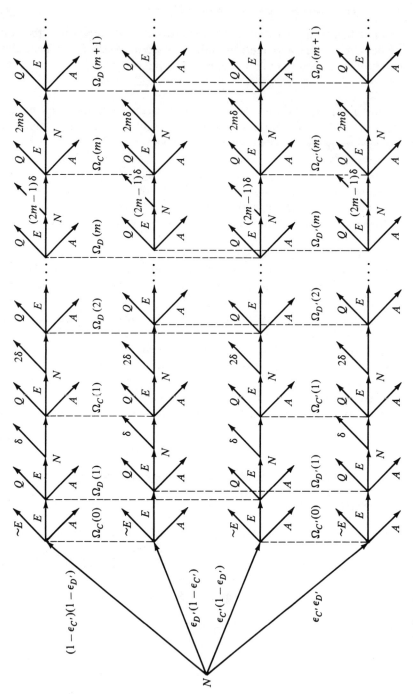

Figure 3.3. Nuclear brinkmanship with two-sided incomplete information.

it would prevail. The irresolute challenger, however, would be willing to take only one step toward the brink, and then only if it were confident enough that the defender would subsequently quit.[11] Similarly, the challenger is uncertain whether it is facing a resolute defender, D', or an irresolute defender, D. The resolute defender would be willing to take up to two steps toward the brink if it were sufficiently confident that that would coerce its adversary into submitting. The irresolute defender would, at most, be willing to take one step toward the brink to coerce the challenger into submitting.[12] Finally, the probability of facing a resolute challenger is $\varepsilon_{C'}$, and the probability of confronting an irresolute challenger is $\varepsilon_C = 1 - \varepsilon_{C'}$. The chances of facing a resolute defender are $\varepsilon_{D'}$, and the likelihood of confronting an irresolute defender is $\varepsilon_D = 1 - \varepsilon_{D'}$. These probabilities are assumed to be common knowledge.

The game's extensive form is depicted in Figure 3.3. Nature begins the game by selecting the types of the states. Starting the game this way with Nature making a random move is a standard modeling technique used to generate the uncertainty associated with the lack of complete information.[13] If Nature plays the top branch, which it will do with probability $\varepsilon_C\varepsilon_D$ or, equivalently, $(1 - \varepsilon_{C'})(1 - \varepsilon_{D'})$, then the irresolute challenger C and the irresolute defender D will actually be facing each other. If Nature takes the branch below this, which will happen with probability $\varepsilon_C\varepsilon_{D'}$, then the irresolute challenger will be confronting the resolute defender D'. If Nature takes the next branch down, which will occur with probability $\varepsilon_{C'}\varepsilon_D$, the resolute challenger C' will be opposing the irresolute defender. Finally, if Nature follows the lowest branch, which it will do with probability $\varepsilon_{C'}\varepsilon_{D'}$, the resolute challenger and resolute defender will be facing each other. Letting Nature start the game with random alternatives that are played with these probabilities formally induces each state's uncertainty about the resolve of its adversary. The challenger, for example, begins play believing that the probability that it is facing the resolute defender D' is $\varepsilon_{D'}$. When, that is, the irresolute challenger is first deciding what to do at $\Omega_C(0)$, it believes that the probability that it is facing the resolute defender D' is $\varepsilon_{D'}$.[14]

---

[11] More formally, the resolve of the resolute challenger will be taken to be greater than 4δ, which implies $M_{C'} \geq 2$. The resolve of the irresolute challenger is less. It satisfies $2\delta < R_C < 4\delta$, which leaves $M_C = 1$.

[12] The level of resolve of the resolute defender satisfies $3\delta < R_{D'} < 5\delta$, so that $M_{D'} = 2$. The resolve of the irresolute defender is less: $\delta < R_D < 3\delta$, which leaves $M_D = 1$.

[13] See the Appendix following Chapter 8 for an introduction to games with incomplete information. For more detailed discussion and some examples, see Harsanyi (1967–8), Kreps and Wilson (1982a), Milgrom and Roberts (1982), and Kreps et al. (1982).

[14] This probability is given by Bayes' rule, which describes how probabilities should be revised in light of new information. According to this rule, the probability that C will be

After the types of the states have been determined, play proceeds as described earlier, with the onus of escalation shifting back and forth until the game ends.

In Figure 3.3, a dashed line connecting two nodes in the tree indicates that these nodes are in the same information set. That is, there is no way for a state to determine if it is at one node or the other. At $\Omega_D(1)$, for example, there is no way for the defender to be certain if it is at the upper node in $\Omega_D(1)$, in which case it is facing the irresolute challenger C, or if it is at the lower node in this information set, in which case it is confronting the resolute challenger C'. Because a state is unable to determine where it is in any given information set, the state is assumed to have beliefs about where it is in this set. A state's beliefs are, moreover, shaped by its adversary's strategies. Suppose, for example, that the resolute challenger is quite likely to challenge the status quo and that the irresolute challenger is very unlikely to dispute the status quo. Then, if the status quo is challenged, so that the defender finds itself having to decide what to do at $\Omega_D(1)$, it will tend to be relatively more confident that it is facing the resolute challenger, who is likely to have challenged the status quo, rather than the irresolute challenger, who is unlikely to have done so. That is, D attaches a relatively high probability to being at the lower node in $\Omega_D(1)$ and a relatively low probability to being at the upper node. Let $\beta_D(m)$ denote the probability with which D believes that it is facing an irresolute challenger at $\Omega_D(m)$. D therefore believes that it is facing a resolute challenger, C', with probability $1 - \beta_D(m)$.

Uncertainty about the resolve of an adversary creates an incentive for developing and maintaining a reputation for being resolute. That, in turn, drives escalation, for to sustain a reputation for being resolute and to derive the benefits of it, an irresolute state must be willing to escalate. To appreciate the value of having a reputation for being resolute, suppose that the states were certain that, say, the challenger's effective resolve was greater than the defender's; then the challenger would challenge the status quo, and the defender would submit. If, conversely, the states were certain that the challenger's effective resolve was less than the defender's, the challenger would not dispute the status quo. An irresolute defender, it would seem, would like to appear resolute. Having a reputation for being resolute is

---

confronting D' at $\Omega_C(0)$ is the same as the probability that C would face D' that was calculated before the game began, namely, $\varepsilon_C\varepsilon_{D'}$, updated in light of the fact that play has reached the information set $\Omega_C(0)$ instead of $\Omega_{C'}(0)$. This latter probability is equal to the sum of the probabilities of reaching each node in $\Omega_C(0)$ or the probability of reaching the upper node, $\varepsilon_C\varepsilon_D$, plus the probability of reaching the lower node, $\varepsilon_C\varepsilon_{D'}$. The probability that C is confronting D' at $\Omega_C(0)$ is therefore $\varepsilon_C\varepsilon_{D'}/[\varepsilon_C\varepsilon_{D'} + \varepsilon_C\varepsilon_D] = \varepsilon_{D'}$. The Appendix following Chapter 8 offers an introduction to Bayesian updating of beliefs.

beneficial. But a price must be paid for these benefits, for to some extent an irresolute defender must be willing to escalate, and that entails running some risk of disaster. The sequential crisis equilibria balance these costs and benefits.

Before describing the equilibria, two remarks are in order. First, note that as with complete information, no state will ever place a positive probability on attacking in a sequential equilibrium. That is, $a_C^*(m) = a_D^*(m) = 0$ for all m. If a state did attack with positive probability, then this state could always improve its payoff by deviating from its strategy by quitting rather than attacking. But if a state can always improve its payoff by deviating from its strategy, then that strategy is not part of a sequential equilibrium. Because the probability of deliberately attacking is zero, the state's strategy at any information set can be characterized by the single probability that the state will escalate at that set.

The second remark simplifies the model further and facilitates the search for the game's equilibria. The simplification is to ensure that the resolve of the resolute challenger C' is so great that it is certain to dispute the status quo and, if necessary, take at least two steps toward the brink in order to prevail. The resolve of the resolute challenger, $R_{C'}$, is high enough so that $e_{C'}^*(0) = 1$, $e_{C'}^*(1) = 1$, and $e_{C'}^*(2) = 1$.[15] (As before, an asterisk denotes an equilibrium strategy or belief.)

The complete statements and derivations of the sequential crisis equilibria are quite cumbersome and are presented in Appendix 3.1 at the end of this chapter. Figure 3.4 summarizes some of the properties of the equilibrium strategies. There are five regions in the $(\varepsilon_{C'}, \varepsilon_{D'})$ plane, where each point in this plane corresponds to a different combination of initial or prior beliefs about the probabilities of facing a resolute challenger, $\varepsilon_{C'}$, and a resolute defender, $\varepsilon_{D'}$. In each of regions (i), (ii), (iii), and (iv) there exists a unique set of sequential equilibrium strategies.[16] (On the borders between regions, multiple equilibria exist.) NSCE denotes the region in which no sequential crisis equilibria exist. In the sequential noncrisis equilibrium that

---

[15]   This assumption simplifies the analysis because it avoids some of the difficulties of deciding what are "reasonable" conjectures or beliefs to hold off the equilibrium path by ensuring that Bayes' rule can be used to derive the states' beliefs at the relevant information sets. See the Appendix following Chapter 8 for a discussion of "reasonable" beliefs and Bayes' rule. This assumption further constrains $R_{C'}$, which has already been assumed to satisfy $R_{C'} > 4\delta$. This constraint is specified in Appendix 3.1, where the game's equilibria are derived.

[16]   Although the sequential crisis equilibrium strategies and beliefs at information sets that are reached with positive probability are unique, the beliefs at unreached information sets can be anything. These beliefs, however, do not affect the equilibrium strategies. See Appendix 3.1 for a discussion of this issue.

Figure 3.4. Types of equilibria.

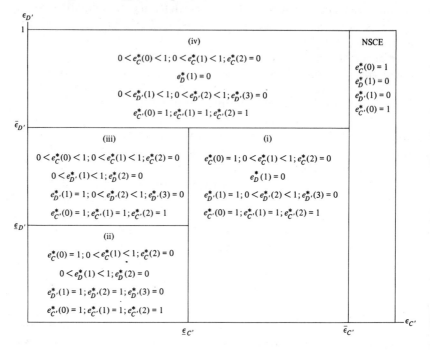

$\epsilon_{D'}$

1

	(iv)	NSCE

(iv)

$0 < e_C^*(0) < 1; 0 < e_C^*(1) < 1; e_C^*(2) = 0$

$e_D^*(1) = 0$

$0 < e_{D'}^*(1) < 1; 0 < e_{D'}^*(2) < 1; e_{D'}^*(3) = 0$

$e_{C'}^*(0) = 1; e_{C'}^*(1) = 1; e_{C'}^*(2) = 1$

NSCE

$e_C^*(0) = 1$
$e_D^*(1) = 0$
$e_{D'}^*(1) = 0$
$e_{C'}^*(0) = 1$

$\bar{\epsilon}_{D'}$

(iii)

$0 < e_C^*(0) < 1; 0 < e_C^*(1) < 1; e_C^*(2) = 0$

$0 < e_{D'}^*(1) < 1; e_{D'}^*(2) = 0$

$e_{D'}^*(1) = 1; 0 < e_{D'}^*(2) < 1; e_{D'}^*(3) = 0$

$e_{C'}^*(0) = 1; e_{C'}^*(1) = 1; e_{C'}^*(2) = 1$

(i)

$e_C^*(0) = 1; 0 < e_C^*(1) < 1; e_C^*(2) = 0$

$e_D^*(1) = 0$

$e_{D'}^*(1) = 1; 0 < e_{D'}^*(2) < 1; e_{D'}^*(3) = 0$

$e_{C'}^*(0) = 1; e_{C'}^*(1) = 1; e_{C'}^*(2) = 1$

$\underline{\epsilon}_{D'}$

(ii)

$e_C^*(0) = 1; 0 < e_C^*(1) < 1; e_C^*(2) = 0$

$0 < e_D^*(1) < 1; e_D^*(2) = 0$

$e_{D'}^*(1) = 1; e_{D'}^*(2) = 1; e_{D'}^*(3) = 0$

$e_{C'}^*(0) = 1; e_{C'}^*(1) = 1; e_{C'}^*(2) = 1$

$\epsilon_{C'}$

$\underline{\epsilon}_{C'}$ $\bar{\epsilon}_{C'}$

does exist, the challenger is certain to dispute the status quo, and neither defender resists: $e_C^*(0) = 1$, and $e_D^*(1) = e_{D'}^*(1) = 0$.[17]

The states' initial strategies are summarized for each region. In region (ii), for example, the irresolute challenger, C, is certain to dispute the status quo, $e_C^*(0) = 1$, and there is some chance that it will then take a step toward the brink if its challenge is resisted, $0 < e_C^*(1) < 1$. The irresolute challenger, however, will never take a second step toward the abyss in this or any other equilibrium. Given the irresolute challenger's resolve, the risk inherent in a

---

[17] To see that these strategies must prevail in any sequential noncrisis equilibrium, note that the probability that the irresolute challenger will dispute the status quo, $e_C^*(0)$, must be positive in a sequential equilibrium. To see this, assume $e_C^*(0) = 0$; then both defenders would be certain that the challenger was resolute if there was a challenge. This and the fact that the resolute challenger's strategy is to escalate imply that both defenders' best replies are to submit: $e_D^*(1) = e_{D'}^*(1) = 0$. But if the defenders are certain not to resist, then the challenger's best response is to dispute the status quo: $e_C^*(0) = 1$. This contradicts the assumption that $e_C^*(0) = 0$, and this contradiction implies that $e_C^*(0) > 0$ in a sequential equilibrium. But in a sequential noncrisis equilibrium there can be no chance of a resisted challenge. This means that $e_D^*(1) = e_{D'}^*(1) = 0$, for if either were positive, there would be some chance of a resisted challenge. Given that $e_D^*(1) = e_{D'}^*(1) = 0$ in any sequential noncrisis equilibrium, C's best reply is to dispute the status quo: $e_C^*(0) = 1$.

second step, 4δ, is too great; so $e_C^*(2) = 0$. The chances that the irresolute defender, D, will resist if challenged are between 0 and 1: $0 < e_D^*(1) < 1$. But the inherent risk of its taking a second step is too large. D therefore will never take this step; so $e_D^*(2) = 0$. The resolute defender in region (ii) is certain to take two steps toward the chasm: $e_{D'}^*(1) = 1$ and $e_{D'}^*(2) = 1$. But after that, the inherent risk of taking a third step is too high. In this equilibrium and the equilibria in other regions, $e_{D'}^*(3) = 0$. Finally, the resolve of the resolute challenger is, by assumption, sufficiently high that it is sure to dispute the status quo and then escalate twice in order to prevail: $e_{C'}^*(0) = 1$, $e_{C'}^*(1) = 1$, and $e_{C'}^*(2) = 1$.

To examine some of the relations among these equilibria, suppose that the probability of facing a resolute challenger is relatively high [i.e., $\varepsilon_{C'} > \bar{\varepsilon}_{C'}$], and the risk of facing a resolute defender is relatively low [i.e., $\varepsilon_{D'} < \underline{\varepsilon}_{D'}$]. In these circumstances, both types of challengers are sure to dispute the status quo: $e_C^*(0) = e_{C'}^*(0) = 1$. Because both types of challengers would behave identically, the defender will learn nothing about the type of the challenger from observing what it does. In particular, the fact that there has actually been a challenge reveals nothing about the challenger. The updated probability that the defender is facing a resolute challenger after a challenge, which, recall, is denoted by $1 - \beta_D(1)$, is the same as the initial probability of facing a resolute challenger: $1 - \beta_D(1) = \varepsilon_{C'}$. Thus, when the prior probability of facing a resolute challenger is high, the updated probability is also high. Indeed, the defender is so confident that the challenger is actually resolute that it never resists the challenge: $e_D^*(1) = e_{D'}^*(1) = 0$.

Now imagine holding the prior probability of facing a resolute defender, $\varepsilon_{D'}$, constant and letting the initial probability of confronting a resolute challenger, $\varepsilon_{C'}$, fall. Graphically, this amounts to approaching region (i) from the right, with $\varepsilon_{D'} < \underline{\varepsilon}_{D'}$. As the prior probability of facing a resolute challenger drops, the defender's expected payoff to resisting a challenge rises if the resolute and irresolute challengers' strategies do not change. At the border between region (i) and the region in which no sequential crisis equilibrium exists, NSCE, the resolute defender may for the first time both resist a challenge and credibly threaten to take a second step toward the brink if the challenger replies to the defender's initial resistance with escalation. Indeed, in the unique sequential crisis equilibrium in region (i), the resolute defender is certain to resist a challenge [$e_{D'}^*(1) = 1$], and there is some chance that it will then take a second step toward the brink: $0 < e_{D'}^*(2) < 1$.

It may at first seem surprising that the resolute defender goes from being unwilling to take a single step toward the abyss to being willing to take two steps rather than only one. But the resolute defender can never be willing to take only one step toward the brink in a sequential crisis equilibrium. If D' were willing to take only one step, then both the resolute challenger and irresolute challenger would know that if they met the defender's resistance with escalation, which they would do at $\Omega_C(1)$ and $\Omega_{C'}(1)$ in Figure 3.3, then the resolute defender, by assumption, would be unwilling to take a second step and would submit. Consequently, both C and C' would escalate, for even the irresolute challenger is sufficiently resolute that it would escalate one step if it were sure that the defender would then quit. But it would make no sense for the resolute defender to escalate one step if the challenger, regardless of type, was then certain to escalate, after which the resolute defender would submit. The best that escalating could bring D' would be the payoff to submitting, $s_{D'}$, and there would be some chance that it could bring the disastrous payoff of $d_{D'}$. But the resolute defender can assure itself of $s_{D'}$ and avoid any risk of disaster by simply not resisting a challenge. If, therefore, the resolute defender is unwilling to take a second step, then it strictly prefers to quit rather than resist a challenge. Thus, being willing to escalate once, but not twice, cannot be part of a sequential crisis equilibrium.

As the defender becomes less and less afraid of facing a resolute challenger [i.e., as $\varepsilon_{C'}$ falls and graphically one moves across (i) to the left], the resolute and irresolute challengers remain certain to dispute the status quo. A challenge still reveals nothing about the actual resolve of the challenger, and the updated probability of facing a resolute challenger after a challenge is the same as the prior probability: $1 - \beta_D(1) = \varepsilon_{C'}$. If the challenge is resisted, the resolute challenger will be certain to escalate: $e_C^*(1) = 0$. But there is some chance that the irresolute challenger will not escalate if its challenge is resisted: $0 < e_C^*(1) < 1$. If, therefore, the challenger takes a step toward the brink after its challenge has been resisted, the defender will update its probability of facing an irresolute challenger. According to Bayes' rule, this updated belief is $\beta_D^*(2) = \beta_D^*(2) = \varepsilon_c e_C^*(1)/ [\varepsilon_{C'} + \varepsilon_c e_C^*(1)]$. As the defender's prior probability of facing a resolute challenger, $\varepsilon_{C'}$, falls in moving across (i), then for a fixed $e_C^*(1)$, the defender is increasingly confident of facing an irresolute challenger.[18] But the more confident the defender is of facing an irresolute challenger, the higher is the defender's expected payoff to taking a second step, for if the defender takes a second step and the challenger really is irresolute, it will quit, and the defender will prevail. In region (i), however, the resolute defender uses a mixed strategy if the challenger takes a step toward the brink after there has been a resisted challenge [i.e., D' uses a mixed strategy at $\Omega_{D'}(2)$]. Mixing means that the resolute defender must be indifferent between acquiescing

---

[18] Recalling that $1 - \varepsilon_C = \varepsilon_{C'}$, then $\partial\beta_D^*(2)/\partial\varepsilon_{C'} = \partial[(1 - \varepsilon_{C'})e_C^*(1)/[\varepsilon_{C'} + (1 - \varepsilon_{C'})e_C^*(1)]]/\partial\varepsilon_{C'} < 0$.

and escalating at $\Omega_{D'}(2)$.[19] Accordingly, the probability that the irresolute challenger will take a step toward the abyss must change in order to offset the falling $\varepsilon_{C'}$ and maintain the resolute defender's indifference. In particular, the irresolute challenger must become less likely to escalate as the prior probability of facing a resolute challenger falls (i.e., as $\varepsilon_{C'}$ decreases). The probability $e_C^*(1)$ falls as one moves across region (i) toward (ii).[20]

Equilibrium (i) formally illustrates an important point. Sometimes states may follow a strategy of bluffing. A state may escalate even if it is certain that its adversary's resolve is greater than its own. The irresolute defender D is so confident that it is facing the resolute challenger C' that it never escalates: $e_D^*(m) = 0$ for all m. Because the resolute defender never escalates, resistance unambiguously signals that the defender is resolute. Thus, the challenger in equilibrium (i) is certain that it is facing the resolute defender if its challenge is actually resisted. Surprisingly, however, C may not submit although it is certain that its adversary is resolute. There is some chance that the irresolute challenger will escalate: $0 < e_C^*(1) < 1$. The justification for this seemingly irrational act is that the resolute defender D' is uncertain of the challenger's resolve. In fact, the resolute defender is so confident that it is facing the resolute challenger that the chances that the resolute defender will submit are sufficiently large that it is worth it to the irresolute challenger C to exploit the resolute defender's uncertainty by escalating. So the irresolute challenger escalates even though it is certain that its adversary's resolve is greater than its own. This underscores an important point that is rarely mentioned in discussions about crisis bargaining and escalation. Of course, a state's beliefs about the resolve of its adversary are important, but so are its beliefs about its adversary's beliefs. If a state believes that its adversary believes that the state is resolute, then the state may escalate even if it is actually irresolute.

Both the probability of facing a resolute challenger and the probability that an irresolute challenger will escalate, $e_C^*(1)$, decrease as one moves to the left across (i). This raises the defender's expected payoff to resisting a challenge. Eventually, the irresolute defender, which initially preferred quitting to resisting, becomes indifferent to quitting and resisting. This defines the border between (i) and (ii).

In region (ii), the irresolute challenger remains certain to dispute the status quo. So updating the prior probability of facing an irresolute challenger does not change this probability: $\beta_D^*(1) = \beta_{D'}^*(1) = \varepsilon_C$. Thus, in moving across (ii) to the left, the probability of facing an irresolute

---

[19] The Appendix following Chapter 8 explains this implication of mixed equilibrium strategies.

[20] That is, $\partial e_C^*(1)/\partial \varepsilon_{C'} > 0$ in region (i).

challenger, given that there has been a challenge, $\beta_D^*(1)$, rises. This means that if the chance that an irresolute challenger will escalate if it meets resistance is fixed [i.e., if $e_C^*(1)$ is fixed], then the defender's expected payoff to resisting a challenge will also rise as it becomes more confident of facing an irresolute challenger. But in this equilibrium the irresolute defender D uses a mixed strategy if there is a challenge; so it must be indifferent between resisting and quitting at $\Omega_D(1)$. Thus, the chances that the irresolute challenger will meet resistance with escalation must rise as the prior probability of facing an irresolute challenger rises in region (ii) in order to keep the irresolute defender indifferent.[21] But if the irresolute defender is indifferent to resisting or quitting, the more resolute defender must strictly prefer resistance. This implies $e_{D'}^*(1) = 1$.

Now consider the consequences of holding the probability of facing a resolute challenger constant and letting the chances of facing a resolute defender increase. Graphically, this amounts to moving upward from (ii) toward (iv). If the prior probability of facing an irresolute defender, ε_D, is falling, and the chance that this defender will resist a challenge, $e_D^*(1)$, does not change, then the challenger will become increasingly confident that the defender is resolute if the defender does, in fact, resist a challenge.[22] This drives down the challenger's expected payoff to escalating, for if the challenger escalates and is actually confronting an irresolute defender, this defender will submit immediately: $e_D^*(2) = 0$. If, however, the defender is resolute, it is sure to escalate: $e_{D'}^*(2) = 1$. Thus, as the chances of facing a resolute defender rise, the expected payoff to escalating at $\Omega_C(1)$ falls as long as the probability that the irresolute defender will resist is fixed. But in equilibrium (ii), the challenger must be indifferent between escalating and submitting if there has been a resisted challenge, because the challenger employs a mixed strategy here: $0 < e_C^*(1) < 1$. This means that as one moves up across (ii) and the prior probability of facing a resolute defender rises, the chances of the irresolute defender resisting a challenge, $e_D^*(1)$, must rise in order to leave the updated probability of facing a resolute defender unchanged if there has been a resisted challenge and thereby keep the irresolute challenger indifferent between escalating and submitting.[23]

Eventually, the defender must be certain to resist if the irresolute challenger is to remain indifferent to escalating or submitting after a resisted challenge. Where this occurs defines the border between regions (ii) and (iii). If the prior probability of facing a resolute defender continues to rise and one moves into region (iii), the irresolute

---

[21] Or, equivalently, $\partial e_C^*(1)/\partial \varepsilon_{C'} < 0$ in region (ii).

[22] More formally, the chances of facing a resolute defender given a resisted challenge, $1 - \beta_C^*(1) = \varepsilon_{D'}/[\varepsilon_{D'} + \varepsilon_D e_D^*(1)]$, are increasing in $\varepsilon_{D'}$.

[23] That is, $\partial e_D^*(1)/\partial \varepsilon_{D'} > 0$.

defender can no longer sustain the irresolute challenger's indifference. The challenger is too confident that the defender is resolute and strictly prefers to quit. But this cannot be an equilibrium, for if the irresolute challenger is certain not to escalate after a resisted challenge, then the defender infers from escalation that the challenger is resolute. In these circumstances, the defender's best strategy is to quit and not escalate as it would in equilibrium (ii). Thus, if the prior probability of facing a resolute defender is too high, equilibrium (ii) collapses, and (iii) emerges.

For the first time there is some chance that the irresolute challenger will not dispute the status quo. As one moves up across (iii), the probability of facing a resolute defender when the challenger is contemplating disputing the status quo, $1 - \beta_C^*(0) = \varepsilon_{D'}$, rises. But in this equilibrium the irresolute challenger must be indifferent between disputing and accepting the status quo. Thus, as the irresolute challenger becomes more confident that the defender is resolute and this tends to reduce the payoff to challenging the status quo, the probability of resistance must fall to keep the irresolute challenger indifferent. In particular, the irresolute defender becomes less and less likely to resist: $e_D^*(1)$ declines as $\varepsilon_{D'}$ rises. The reason that the resolute defender does not also become less likely to escalate is that because it is more resolute, it strictly prefers to resist whenever the less resolute defender is, as in region (iii), indifferent between resisting and acquiescing. Because the irresolute defender uses a mixed strategy and must therefore be indifferent between resisting and submitting if challenged, the combined probability that the irresolute challenger will dispute the status quo, $e_C^*(0)$, and the chances that it will subsequently escalate if its challenge is resisted, $e_C^*(1)$, must keep the irresolute defender indifferent. The former probability contributes to this by affecting the irresolute defender's beliefs about the resolve of the challenger if there is actually a challenge. The less likely the irresolute challenger is to mount a challenge, the more confident the defender is that the challenger is resolute if there is really a challenge. The chances that the irresolute defender will escalate if its challenge is resisted, $e_C^*(1)$, influences the irresolute defender's expected payoff to resisting by affecting the payoff to escalating if the challenger is actually irresolute. The more likely this challenger is to escalate, the lower the expected payoff to resisting a challenge.

As the prior probability of confronting a resolute defender rises and one moves upward across (iii), the chances that the irresolute defender will resist fall. Finally, the irresolute defender must be certain to quit [i.e., $e_D^*(1) = 0$] in order to keep the irresolute challenger indifferent between disputing and accepting the status quo. This defines the border between (iii) and (iv). If the initial chances of confronting a resolute defender rise still further, then in region (iv) the irresolute challenger is too fearful of a resolute defender and now strictly prefers to quit. But this means that if there is a challenge, the defenders are sure that the challenger is resolute and therefore prefer quitting to resisting. Equilibrium (iii) collapses, and (iv) emerges. The resolute defender in (iv) plays a role like the one that the irresolute defender played in (iii). The resolute defender's strategy keeps the irresolute challenger indifferent between disputing and accepting the status quo and between escalating and quitting if there is a resisted challenge.

Resolve, misperception, the status quo, and the dynamics of escalation

How do changes in the level of resolve, in the degree of misperception, and in the value of the status quo affect crisis stability and the dynamics of escalation in the model? The equilibrium strategies just described and fully specified in Appendix 3.1 make it possible to begin to study these effects. For example, the consequences of the challenger's having a greater stake in the status quo may be determined by examining how the states' strategies change as q_C varies. To some extent, an analysis of changes in the level of resolve, in the degree of misperception, and in the value of the status quo is complicated by the existence of four equilibria that tend to be inversely related. An increase in the irresolute challenger's resolve due to a higher return to prevailing (i.e., to an increase in w_C) makes the irresolute defender D less likely to resist a challenge in equilibrium (ii) but more likely to do so in equilibrium (iii). Nevertheless, the four equilibria do support some generalizations. The characterization of a brinkmanship crisis as a contest of resolve can be misleading. Moreover, reducing the level of misperception may reduce, not increase, crisis stability. Finally, an increase in the irresolute potential challenger's stake in the status quo does make a crisis less likely, as one might intuitively expect, but not necessarily by making the potential challenger less likely to dispute the status quo. Rather, stability may increase because the defender is less likely to resist a challenge.

Before taking up this examination, two preliminary observations are in order. First, the model is very simple, and the states use mixed strategies in the sequential crisis equilibria. This makes the empirical significance of the interactions that will be discussed difficult to assess.[24] Are the interactions artifacts of the model, or do they reflect an underlying empirical phenomenon? Absent empirical evaluation, the development of richer, better models may shed some light on this. If these interactions exist in a wide variety of models, one may be more confident that the interactions are

---

[24] For a discussion of some of the issues involved in interpreting mixed equilibria, see Luce and Raiffa (1957), Harsanyi (1973), Harsanyi and Selten (1988), and the Appendix that follows Chapter 8.

not artifacts of a particular model. But for now, the empirical significance of these interactions must remain tentative.[25]

The second observation is that although each state is uncertain of its adversary's resolve, as modeled by letting Nature begin the game by randomly selecting the levels of resolve, the phenomenon being modeled is a crisis in which each state's resolve, though unknown to its adversary, is fixed. Viewed in this way, the equilibria describe the escalatory dynamics of four different types of crises. These types are described by the types of states that are actually facing each other in the crisis. For example, in a crisis in which both states are actually irresolute, escalation follows the dynamic specified by the strategies of C and D. If, however, the actual crisis involves two resolute states, then the interaction of the strategies of C' and D' will determine the pattern of escalation. Let (C, D), (C, D'), (C', D), and (C', D') denote these crises.

Although there are four distinct types of crises, and each has its own escalatory dynamic, it is important to realize that these types of crises cannot be separated completely. They are linked by the states' beliefs. For example, an actual crisis of type (C, D) is linked to (C, D') because the actual challenger, C, is uncertain of the type of its adversary. C does not know if it is facing the irresolute defender D or the resolute defender D'. That is, C does not know if it is in (C, D) or (C, D'). Indeed, C believes that it is in (C, D) with probability ε_D and in (C, D') with probability $\varepsilon_{D'}$. Similarly, the beliefs of D link the actual crisis (C, D) to (C', D). This linkage means that a crisis cannot be described solely in terms of the resolve of the states actually in the crisis. The states' beliefs about the levels of resolve or, more generally, the potential types of their adversaries are also integral parts of the description of a crisis.

Crisis stability

The existence of different types of crises naturally leads to questions about their relative stability. Intuition suggests that a crisis in which both states are resolute should be more likely to end in war and hence should be less stable than a crisis in which only one state is resolute. Furthermore, a crisis

---

[25] Indeed, Nalebuff (1986) offers a model of brinkmanship in which each state's adversary may come from a continuum of types rather than just being one of two types as in the current model. With a continuum of types, there is a pure-strategy equilibrium, and the interactions in it are quite different from those in the model developed here. For example, the state with the greatest resolve always prevails, and there is no bluffing. But in the model about to be examined, the state with the greatest resolve does not always prevail, and, as already shown, there is bluffing in that a state may escalate even though it is certain that its adversary's resolve is greater than its own.

in which one state is resolute should be less stable than a crisis in which neither state is resolute. As will be shown, the model supports this intuition.

Crisis stability usually is taken to be a measure of the likelihood that a crisis will end in war. The more stable the crisis, the less likely is war. This idea is easily formalized in the model. For example, the probability that a crisis of, say, type (C, D') will end in war is the probability that the first step toward the brink will immediately lead to disaster, which is δ, plus the probability that after the first step does not lead immediately to disaster, a second step will be taken, and it will lead directly to disaster, which is $(1 - \delta)e_C^*(1)2\delta$, plus the probability that after the first and second steps do not lead directly to disaster, a third step will be taken, and it will lead to disaster, $(1 - \delta)e_C^*(1)(1 - 2\delta)e_D^*(2)3\delta$. Because the crisis is of type (C, D'), no one is willing to run the risk of a fourth step; so there is no additional risk. Pulling all of this together and letting $P_W((C, D'))$ denote the probability that the crisis will end in disaster, then

$$P_W((C, D')) = \delta + (1 - \delta)e_C^*(1)2\delta + (1 - \delta)e_C^*(1)(1 - 2\delta)e_{D'}^*(2)3\delta$$

The probability that a crisis will not end in disaster is $1 - P_W$, and this will be taken as the measure of crisis stability.

P_W is calculated from the point in the game tree in Figure 3.2 at which Nature first has a chance to play disaster. At this point, there is a crisis: There has been a resisted challenge. Calculating P_W in this way raises an issue that will become important later, but should be introduced here because it affects the way that P_W is calculated. The probability that a situation of type (C, D') will end in disaster will not be calculated from where Nature first has a chance to impose disaster. Rather, this probability will be calculated from the point in the game tree after Nature has chosen the types to be C and D', but before the states actually begin to play. Put another way, *situational stability* is evaluated from the point at which a potential challenger is deciding whether or not to exploit the situation by challenging the status quo. It is the probability that a situation will not escalate to disaster. For a (C, D') situation, this probability will be calculated from $\Omega_C(0)$. Letting S_W denote the probability $e_C^*(0)e_{D'}^*(1)P_W$, then $1 - S_W$ measures situational stability. In general, situational stability will not equal crisis stability, and, more important, changes in the model's parameters that, for example, increase situational stability may not increase crisis stability. Thus, the distinction between crisis stability and situational stability or, more generally, the distinction between statements made about a historical sample that includes only crises and statements about a historical sample that includes situations that could have become crises, but did not, is sometimes crucial. Indeed, this distinction will play an important role in the discussion of the effects of changes in the degree of misperception on stability, as well as in the analysis of the distribution of crises. However, the following conclusions about the relative stability of the four types of crises hold for both crisis stability and situational stability.

The types of crises and situations may be ranked by noting that a resolute state is always at least as likely to escalate as its irresolute counterpart, and sometimes it is more likely to escalate. This implies that a severe crisis that entails a grave conflict of interest because both sides are resolute is more dangerous and less stable than a crisis in which only one state is resolute. A minor crisis in which neither state is resolute is less dangerous and more stable than one in which one or both states are resolute. Symbolically, $P_W((C', D')) > P_W((C', D)) > P_W((C, D))$, and $P_W((C', D')) > P_W((C, D')) > P_W((C, D))$.[26] The model agrees with the intuitive ranking of these crises' relative stability.

Resolve

Brinkmanship crises often are described as contests of resolve and competitions in taking risks (Schelling 1966; Jervis 1979–80, 1984). The effect of such description is that it shifts the emphasis away from a contest of military strength, which was central to the classical logic of war, and focuses it on each state's resolve, that is, on each state's willingness to run the risk of disaster. In this way, the description of a crisis as a contest of resolve captures much of the essence of brinkmanship and the approach to nuclear deterrence based on the strategy that leaves something to chance and the array of risk. But the model indicates that this description may also be misleading if it is used to draw inferences about the dynamics of brinkmanship crises. The description suggests many propositions that do not hold in the model.

One of these propositions is that the state "willing to run the greatest risks will prevail" (Jervis 1979–80, p. 631). Recall that the irresolute challenger C in equilibrium (i) is certain that it is facing a more resolute adversary if its challenge is resisted. Nevertheless, C exploits the defender's uncertainty about the challenger's resolve by escalating with probability $e_C^*(1) > 0$. The irresolute challenger, certain that its adversary's resolve is

[26] To see this, note that

$$P_W((C', D')) = \delta + (1-\delta)e_C^*(1)2\delta + (1-\delta)e_C^*(1)(1-2\delta)e_{D'}^*(2)3\delta$$
$$+ (1-\delta)e_C^*(1)(1-2\delta)e_D^*(2)(1-3\delta)e_{C'}^*(2)4\delta$$

and $P_W((C', D)) = \delta + (1-\delta)e_C^*(1)2\delta$. This implies $P_W((C', D')) > P_W((C', D))$. But $P_W((C, D)) = \delta + (1-\delta)e_C^*(1)2\delta$. So $P_W((C', D)) > P_W((C, D))$ because $e_C^*(1) > e_C^*(1)$.

greater, is playing a strategy of pure bluff. But in a (C, D') crisis, C will prevail with probability $(1 - \delta)e_C^*(1)(1 - 2\delta)(1 - e_{D'}^*(2))$ in equilibrium (i). Sometimes bluffing works, and the state with the least resolve prevails.[27]

A second inference suggested by the notion of a contest of resolve and, somewhat more formally, by critical-risk models of crisis bargaining is that the greater the resolve of a state's adversary, the less likely that state is to escalate (Ellsberg 1959; Jervis 1972, 1978; Snyder and Diesing 1977). The reasoning here is that the greater an adversary's resolve, the more likely it is to stand firm, and thus the greater the risk of disaster if the state also stands firm. This greater risk of disaster then makes the state less likely to stand firm. This argument does not hold in the brinkmanship model. An increase in an adversary's resolve may make a state more, not less, likely to escalate. In equilibria (ii) and (iii), an increase in D's resolve makes C more likely to escalate.[28]

This difference is troubling. The argument that the greater an adversary's resolve, the less likely a state should be to escalate seems to follow. Yet this conclusion does not hold in the model. What accounts for the disparity between this argument and its formal counterpart? The model makes it possible to trace the various factors at work more clearly, and this shows that the former argument, on closer examination, leaves out important interactions. Suppose, as argued, that an increase in the irresolute defender's level of resolve R_D made it more likely to escalate, and therefore the irresolute challenger C less likely to escalate at $\Omega_C(1)$ in the face of resistance. This, however, is not the end of the analysis of the effects of the increase in R_D. Consider C's original decision of whether or not to dispute the status quo. With the irresolute defender more likely to resist, and C less likely to meet resistance with escalation, the challenger's payoff to disputing the status quo decreases. This makes C less likely to dispute the status quo. But the irresolute challenger's being less likely to dispute the status quo affects the defender's beliefs about the challenger's resolve. Because the irresolute challenger is less likely to dispute the status quo, the irresolute defender will be less confident that it is facing the irresolute challenger and more confident that it is confronting the resolute challenger if there is a challenge to the status quo. Being less confident of facing the irresolute challenger reduces the irresolute defender's expected payoff to resisting and tends to make it less likely to resist. But if the irresolute defender is now less likely to resist a challenge, the payoff to mounting a challenge rises, and the irresolute challenger will have an incentive to alter its strategy. This, in turn,

---

[27] See, however, Nalebuff (1986) for a model of brinkmanship in which the state with the greatest resolve does prevail.

[28] More formally, $\partial e_C^*(1)/\partial R_D > 0$.

will give the irresolute defender an incentive to change its strategy, and so on and so forth. The argument that the greater an adversary's resolve, the less likely a state is to escalate leaves out the complicated interactions between strategies and beliefs that are summarized in the equilibrium strategies.

The effects of changes in an adversary's resolve may also differ depending on the stage of the crisis. In equilibrium (iii), an increase in D's resolve in a (C, D) crisis makes the irresolute challenger C initially less likely to exploit the situation. But if the challenger overcomes its greater initial reluctance to dispute the status quo, it will pursue its challenge more tenaciously in that it is more likely to escalate if its reluctantly made challenge is resisted. That is, an increase in R_D reduces $e_C^*(0)$, but raises $e_C^*(1)$.[29]

Another proposition that might easily be thought to follow from the description of a crisis as a contest of resolve is that a state should be more likely to prevail the greater its resolve. The greater a state's resolve, the argument might go, the less likely its adversary is to stand firm, and consequently the more likely the state is to prevail. Again, the model indicates that this argument is problematic. It also leaves out many complicating interactions between a state's strategies and its adversary's beliefs. When, as has just been shown, these interactions are taken into account, an increase in a state's level of resolve may make an adversary more likely to escalate in the model. But the more likely a state's adversary is to escalate, the less likely this state is to prevail. Having greater resolve may not make prevailing more likely.[30]

Perhaps the least demanding proposition suggested by the notion of a contest of resolve is that the states' levels of resolve summarize enough information about the payoff structure of the situation to determine their strategies.[31] That is, the states' strategies should depend on a combination of payoffs that can be reduced to an expression involving only the states' levels of resolve. But even that is not the case. In equilibrium (iii), for example, $e_D^*(1)$ and $e_D^*(2)$ depend on a combination of the payoffs of C that cannot be reduced to an expression involving only the states' levels of resolve. In the contest of resolve, resolve does not even fully describe the dynamics of the contest.

In sum, many propositions that seem to follow from the description of a contest of resolve do not hold in the model. Describing a brinkmanship crisis as a contest of resolve may obscure more than it clarifies.

---

[29] $\partial e_C^*(0)/\partial R_D < 0$, but $\partial e_C^*(1)/\partial R_D > 0$.

[30] More formally, the probability that D will prevail in equilibrium (ii) is the probability of facing the irresolute challenger times the probability of its submitting after a resisted challenge. That is, $\varepsilon_C e_D^*(1)(1 - \delta)(1 - e_C^*(1))$, and this decreases as R_D increases.

[31] In other words, the states' levels of resolve are sufficient statistics for their payoffs.

Misperception and crisis stability

The situation actually facing a state can be distinguished in the model from the situation that the state believes itself to be facing. Indeed, the model offers a natural measure of the degree to which a state misperceives its situation. This measure, in turn, makes it possible to examine the effects of changes in the level of misperception on crisis stability. To see how misperception will be measured, suppose, for example, that the irresolute challenger C and the irresolute defender D are actually facing each other. At $\Omega_C(0)$, the irresolute challenger believes that it is facing the resolute defender D' with probability $\varepsilon_{D'}$. Because the challenger is actually facing the irresolute defender D, the strength of its belief that it is facing the resolute defender D' (i.e., the value of $\varepsilon_{D'}$) measures the degree of the challenger's misperception about the type of its adversary. Conversely, had the challenger actually been facing the resolute defender D', then $\varepsilon_D = 1 - \varepsilon_{D'}$ would have measured the degree of misperception. Given the types of adversaries actually facing each other, the probabilities $\varepsilon_{C'}$ and $\varepsilon_{D'}$ measure their initial misperceptions. As the crisis escalates, each state revises its beliefs about its adversary in light of its actions, and this affects the degree of misperception.

Three important qualifications to this formulation of misperception must be noted before the effects of misperception are examined. First, although misperception may connote making a perceptual mistake, that is not the case here. Misperception in this context means only that a state attaches some positive probability to being in a situation that in fact it is not in. Nevertheless, the probabilities representing the state's beliefs are not mistaken in that they fully incorporate the information the state has about its situation.

The second qualification is that the probabilities $\varepsilon_{C'}$ and $\varepsilon_{D'}$ are assumed to be common knowledge. That is, each state knows the values of these probabilities, knows that the other state knows them, knows that the other state knows that it knows them, and so forth. Consequently, each state knows how badly its adversary misperceives it. For example, irresolute challenger C, knowing its type, knows that its adversary's degree of misperception is $\varepsilon_{C'}$, because C knows that its adversary believes it is facing the resolute challenger C' with probability $\varepsilon_{C'}$. This assumed knowledge of the other's degree of misperception may be a serious limitation of this formulation of misperception.

Third, recall that the model has been simplified by assuming that there are only two possible types of adversaries. With only two possible types, it is natural to measure misperception by the strength of a state's belief that it is facing one type when it is actually facing the other type of adversary. And because a single probability can be used to measure the level of misperception in this simple case, it is also natural to say that the greater this probability, the greater the level of misperception. But suppose one wanted to examine the consequences of changes in the degree of misperception in a more general context in which there were more than two possible types of adversaries. As in the simpler case, this more general case could be modeled by assuming that each state begins the game with an initial probability distribution defining its initial beliefs about the probability of its facing any particular type of adversary. The effects of different initial beliefs could then be studied by beginning the game with a different probability distribution defined over the possible types of adversaries. But given two different initial probability distributions, what does it mean to say that misperception is greater in one than in the other? If the answer to this question is to be well defined, it must be possible to rank probability distributions along a single dimension, that of a greater or lesser degree of misperception. But probability distributions may differ in many dimensions. Characterizing a normal probability distribution, for example, requires two dimensions: a mean and variance. Whether or not the many dimensions along which probability distributions may vary can be condensed into a single dimension that might sensibly be said to represent misperception is unclear. Assuming that there are only two possible types of adversaries finesses this problem in the simple models studied here. In a less restrictive setting, as in much of the existing work on the effects of misperception (Jervis 1977; Lebow 1981; Jervis et al. 1985), a natural measure of misperception is lacking, the precise meaning of a general increase in the level of misperception is unclear, and consequently one cannot study the effects of a general increase in misperception.

In the simpler case in which there is a well-defined measure of misperception, the model indicates that there is no reason to believe that crisis bargaining reduces misperception and that crises end when perceptions are sufficiently clear. Indeed, misperception often will become worse during a crisis. The equilibrium strategies and beliefs show that as the crisis unfolds, the states usually become more confident that they are facing resolute adversaries. Thus, if the crisis actually involves an irresolute state, say the crisis is of type (C, D), then the longer the crisis lasts, the greater the degree of misperception will become. C, for example, will become increasingly confident that it is facing D', whereas it is actually facing D.

Turning to the effects of changes in the initial level of misperception, there would be no crises if misperception could be completely eliminated. Each state would know its adversary's resolve, and with complete information, Proposition 3.1 shows that there would be no crises. But what if misperception is reduced but not eliminated? Table 3.1 summarizes the effects of small reductions in the degree of misperception on crisis and situational stability. (Crisis stability, it will be recalled, is a measure of the probability that the game will end in disaster once there has been a resisted challenge, whereas situational stability is the probability of disaster once Nature has selected the states' types, but before the potential challenger decides whether or not to dispute the status quo.) These effects are derived by evaluating the signs of the partial derivatives of the probability of war with respect to $\varepsilon_{C'}$ and $\varepsilon_{D'}$. Suppose, for example, the irresolute challenger C and the irresolute defender D are facing each other. P_W is the probability that a crisis of this type will end in war, and $P_W = \delta + (1 - \delta)e_C^*(1)2\delta$. The probability of the situation ending in war, S_W, is $e_C^*(0)e_D^*(1)P_W$. Now in equilibrium (iii), S_W rises as the prior probability of facing a resolute defender, $\varepsilon_{D'}$, falls: $\partial S_W/\partial \varepsilon_{D'} < 0$. The situation becomes less stable as $\varepsilon_{D'}$ decreases. But C, while actually facing D, believes that it is facing D' with probability $\varepsilon_{D'}$. As $\varepsilon_{D'}$ decreases, therefore, C's misperception decreases. The situation thus becomes less stable as misperception decreases, and a minus sign appears in the cell in the column under equilibrium (iii) and "Situation" and in row C in the (C, D) crisis rows. The other cells are evaluated in the same way: A plus sign denotes an increase in stability due to a decrease in misperception; a minus sign denotes a decrease in stability; a zero denotes no effect. Table 3.1 shows that except for C', which has been constructed so that it plays the trivial strategy of always escalating, reducing a state's misperception can be destabilizing as well as stabilizing. The effects of more accurate perceptions depend very much on the situation that is perceived more clearly.

An overdrawn example will demonstrate that reducing misperceptions

Table 3.1. *Effects of reducing misperception on crisis stability and situational stability*

Type of crisis		(i) Situation	(i) Crisis	(ii) Situation	(ii) Crisis	(iii) Situation	(iii) Crisis	(iv) Situation	(iv) Crisis
(C, D)	C	0	0	+	0	−	0	−	0
	D	+	+	−	−	+	0	+	0
(C, D')	C	0	0	0	0	+	+	+	0
	D'	+	+	−	−	+	0	+	0
(C', D)	C'	0	0	+	0	−	0	0	0
	D	0	0	0	0	0	0	0	0
(C', D')	C'	0	0	0	0	+	+	+	0
	D'	0	0	0	0	0	0	0	0

can reduce stability by making war more likely. Suppose that the defender is actually facing an irresolute challenger. But the defender also misperceives the resolve of the challenger and is very confident that the challenger is resolute. Given this misperception, the defender, as in the NSCE region in Figure 3.4, may not resist a challenge to the status quo. There will be no crisis and no chance of war. If, however, the challenger more accurately perceives the defender's low level of resolve, so that $\varepsilon_{C'} < \bar{\varepsilon}_{C'}$ in Figure 3.4, the defender may resist. This creates a crisis and some chance of war. More accurate perceptions in this case will have reduced stability.

The status quo

Detente and linkage politics are based in part on the belief that the greater the stake a potential challenger has in the status quo, the less likely this state is to put this more valuable stake at risk by challenging the status quo (Litwak 1984, pp. 89–96). Although this is an assertion about foreign policy, not about crisis bargaining, it has an obvious parallel in crisis bargaining. The greater the challenger's stake in the status quo, the less likely it will be to dispute the status quo. In the model, this parallel does not hold. An increase in the value of the status quo to the potential challenger has a more complicated effect on the escalatory dynamics. An increase in the challenger's stake in the status quo that is large enough to shift the equilibrium from one type to another may make a challenge less likely. But at least for small increases in the value of the status quo that do not affect the type of the equilibrium, a potential challenger is not less likely to make a challenge. Rather, the defender is less likely to resist.

To see formally that an increase in the value of the status quo that shifts the type of equilibrium may make a challenge less likely, consider first the effect of a large increase in the value of the status quo in equilibrium (ii). In (ii), the challenger disputes the status quo with probability 1: $e_C^*(0) = 1$. But if q_C rises, so that $\varepsilon_{D'}$, which in (ii) was less than $\varepsilon_{D'}$ in Figure 3.4, is now between $\bar{\varepsilon}_{D'}$ and $\underline{\varepsilon}_{D}$, then (iii) will now exist. But $e_C^*(0) < 1$ in (iii). Thus, the increase in the challenger's stake has reduced the probability of a challenge to the status quo.

Now consider the effects of an increase in the challenger's stake that does not shift the equilibrium. The strategies $e_C^*(0)$ and $e_C^*(1)$ do not depend on q_C.[32] Changes in q_C do not affect C's strategy. An increase in the challenger's stake in the status quo does not leave the challenger less likely to dispute the status quo. The strategies that may be affected by changes in q_C are $e_D^*(1)$, $e_{D'}^*(1)$, and $e_{D'}^*(2)$. When they are, an increase in q_C makes D and

---

[32] The Appendix following Chapter 8 discusses this property of mixed-strategy equilibria.

D' less likely to escalate if challenged. Crises thus become less likely, but only because resistance is less likely.

As with arguments assessing the effects of changes in the levels of resolve, an apparently compelling argument about the effect of the potential challenger's having a greater stake in the status quo does not hold in the model. A greater stake may not make a challenge less likely. As before, the disparity between this argument and its formal counterpart seems to arise at least in part because the former leaves out important interactions between the states' strategies and their adversaries' beliefs that the model illuminates. To trace these interactions, suppose the potential challenger's stake in the status quo q_C rises. Given the defender's strategy, the irresolute challenger C is less likely to dispute the status quo.[33] But this is not the end of the analysis. Because the irresolute challenger is less likely to dispute the status quo, the defender is more confident that the challenger is resolute if there is in fact a challenge. The higher probability of facing a resolute challenger reduces the defender's payoff to resisting a challenge, and this makes resistance less likely.[34] If, however, the defender is less likely to resist, a challenge to the status quo offers a higher payoff and is more likely to be made.[35] The irresolute C is more likely to escalate. This makes the defender more confident of facing the irresolute challenger and increases the defender's payoff to resisting. And so it goes, until in equilibrium neither state wants to deviate from its strategy given its beliefs and its adversary's strategy. The simple argument that an increase in the challenger's stake in the status quo makes a challenge less likely leaves out all of these interactions.

The distribution of crises

One consequence of the nuclear revolution is that crises "should be in peripheral areas where neither side's stake is very high" (Jervis 1986, p. 695). The model provides some weak support for the argument that the states' stakes in a brinkmanship crisis will be small. In the model, the challenger in a crisis is more likely to be irresolute than resolute. This immediately implies that crises in which both states are resolute are less likely than crises in which at least one state is irresolute. Crises entailing a severe conflict of interest should be relatively less frequent.

---

[33] More formally, if C is originally using a mixed strategy at $\Omega_C(0)$, then it is indifferent to accepting the status quo or disputing it. An increase in q_C therefore implies that C will strictly prefer to accept the status quo. The strategy $e_C(0) = 0$ is now C's best reply.

[34] With $e_C(0) = 0$, the defender is certain that it is facing the resolute challenger C' if there is a challenge: $\beta_D(1) = 0$. The defender's best reply is therefore to submit: $e_D(1) = e_{D'}(0) = 0$.

[35] If the defender is certain to submit, i.e., if $e_D(0) = e_{D'}(1) = 0$, then the irresolute challenger's payoff to disputing the status quo is greater than the payoff to accepting it. C's best reply is $e_C(0) = 1$.

To show this, suppose that the probabilities ε_C, $\varepsilon_{C'}$, ε_D, and $\varepsilon_{D'}$ measure the distribution of interests in the international system. That is, there is a mild conflict of interest underlying a situation of type (C, D), a relatively more severe conflict underlying the situations (C, D') and (C', D), in which one of the states is resolute, and a severe conflict of interest underlying the situation (C', D'), in which both states are resolute. Then the probabilities ε_C, $\varepsilon_{C'}$, ε_D, and $\varepsilon_{D'}$ define the distribution of the underlying conflicts of interest in the system. The probability of a situation of type (C, D) is $\varepsilon_C\varepsilon_D$, that for (C, D') is $\varepsilon_C\varepsilon_{D'}$, that for (C', D) is $\varepsilon_{C'}\varepsilon_D$, and that for (C', D') is $\varepsilon_{C'}\varepsilon_{D'}$.

The demonstration that the challenger is more likely to be irresolute in a crisis begins by letting Π denote the probability of a crisis (i.e., of a resisted challenge). This is given by the probability that the irresolute challenger is actually in the crisis, which is ε_C, multiplied by the probability that it will escalate, $e_C^*(0)$, multiplied by the probability that the resolute or irresolute defender will escalate, which is $\varepsilon_D e_D^*(1) + \varepsilon_{D'} e_{D'}^*(1)$, plus the probability that the resolute challenger is actually in the crisis, multiplied by the probability that it will escalate, and then multiplied by the probability that the irresolute or resolute defender will escalate. Bringing all of this together leaves

$$\Pi = \varepsilon_C e_C^*(0)[\varepsilon_D e_D^*(1) + \varepsilon_{D'} e_{D'}^*(1)] + \varepsilon_{C'}[\varepsilon_D e_D^*(1) + \varepsilon_{D'} e_{D'}^*(1)]$$

The probability of an irresolute challenger given a crisis, according to Bayes' rule, is the probability of an irresolute challenger disputing the status quo and the defender resisting divided by the probability of there being a crisis. This is

$$(1 - \varepsilon_{C'}) e_C^*(0)[(1 - \varepsilon_{D'}) e_D^*(1) + \varepsilon_{D'} e_{D'}^*(1)] / \Pi$$

Similarly, the probability of a resolute challenger is the probability of a resolute challenger mounting a challenge that is resisted divided by the probability of there being a crisis. This is

$$\varepsilon_{C'}[(1 - \varepsilon_{D'}) e_D^*(1) + \varepsilon_{D'} e_{D'}^*(1)] / \Pi$$

One can then show that $(1 - \varepsilon_{C'}) e_C^*(0) > \varepsilon_{C'}$, and this implies that the challenger is more likely to be irresolute.[36]

---

[36] To see that $(1 - \varepsilon_{C'}) e_C^*(0) > \varepsilon_{C'}$, note that greatest lower bound for the expression for $(1 - \varepsilon_{C'}) e_C^*(0)/\varepsilon_{C'}$ in equilibrium (iv) is obtained by evaluating this expression at the least upper bound of $R_{D'}$, which is 5δ. Substituting this value for $R_{D'}$ in the inequality $(1 - \varepsilon_{C'}) e_C^*(0)/\varepsilon_{C'} > 1$ gives a relation in δ that will be satisfied if δ is restricted to be less than 0.10. This restriction on δ merely means that the least resolute state, D, is not willing to hazard a chance of disaster of more than 30 percent. Thus, if $\delta < 0.10$, a challenger is more likely to be irresolute in equilibrium (iv). A similar argument shows that this restriction on δ ensures that the challenger is more likely to be irresolute in equilibrium (iii). In equilibria (i) and (ii), $e_C^*(0) = 1$; so it suffices to show $\varepsilon_{C'} < \frac{1}{2}$. But the bounds on $\varepsilon_{C'}$ ensure that this also holds if $\delta < 0.10$.

The fact that the challenger is more likely to be irresolute immediately leads to the conclusion that crises entailing a severe conflict of interest will be relatively less frequent. That is, the probability of a severe conflict of interest underlying a situation that actually becomes a crisis will be less than $\frac{1}{2}$. To establish this, note that this probability will be less than $\frac{1}{2}$ if and only if the probability of a severe crisis, $\varepsilon_{C'}\varepsilon_{D'}e^*_{D'}(1)$, is less than the probability of the crisis not being severe, which is $\Pi - \varepsilon_{C'}\varepsilon_{D'}e^*_{D'}(1)$. But

$$
\begin{aligned}
\Pi - \varepsilon_{C'}\varepsilon_{D'}e^*_{D'}(1) &= (1 - \varepsilon_{C'})(1 - \varepsilon_{D'})e^*_C(0)e^*_D(1) \\
&\quad + \varepsilon_{D'}(1 - \varepsilon_{C'})e^*_C(0)e^*_{D'}(1) + \varepsilon_{C'}(1 - \varepsilon_{D'})e^*_D(1) \\
&> \varepsilon_{C'}(1 - \varepsilon_{D'})e^*_D(1) + \varepsilon_{C'}\varepsilon_{D'}e^*_{D'}(1) + \varepsilon_{C'}(1 - \varepsilon_{D'})e^*_D(1) \\
&> \varepsilon_{C'}\varepsilon_{D'}e^*_{D'}(1)
\end{aligned}
$$

where the first inequality follows because $(1 - \varepsilon_{C'})e^*_C(0) > \varepsilon_{C'}$. Thus, given a crisis, the probability of its entailing a severe conflict of interest is less than the probability of its not entailing a severe conflict.

The fact that a challenger is less likely to be resolute and that a crisis is less likely to be severe may lead to a kind of selection bias, and this illustrates the importance of distinguishing between statements about crises and statements about situations. Suppose one wanted to assess the underlying distribution of interests in the system. In effect, this amounts to trying to determine the probability distribution of the points in the $(\varepsilon_{C'}, \varepsilon_{D'})$ plane in Figure 3.4. But, clearly, if one's sample consists solely of crises, perhaps because history naturally focuses attention on them and not on situations that could have become crises but did not, then any situation in the no-sequential-crisis-equilibrium (NSCE) region will not be included in the sample. And those situations that will be excluded are those in which the probability of facing a resolute challenger is high; that is, situations in which $\varepsilon_{C'} > \bar{\varepsilon}_{C'}$ will be excluded from a sample consisting only of crises. These excluded cases, moreover, are those in which a severe conflict of interest is more likely.

The dynamics of brinkmanship escalation

The doctrine of massive retaliation foundered on the credibility problem created by the nuclear revolution. If no state would ever deliberately launch a massive nuclear attack first because the cost of doing so would be too great, then the threat to do so would seem inherently incredible. The strategy that leaves something to chance solved that problem, at least in principle. It linked the use or threatened use of force to states' attempts to secure their interests through an array of risk. In this approach to deterrence, states act in ways that raise the risk that they will lose collective control of the crisis and that the crisis will end in the utter devastation of a general nuclear exchange. The brinkmanship analogy, in turn, offered some insight into the dynamics of crisis bargaining when force and political ends were related in this way. This chapter has sought to extend the insights derived from this analogy by formalizing it.

The model supports some of the inferences that might be drawn from this analogy and from the description of a brinkmanship crisis as a contest of resolve. But the model also contradicts many of the conclusions suggested by this analogy and description. The model agrees with the analogy that crises involving a grave conflict of interest are the least stable and the most dangerous, whereas crises in which there is only a minor conflict of interest are the most stable and least dangerous. However, the model contradicts the analogy's suggestion that the state with the greatest resolve will prevail, or that the greater an adversary's resolve, the less likely a state is to escalate. Indeed, an increase in the defender's resolve in the model may make an irresolute challenger more likely to escalate after resistance. Contrary to what might be presumed to follow from the description of a brinkmanship crisis as a contest of resolve, a state may be less, not more, likely to prevail the greater its resolve. Describing a brinkmanship crisis as a contest of resolve may obscure as much as it clarifies.

Because the situation actually facing a state may be distinguished from the situation a state believes itself to be facing, certain aspects of the role of misperception in crisis bargaining can be formalized. The formalization indicates that misperception may become worse during a crisis. Although there would be no crises if misperception could be completely eliminated, reducing but not eliminating misperception can be stabilizing or destabilizing.

Increasing a potential challenger's stake in the status quo would seem to enhance stability by reducing the likelihood of a challenge to the status quo, for to do so would be to risk a more valuable stake. The model has shown this assertion to be problematic. The challenger's having a greater stake in the status quo does make a crisis less likely, but not necessarily because the potential challenger is less likely to challenge the status quo. Rather, the challenged state may be more likely to submit.

Some weak statements about the distribution of crises may also be made. Given a crisis, a challenger is, surprisingly, more likely to be irresolute than resolute. A severe crisis, moreover, is less likely than a crisis that is not severe.

What seems to account, at least in part, for the inconsistencies between the arguments based on brinkmanship and the image of a contest of resolve and the more formal counterparts of those arguments that are developed here is that the former often leave out important interactions between the states' strategies and their beliefs. The model, for example, illustrates that an initial change in one state's strategy could alter the other state's beliefs. Different beliefs may lead to a new strategy, and that, in turn, leads the first state to change its strategy. Often these interacting factors point to opposite directions. If an irresolute state becomes more likely to escalate, that tends to reduce an adversary's expected payoff to escalating and makes the adversary less likely to escalate. But there is an opposing influence. By being more likely to escalate, the irresolute state also affects its adversary's beliefs. The more likely an irresolute state is to escalate, the more confident an adversary is of facing the irresolute state. This greater confidence increases the adversary's payoff to escalating and tends to make the adversary more likely to escalate. The formal arguments keep track of these factors and balance the opposing influences in ways that their less formal counterparts cannot.

The point, however, is not tnat the conclusions derived from the formal model developed here are better than other conclusions. Indeed, different models are likely to keep track of and weigh the competing factors differently.[37] Whether the simple brinkmanship analogy, the model examined here, or some other models offer better conclusions should ultimately be judged with empirical evidence. The point is that the dynamics of crisis bargaining are enormously complicated, and simple generalizations that may at first seem quite compelling may in the end be misleading.

In the approach to nuclear deterrence based on the strategy that leaves something to chance, the use or threatened use of force is related to states' attempts to further their ends through the array of risk. Limited options that, if exercised, will create different levels of autonomous risk bridge the gap between doing too much by launching a massive nuclear attack and doing too little by acquiescing to an adversary's challenge to the status quo. The formal model of brinkmanship developed in this chapter is a step toward understanding this approach. But some of the model's simplifying assumptions make it impossible to examine crucial aspects of this approach.

In particular, it is natural to ask what the effects are of having to take larger or more dangerous steps toward the brink when escalating. Does it make any difference if a state can take relatively small steps that will generate small incremental risks of losing collective control or if a state can take only large steps that will entail greater incremental risks? Are smaller incremental risks associated with greater stability or less?

The model studied in this chapter cannot address these questions adequately. To simplify the analysis, the model presumed that regardless of

---

[37] See Nalebuff (1986) for a contrasting model of brinkmanship.

the size of the incremental risk δ, both the irresolute challenger and defender would be willing to take at most one step toward the brink, whereas the resolute defender would be willing to take no more than two steps. This assumption means that δ and the states' levels of resolve are not independent. As the incremental δ varies, the states' levels of resolve may also have to change in order to keep the maximum number of steps that the states might be willing to take constant.[38] But to trace the effects of having different incremental risks, one would like δ to be independent of the states' levels of resolve so that the former might be varied while the latter is held constant. This cannot be done in the present model. Developing a model in which this can be done is the task of the next chapter. In that model of longer brinkmanship crises, the states may be willing to take several steps toward the brink, and the size of the incremental risk will be independent of the maximum number of steps the states are willing to take.

Appendix 3.1

This appendix derives the sequential crisis equilibria of the brinkmanship game when there is two-sided incomplete information. In this game, there are four generic types of potential sequential crisis equilibria: (i), (ii), (iii), and (iv). Generically, only one of these equilibria can exist at a time, and which one that will be, if any,[39] will depend on the initial beliefs of the states (i.e., on the values of $\varepsilon_{C'}$ and $\varepsilon_{D'}$). The sequential crisis equilibrium strategies in (i) are

$$e_C^*(0) = 1$$

$$e_C^*(1) = \left(\frac{\varepsilon_{C'}}{1-\varepsilon_{C'}}\right)\left[\frac{[1-(1-3\delta)(1-4\delta)][1-R_{D'}]}{R_{D'}-3\delta}\right]$$

$$e_C^*(m) = 0 \quad \forall m \geq 2$$

$$e_D^*(m) = 0 \quad \forall m \geq 1$$

$$e_{D'}^*(1) = 1$$

$$e_{D'}^*(2) = \frac{R_C - 2\delta}{(1-2\delta)[(1-3\delta)R_C + 3\delta]}$$

$$e_{D'}^*(m) = 0 \quad \forall m \geq 3$$

$$e_{C'}^*(m) = 1 \quad \forall m \leq M_{C'}$$

$$e_{C'}^*(m) = 0 \quad \forall m > M_{C'}$$

[38] More specifically, the model is based on the assumption that $M_D = 1$, $M_C = 1$, $M_{D'} = 2$, and $M_{C'} \geq 2$. This then defines the following relations between δ and the states' levels of resolve: $\delta < R_D < 3\delta$, $2\delta < R_C < 4\delta$, $3\delta < R_{D'} < 5\delta$, and $4\delta < R_{C'}$. So as δ varies, R_D, R_C, $R_{D'}$, and $R_{C'}$ may also have to change in order to continue to satisfy these relations.

[39] If $\varepsilon_{C'}$ and $\varepsilon_{D'}$ do not satisfy the necessary constraints, then no sequential crisis equilibria exist. Only sequential noncrisis equilibria exist.

and they have these relevant[40] beliefs:

$$\beta_C^*(0) = \beta_{C'}^*(0) = 1 - \varepsilon_{D'}$$
$$\beta_C^*(1) = \beta_{C'}^*(1) = 0$$
$$\beta_C^*(2) = \beta_{C'}^*(2) = 0$$
$$\beta_D^*(1) = \beta_{D'}^*(1) = 1 - \varepsilon_{C'}$$
$$\beta_D^*(2) = \beta_{D'}^*(2) = \frac{[1 - (1 - 3\delta)(1 - 4\delta)](1 - R_{D'})}{(1 - 3\delta)[(1 - 4\delta)R_{D'} + 4\delta]}$$

Equilibrium (i) exists only if

$$\underline{\varepsilon}_{C'} < \varepsilon_{C'} < \bar{\varepsilon}_{C'} \qquad \varepsilon_{D'} < \bar{\varepsilon}_{D'}$$

where

$$\underline{\varepsilon}_{C'} = \left[\frac{R_D - \delta}{(1 - \delta)[(1 - 2\delta)R_D + 2\delta]}\right]\left[\frac{R_{D'} - 3\delta}{(1 - 3\delta)[(1 - 4\delta)R_{D'} + 4\delta]}\right]$$

$$\bar{\varepsilon}_{C'} = \left[\frac{R_{D'} - \delta}{(1 - \delta)[(1 - 2\delta)R_{D'} + 2\delta]}\right]\left[\frac{R_{D'} - 3\delta}{(1 - 3\delta)[(1 - 4\delta)R_{D'} + 4\delta]}\right]$$

$$\bar{\varepsilon}_{D'} = \frac{w_C - q_C}{w_C - d_C}\left(\frac{1}{(1 - \delta)R_C + \delta}\right)$$

The sequential crisis equilibrium strategies in (ii) are

$$e_C^*(0) = 1$$
$$e_C^*(1) = 1 - \left(\frac{1}{1 - \varepsilon_{C'}}\right)\frac{[1 - (1 - \delta)(1 - 2\delta)][1 - R_D]}{(1 - \delta)[(1 - 2\delta)R_D + 2\delta]}$$
$$e_C^*(m) = 0 \quad \forall\, m \geq 2$$
$$e_D^*(1) = \left(\frac{\varepsilon_{D'}}{1 - \varepsilon_{D'}}\right)\left(\frac{\beta_C^*(1)}{1 - \beta_C^*(1)}\right)$$
$$e_D^*(m) = 0 \quad \forall\, m \geq 2$$
$$e_{D'}^*(1) = 1$$
$$e_{D'}^*(2) = 1$$
$$e_{D'}^*(m) = 0 \quad \forall\, m \geq 3$$
$$e_{C'}^*(m) = 1 \quad \forall\, m \leq M_{C'}$$
$$e_{C'}^*(m) = 0 \quad \forall\, m > M_{C'}$$

---

[40] Because both C and C' always submit for $m > M_{C'}$, and both D and D' always submit for $m > M_{D'}$, the beliefs off the equilibrium path at $\Omega_C(m)$ and $\Omega_{C'}(m)$ and at $\Omega_D(m)$ and $\Omega_{D'}(m)$ can be anything. These arbitrary beliefs, however, do not affect the states' strategies, and in that sense they are irrelevant.

and they have these relevant beliefs:

$$\beta_C^*(0) = \beta_{C'}^*(0) = 1 - \varepsilon_{D'}$$

$$\beta_C^*(1) = \beta_{C'}^*(1) = \frac{[1 - (1 - 2\delta)(1 - 3\delta)][1 - R_C]}{(1 - 2\delta)[(1 - 3\delta)R_C + 3\delta]}$$

$$\beta_C^*(2) = \beta_{C'}^*(2) = 0$$

$$\beta_D^*(1) = \beta_{D'}^*(1) = 1 - \varepsilon_{C'}$$

$$\beta_D^*(2) = \beta_{D'}^*(2) = (1 - \varepsilon_{C'})e_C^*(1)/[\varepsilon_{C'} + (1 - \varepsilon_{C'})e_C^*(1)]$$

$$\beta_D^*(3) = \beta_{D'}^*(3) = 0$$

Equilibrium (ii) exists only if

$$\varepsilon_{C'} < \underline{\varepsilon}_{C'} \qquad \varepsilon_{D'} < \underline{\varepsilon}_{D'}$$

where

$$\underline{\varepsilon}_{D'} = \frac{w_C - q_C}{w_C - d_C}\left(\frac{1}{(1 - \delta)R_C + \delta}\right)\left(\frac{R_C - 2\delta}{(1 - 2\delta)[(1 - 3\delta)R_C + 3\delta]}\right)$$

The sequential crisis equilibrium strategies in (iii) are

$$e_C^*(0) = \frac{\varepsilon_{C'}}{1 - \varepsilon_{C'}}\left(\frac{1}{1 - \beta_{D'}^*(2)}\right)\left[\frac{[1 - (1 - \delta)(1 - 2\delta)][1 - R_D]}{R_D - \delta} + \beta_{D'}^*(2)\right]$$

$$e_C^*(1) = \frac{\beta_{D'}^*(2)[R_D - \delta]}{[1 - (1 - \delta)(1 - 2\delta)][1 - R_D] + \beta_{D'}^*(2)[R_D - \delta]}$$

$$e_C^*(m) = 0 \quad \forall m \geq 2$$

$$e_D^*(1) = 1 - \frac{1}{1 - \varepsilon_{D'}}\left[1 - \left(\frac{w_C - q_C}{w_C - d_C}\right)\frac{1}{(1 - \delta)R_C + \delta}\right]$$

$$e_D^*(m) = 0 \quad \forall m \geq 2$$

$$e_{D'}^*(1) = 1$$

$$e_{D'}^*(2) = \left(\frac{1}{\varepsilon_{D'}}\right)\left(\frac{w_C - q_C}{w_C - d_C}\right)\left[\frac{1}{(1 - \delta)R_C + \delta}\right]$$

$$\times \frac{R_C - 2\delta}{(1 - 2\delta)[(1 - 3\delta)R_C + 3\delta]}$$

$$e_{D'}^*(m) = 0 \quad \forall m > 2$$

$$e_{C'}^*(m) = 1 \quad \forall m \leq M_{C'}$$

$$e_{C'}^*(m) = 0 \quad \forall m > M_{C'}$$

and they have these relevant beliefs:

$$\beta_C^*(0) = \beta_{C'}^*(0) = 1 - \varepsilon_{D'}$$

$$\beta_C^*(1) = \beta_{C'}^*(1) = 1 - \varepsilon_{D'}\left(\frac{w_C - d_C}{w_C - q_C}\right)[(1+\delta)R_C + \delta]$$

$$\beta_C^*(2) = \beta_{C'}^*(2) = 0$$

$$\beta_D^*(1) = \beta_{D'}^*(1) = \frac{[1 - (1-\delta)(1-2\delta)][1 - R_D] + \beta_D^*(2)[R_D - \delta]}{(1-\delta)[(1-2\delta)R_D + 2\delta]}$$

$$\beta_D^*(2) = \beta_{D'}^*(2) = \frac{[1 - (1-3\delta)(1-4\delta)][1 - R_{D'}]}{(1-3\delta)[(1-4\delta)R_{D'} + 4\delta]}$$

$$\beta_{D'}^*(3) = \beta_{D'}^*(3) = 0$$

Equilibrium (iii) exists only if

$$\varepsilon_{C'} < \underline{\varepsilon}_{C'} \qquad \underline{\varepsilon}_{D'} < \varepsilon_{D'} < \bar{\varepsilon}_{D'}$$

The sequential crisis equilibrium strategies in (iv) are

$$e_C^*(0) = \frac{\varepsilon_{C'}}{1 - \varepsilon_{C'}}\left(\frac{1}{1 - \beta_{D'}^*(2)}\right)\left[\frac{[1 - (1-\delta)(1-2\delta)][1 - R_{D'}]}{R_{D'} - \delta} + \beta_{D'}^*(2)\right]$$

$$e_C^*(1) = \frac{\beta_{D'}^*(2)[R_{D'} - \delta]}{[1 - (1-\delta)(1-2\delta)][1 - R_{D'}] + \beta_{D'}^*(2)[R_{D'} - \delta]}$$

$$e_C^*(m) = 0 \quad \forall m \geq 2$$

$$e_D^*(m) = 0 \quad \forall m \geq 1$$

$$e_{D'}^*(1) = \left(\frac{1}{\varepsilon_{D'}}\right)\left(\frac{w_C - q_C}{w_C - d_C}\right)\frac{1}{(1-\delta)R_C + \delta}$$

$$e_{D'}^*(2) = \frac{R_C - 2\delta}{(1-2\delta)[(1-3\delta)R_C + 3\delta]}$$

$$e_{D'}^*(m) = 0 \quad \forall m \geq 3$$

$$e_{C'}^*(m) = 1 \quad \forall m \leq M_{C'}$$

$$e_{C'}^*(m) = 0 \quad \forall m > M_{C'}$$

and they have these relevant beliefs:

$$\beta_C^*(0) = \beta_{C'}^*(0) = 1 - \varepsilon_{D'}$$

$$\beta_C^*(1) = \beta_{C'}^*(1) = 0$$

$$\beta_C^*(2) = \beta_{C'}^*(2) = 0$$

$$\beta_D^*(1) = \beta_{D'}^*(1) = (1 - \varepsilon_{C'})e_C^*(0)/[\varepsilon_{C'} + (1 - \varepsilon_{C'})e_C^*(0)]$$

$$\beta_D^*(2) = \beta_{D'}^*(2) = \frac{[1 - (1-3\delta)(1-4\delta)][1 - R_{D'}]}{(1-3\delta)[(1-4\delta)R_{D'} + 4\delta]}$$

Equilibrium (iv) exists only if

$$\varepsilon_{C'} < \bar\varepsilon_{C'} \qquad \varepsilon_{D'} > \bar\varepsilon_{D'}$$

These equilibria are derived through backward programming. As noted earlier, no state can attach a positive probability to attacking at any information set. Accordingly, determining the sequential equilibria means specifying $e_C^*(m)$ and $e_{C'}^*(m)$ for $0 \le m \le K/2$, $e_D^*(m)$ and $e_{D'}^*(m)$ for $1 \le m \le K/2$, and a consistent set of beliefs, where an asterisk denotes an equilibrium condition.

Recall that M_C, which is assumed to be equal to 1, is the last step C can take before the inherent risk of slipping over the brink becomes too large: M_C is the largest integer m such that $2m\delta < R_C$. Thus, C's best reply at $\Omega_C(m)$ for $m > M_C = 1$ is to submit: $e_C^*(m) = 0$. Similarly, $e_D^*(m) = 0$ for $m > M_D$, where M_D is taken to be 1; $e_{D'}^*(m) = 0$ for $m > M_{D'}$, where $M_{D'}$ is equal to 2; and $e_{C'}^*(m) = 0$ for $m > M_{C'} \ge 2$. Now note that if C' escalates at $\Omega_{C'}(m)$ for $M_{C'} \ge m \ge 2$, its adversary, regardless of type, will not subsequently escalate. The risk is too high. But then the definition of $M_{C'}$ implies that the payoff to C' of escalating at these information sets is greater than the return to submitting. So $e_{C'}^*(m) = 1$ for $M_{C'} \ge m \ge 2$.

The game has been simplified by assuming that C' will escalate at $\Omega_{C'}(0)$, $\Omega_{C'}(1)$, and $\Omega_{C'}(2)$, regardless of what its adversary does. That, it was observed, might further restrict $M_{C'}$ beyond the existing constraint that $M_{C'} \ge 2$. To define this constraint and ensure that it can be satisfied, note that the worst that can happen to C' is that it will be facing a resolute adversary that will escalate with probability 1 at $\Omega_{D'}(1)$ and $\Omega_{D'}(2)$. Because $M_{D'} = 2$, the resolute adversary D' will then submit. To ensure that C' will escalate at $\Omega_{C'}(0)$, $\Omega_{C'}(1)$, and $\Omega_{C'}(2)$ in this worst case, it will suffice to assume that

$$R_{C'} > 1 - (1 - \delta)(1 - 2\delta)(1 - 3\delta)(1 - 4\delta) + (q_{C'} - s_{C'})/(w_{C'} - d_{C'})$$

For any $\delta < \tfrac{1}{4}$, this can always be done with suitable choices of $w_{C'}$, $q_{C'}$, $s_{C'}$, and $d_{C'}$. Finally, observe that whenever that inequality is satisfied, $R_{C'} > 4\delta$, and therefore $M_{C'} \ge 2$.

The only strategies left to be specified are those at $\Omega_C(0)$, $\Omega_C(1)$, $\Omega_D(1)$, $\Omega_{D'}(1)$, and $\Omega_{D'}(2)$. To find these, begin by considering the problem facing D' if the crisis reaches $\Omega_{D'}(2)$. If D' is facing C, escalation brings $3\delta d_{D'} + (1 - 3\delta)w_{D'}$. If, however, D' is facing C', escalation yields $3\delta d_{D'} + (1 - 3\delta)[4\delta d_{D'} + (1 - 4\delta)s_{D'}]$. But D' is uncertain whether it is facing C or C', and so its expected payoff to escalation is

$$\beta_{D'}(2)[3\delta d_{D'} + (1 - 3\delta)w_{D'}] + (1 - \beta_{D'}(2))$$
$$\times [3\delta d_{D'} + (1 - 3\delta)[4\delta d_{D'} + (1 - 4\delta)s_{D'}]]$$

where, recall, $\beta_{D'}(2)$ is the probability of facing an irresolute challenger at $\Omega_{D'}(2)$.

Let $B_{D'}(2)$ be the value of $\beta_{D'}(2)$ that leaves D' indifferent between submitting and escalating at $\Omega_{D'}(2)$. Then,

$$B_{D'}(2) = \frac{[1-(1-3\delta)(1-4\delta)][1-R_{D'}]}{(1-3\delta)[(1-4\delta)R_{D'}+4\delta]}$$

So the best response of D' at $\Omega_{D'}(2)$ is $e_{D'}(2)=1$ if $\beta_{D'}(2) > B_{D'}(2)$, $e_{D'}(2) \in [0,1]$ if $\beta_{D'}(2) = B_{D'}(2)$, and $e_{D'}(2) = 0$ if $\beta_{D'}(2) < B_{D'}(2)$.

Beliefs are given by Bayes' rule where this rule can be applied. For $\Omega_{D'}(2)$, this means

$$\beta_{D'}(2) = \frac{(1-\varepsilon_{C'})e_C(0)e_C(1)}{(1-\varepsilon_{C'})e_C(0)e_C(1)+\varepsilon_{C'}e_{C'}(0)e_{C'}(1)}$$

Recalling that $e_{C'}^*(0) = e_{C'}^*(1) = 1$ in equilibrium, substituting for $\beta_{D'}(2)$ shows that D's best reply is

$$e_{D'}(2)=1 \qquad \text{if } e_C(1)e_C(0) > \left[\frac{\varepsilon_{C'}}{1-\varepsilon_{C'}}\right]\left[\frac{B_{D'}(2)}{1-B_{D'}(2)}\right]$$

$$e_{D'}(2)\in[0,1] \quad \text{if } e_C(1)e_C(0) = \left[\frac{\varepsilon_{C'}}{1-\varepsilon_{C'}}\right]\left[\frac{B_{D'}(2)}{1-B_{D'}(2)}\right]$$

$$e_{D'}(2)=0 \qquad \text{if } e_C(1)e_C(0) < \left[\frac{\varepsilon_{C'}}{1-\varepsilon_{C'}}\right]\left[\frac{B_{D'}(2)}{1-B_{D'}(2)}\right]$$

Now observe that there must always be some chance that the resolute defender will escalate at $\Omega_{D'}(2)$ in a sequential crisis equilibrium: $e_D^*(2)$ must be greater than zero. To see this, assume that $e_D^*(2) = 0$. Because D' is certain to submit at $\Omega_{D'}(2)$, C's best reply at $\Omega_C(1)$ is to escalate: $e_C(1) = 1$. This implies that D' should not resist: $e_{D'}(1) = 0$. It would make no sense for D' to resist at $\Omega_{D'}(1)$ if C and C' were certain to escalate at $\Omega_C(1)$ and $\Omega_{C'}(1)$, after which D' would be certain to quit. D' could do better simply by not resisting. Similarly, the irresolute defender will not resist: $e_D(1) = 0$. But this is a contradiction: If $e_D(1) = e_{D'}(1) = 0$, no challenge is resisted, and there is no crisis.

The fact that $e_D^*(2) > 0$ implies that

$$e_C(1)e_C(0) \geq [\varepsilon_{C'}/(1-\varepsilon_{C'})][B_{D'}(2)/(1-B_{D'}(2))]$$

in any sequential crisis equilibrium. Finding these equilibria requires consideration of two cases. Equality is assumed to hold in the first and yields equilibria (i), (iii), and (iv). Inequality is presumed in the second, and this gives equilibrium (ii).

Case I: $e_C(1)e_C(0) = [\varepsilon_{C'}/(1-\varepsilon_{C'})][B_{D'}(2)/(1-B_{D'}(2))]$

Consider the problem facing the irresolute challenger C after a resisted challenge [i.e., at $\Omega_C(1)$]. The payoff to escalation is

$$\beta_C(1)[2\delta d_C + (1-2\delta)w_C] + (1-\beta_C(1))$$
$$\times [2\delta d_C + (1-2\delta)[(1-e_{D'}(2))w_C + e_{D'}(2)[3\delta d_C + (1-3\delta)s_C]]]$$

Let $\hat{e}_{D'}(2)$ be the strategy of D' at $\Omega_{D'}(2)$ that leaves C indifferent to submitting and escalating. Then,

$$\hat{e}_{D'}(2) = [R_C - 2\delta]/[(1-\beta_C(1))(1-2\delta)[(1-3\delta)R_C + 3\delta]]$$

The expression for $\hat{e}_{D'}(2)$ may be simplified by substituting for $\beta_C(1)$. By Bayes' rule,

$$\beta_C(1) = (1-\varepsilon_{D'})e_D(1)/[(1-\varepsilon_{D'})e_D(1) + \varepsilon_{D'}e_{D'}(1)]$$

This gives

$$\hat{e}_{D'}(2) = \left[1 + \left(\frac{1-\varepsilon_{D'}}{\varepsilon_{D'}}\right)\frac{e_D(1)}{e_{D'}(1)}\right]\left[\frac{R_C - 2\delta}{(1-2\delta)[(1-3\delta)R_C + 3\delta]}\right]$$

Because the irresolute defender always quits at $\Omega_D(2)$, C's best response at $\Omega_C(1)$ depends only on what the resolute defender does at $\Omega_{D'}(2)$. Consequently, C's best response at $\Omega_C(1)$ is $e_C(1) = 0$ if $e_{D'}(2) > \hat{e}_{D'}(2)$, $e_C(1) \in [0,1]$ if $e_{D'}(2) = \hat{e}_{D'}(2)$, and $e_C(2) = 1$ if $e_{D'}(2) < \hat{e}_{D'}(2)$.

Now turn to the problem facing D at $\Omega_D(1)$. Let $\hat{e}_C(1)$ be the value of $e_C(1)$ that makes D indifferent to escalating and submitting. Then $\hat{e}_C(1)$ satisfies

$$s_D = \beta_D(1)[\delta d_D + (1-\delta)[(1-\hat{e}_C(1))w_D + \hat{e}_C(1)[2\delta d_D + (1-2\delta)s_D]]]$$
$$+ (1-\beta_D(1))[\delta d_D + (1-\delta)[2\delta d_D + (1-2\delta)s_D]]$$

and this is given by

$$\hat{e}_C(1) = 1 - \frac{[1-(1-\delta)(1-2\delta)][1-R_D]}{\beta_D(1)(1-\delta)[(1-2\delta)R_D + 2\delta]}$$

Substituting for $\beta_D(1)$ yields

$$\hat{e}_C(1) = 1 - \left[1 + \left(\frac{\varepsilon_{C'}}{1-\varepsilon_{C'}}\right)\frac{1}{e_C(0)}\right]\left[\frac{[1-(1-\delta)(1-2\delta)][1-R_D]}{(1-\delta)[(1-2\delta)R_D + 2\delta]}\right]$$

D's best reply at $\Omega_D(1)$ is $e_D(1) = 0$ if $e_C(1) > \hat{e}_C(1)$, $e_D(1) \in [0,1]$ if $e_C(1) = \hat{e}_C(1)$, and $e_D(1) = 1$ if $e_C(1) < \hat{e}_C(1)$.

D' faces a similar problem at $\Omega_{D'}(1)$. Recalling that D' is indifferent between submitting and escalating at $\Omega_{D'}(2)$, because $\beta_{D'}(2) = B_{D'}(2)$ in Case I, then the value of $e_C(1)$ that will leave D' indifferent to escalating and submitting, which will be denoted by $\tilde{e}_C(1)$, is

$$\tilde{e}_C(1) = 1 - \left[1 + \left(\frac{\varepsilon_{C'}}{1-\varepsilon_{C'}}\right)\frac{1}{e_C(0)}\right]\left[\frac{[1-(1-\delta)(1-2\delta)][1-R_{D'}]}{(1-\delta)[(1-2\delta)R_{D'} + 2\delta]}\right]$$

The best response for D' at $\Omega_{D'}(1)$ is $e_{D'}(1) = 0$ if $e_C(1) > \tilde{e}_C(1)$, $e_{D'}(1) \in [0, 1]$ if $e_C(1) = \tilde{e}_C(1)$, and $e_{D'}(1) = 1$ if $e_C(1) < \tilde{e}_C(1)$.

These best-reply correspondences will now be used to find points that will be the best responses to themselves. Note that $\hat{e}_C(1)$ and $\tilde{e}_C(1)$ are increasing in $e_C(0)$. Because $\delta < R_D < 3\delta$ and $3\delta < R_{D'} < 5\delta$, it is easy to show that for any $e_C(0)$, $\tilde{e}_C(1) > \hat{e}_C(1)$. Figure A3.1 graphs $\hat{e}_C(1)$ and $\tilde{e}_C(1)$ and the constraint Z, that defines Case I. That is, Z is the curve given by

$$e_C(1)e_C(0) = [\varepsilon_{C'}/(1 - \varepsilon_{C'})][B_{D'}(2)/(1 - B_{D'}(2))]$$

Because in Case I this constraint must be satisfied, only points along Z need be considered as potential equilibria.

Let H' be the value of $e_C(0)$ at which $\tilde{e}_C(1)$ satisfies the constraint, and let H be the value of $e_C(0)$ at which $\hat{e}_C(1)$ satisfies the constraint. Because $\hat{e}_C(1) < \tilde{e}_C(1)$ for any $e_C(0)$, and because $e_C(1)$ is decreasing in $e_C(0)$ along Z, $H' < H$.

H' and H make it possible to specify the best replies of D and D' at $\Omega_D(1)$ and $\Omega_{D'}(1)$. Considering only points along Z, then if, for example, $e_C(0) < H$, it must be that $e_C(1) > \hat{e}_C(1)$. But this means that the best reply of D is $e_D(1) = 0$. Indeed, the best-reply correspondence of D at $\Omega_D(1)$ is given by $e_D(1) = 0$ if $e_C(0) < H$, $e_D(1) \in [0, 1]$ if $e_C(0) = H$, and $e_D(1) = 1$ if $e_C(0) > H$. Similarly, the best-reply correspondence of D' at $\Omega_{D'}(1)$ is given by $e_{D'}(1) = 0$ if $e_C(0) < H'$, $e_{D'}(1) \in [0, 1]$ if $e_C(0) = H'$, and $e_{D'}(1) = 1$ if $e_C(0) > H'$.

In a sequential crisis equilibrium there must be some chance of a challenge being resisted. This means that $e_C(0) \geq H'$, because if $e_C(0) < H'$, then $e_D(1) = 0$ and $e_{D'}(1) = 0$. Thus, the search for sequential crisis equilibria may be limited to points along Z for which $e_C(0) \geq H'$. If, moreover, $e_C(0) = H'$, then $e_{D'}(1) > 0$; otherwise, $e_{D'}(1) = e_D(1) = 0$.

Figure A3.1. $\hat{e}_C(1)$ and $\tilde{e}_C(1)$.

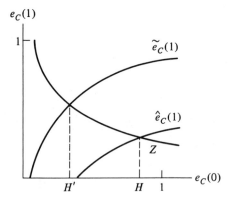

Now consider C's best response if the game reaches $\Omega_C(1)$. This depends on a comparison of $e_{D'}(2)$ and $\hat{e}_{D'}(2)$. This comparison may be transformed into one between $e_{D'}(2)$ and $e_C(0)$. Recall that $\hat{e}_{D'}(2)$ is a function of $e_D(1)/e_{D'}(1)$. But in equilibrium, $e_D(1)$ and $e_{D'}(1)$ will be best replies to other strategies. Indeed, as was just demonstrated, these best replies are functions of $e_C(0)$. If, for example, $H' \leq e_C(0) < H$, the best replies of D and D' at $\Omega_D(1)$ and $\Omega_{D'}(1)$ are $e_D(1) = 0$ and $e_{D'}(1) > 0$. Hence, $\hat{e}_{D'}(2)$ evaluated at these best responses is

$$[R_C - 2\delta]/[(1 - 2\delta)[(1 - 3\delta)R_C + 3\delta]]$$

Let L' be this value, and let L be the value of $\hat{e}_{D'}(2)$ evaluated at $e_D(1) = e_{D'}(1) = 1$. Then the transformed best-reply correspondence for C at $\Omega_C(1)$ is

1	if $(e_C(0), e_{D'}(2)) \in [H', H) \times [0, L')$
$[0, 1]$	if $(e_C(0), e_{D'}(2)) \in [H', H) \times \{L'\}$
0	if $(e_C(0), e_{D'}(2)) \in [H', H) \times (L', 1]$
1	if $(e_C(0), e_{D'}(2)) \in \{H\} \times [0, L')$
$[0, 1]$	if $(e_C(0), e_{D'}(2)) \in \{H\} \times [L', L]$
0	if $(e_C(0), e_{D'}(2)) \in \{H\} \times (L, 1]$
1	if $(e_C(0), e_{D'}(2)) \in (H, 1] \times [0, L')$
$[0, 1]$	if $(e_C(0), e_{D'}(2)) \in (H, 1] \times \{L'\}$
0	if $(e_C(0), e_{D'}(2)) \in (H, 1] \times (L', 1]$

This correspondence is illustrated in Figure A3.2 and will be called BR. Figure A3.2 also shows the constraining curve Z, which has now become a surface, Σ.

Remember that the problem is to specify the equilibrium strategies at $\Omega_C(0), \Omega_C(1), \Omega_D(1), \Omega_{D'}(1)$, and $\Omega_{D'}(2)$. The first of these to fall out is $e_{D'}^*(2)$. If a sequential crisis equilibrium exists, it must be in the intersection of BR and Σ. But at all points of intersection, $0 < e_C(1) < 1$. To see this, recall that Z approaches 0 asymptotically from above; so $e_C(1) > 0$. Over $H' \leq e_C(0) \leq 1$, $e_C(1)$ attains its maximum on Σ at $e_C(0) = H'$. But from the definition of H', $e_C(1) < 1$ at $e_C(0) = H'$. Because $0 < e_C(1) < 1$, the best-reply correspondence for C at $\Omega_C(1)$ implies $e_{D'}(2) = \hat{e}_{D'}(2)$. In a sequential crisis equilibrium, $e_{D'}^*(2) = \hat{e}_{D'}(2)$. [Of course, $\hat{e}_{D'}(2)$ is still a function of $e_D(1)$ and $e_{D'}(1)$; so a complete determination of $\hat{e}_{D'}(2)$ awaits their specification.]

At this point it is necessary to consider two subcases. In the first, $e_C(0) \geq H$, and this will yield equilibrium (iii). The second subcase is defined by $H' \leq e_C(0) < H$, and this will give equilibria (i) and (iv).

The specification of (iii) begins by noting that because $e_C(0) \geq H > H'$ in

the first subcase, then $e_D^*(1) = 1$. Moreover, $1 \geq e_C(0) \geq H$. Accordingly, it is
assumed that $H < 1$. (The possibility that $H = 1$ is disregarded because it has
measure zero.) But $H < 1$ implies that $e_C(0) < 1$. Arguing by contradiction,
assume $e_C(0) = 1$. Because $e_C(0) = 1 > H$, $e_D(1) = 1$. Moreover, $e_C(0) = 1$
implies that the payoff to C from exploiting the situation at $\Omega_C(0)$ is at least
as great as the value of the status quo. This leaves

$$q_C \leq (1 - \varepsilon_{D'})(\delta d_C + (1 - \delta)s_C) + \varepsilon_{D'}(\delta d_C + (1 - \delta)s_C)$$

where the expression for the return to exploiting the situation has been
simplified by taking $e_D(1) = e_{D'}(1) = 1$ and noting that because $0 < e_C(1) < 1$,
C is randomizing at $\Omega_C(1)$, which means that the expected payoff if this
information set is reached is s_C. The right side of this is less than s_C. This,
however, is a contradiction, because $q_C > s_C$. Hence, $H < 1$ means $0 < H' <
e_C(0) < 1$.

Because $0 < e_C(0) < 1$, C must be indifferent to accepting the status quo
and exploiting the situation. This leads directly to an expression for $e_D^*(1)$.
Indifference implies

$$q_C = (1 - \varepsilon_{D'})[(1 - e_D^*(1))w_C + e_D^*(1)[\delta d_C + (1 - \delta)s_C]] + \varepsilon_{D'}[\delta d_C + (1 - \delta)s_C]$$

Figure A3.2. The best-reply correspondences.

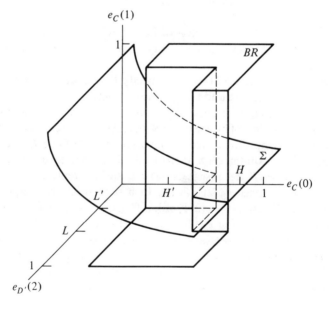

This gives

$$e_D^*(1) = 1 - \frac{1}{1 - \varepsilon_{D'}}\left[1 - \left(\frac{w_C - q_C}{w_C - d_C}\right)\left(\frac{1}{(1 - \delta)R_C + \delta}\right)\right]$$

This expression and the fact that $e_{D'}^*(1) = 1$ may be used to complete the specification of $e_{D'}^*(2)$. The result is the expression reported earlier for equilibrium (iii).

The expression for $e_D^*(1)$ places a restriction on the relation among the variables $\varepsilon_{D'}$, q_C, R_C, and δ. Examining it carefully yields the last two strategies that remain to be determined, $e_C^*(0)$ and $e_C^*(1)$. The expression for $e_D^*(1)$ implies $e_D^*(1) < 1$. The best-reply correspondence for D at $\Omega_D(1)$ shows that $e_C(0) \leq H$ if $e_D^*(1) < 1$. But $e_C(0)$ has also been restricted to being larger than or equal to H. Thus, $e_C^*(0) = H$. H, in turn, is the value of $e_C(0)$ that satisfies the constraint

$$\hat{e}_C(1) = [\varepsilon_{C'}/(1 - \varepsilon_{C'})][B_{D'}(2)/(1 - B_{D'}(2))][1/e_C(0)]$$

Solving this for $e_C(0)$ gives the expression for $e_C^*(0)$ described earlier. Substituting $e_C^*(0)$ for $e_C(0)$ in the constraint defining Case I yields the expression for $e_C^*(1)$.

The expressions for the states' beliefs are obtained by Bayes' rule and by substituting the expressions for the equilibrium strategies that have just been derived.

A sequential equilibrium will exist as long as the expressions for $e_C^*(0)$, $e_C^*(1)$, $e_D^*(1)$, and $e_{D'}^*(2)$ satisfy the constraints $0 \leq e_C^*(0) \leq 1, 0 \leq e_C^*(1) \leq 1, 0 \leq e_D^*(1) \leq 1$, and $0 \leq e_{D'}^*(2) \leq 1$. The first two constraints are satisfied because $0 < H < 1$. Only $H < 1$ is binding, and this gives the restriction on $\varepsilon_{C'}$ noted earlier. The expression for $e_D^*(1)$ is always less than 1, and $e_D^*(1) \geq 0$ yields the upper bound on $\varepsilon_{D'}$ defined earlier for equilibrium (iii). Finally, examining the expression for $e_{D'}^*(2)$ after substituting the expression for $e_D^*(1)$ gives the lower bound on $\varepsilon_{D'}$.

Now consider the second subcase, in which $H' \leq e_C(0) < H$. If $e_C^*(0) < 1$, equilibrium (iv) results. If $e_C^*(0) = 1$, equilibrium (i) obtains.

Assume $e_C(0) < 1$. This implies $e_C^*(0) = H'$. Arguing by contradiction to establish this, assume $H' < e_C(0)$. Because $H' < e_C(0) < H$, the best reply for D is $e_D(1) = 0$, and the best reply for D' is $e_{D'}(1) = 1$. But $0 < H' < e_C(0) < 1$ means that C is mixing at $\Omega_C(0)$. C must therefore be indifferent to the payoffs to exploiting and not exploiting the situation. And, as has already been shown, $0 < e_C(1) < 1$ for $H' < e_C(0) < 1$; so C is also mixing at $\Omega_C(1)$. All of this requires

$$q_C = (1 - \varepsilon_{D'})w_C + \varepsilon_{D'}[\delta d_C + (1 - \delta)s_C]$$

where this expression has been calculated given that $e_D(1) = 0$ and $e_{D'}(1) = 1$ and that C's expected payoff on reaching $\Omega_C(1)$ is s_C because C is mixing here. The relation among w_C, q_C, s_C, and d_C defined by this equality is an event of measure zero, and disregarding it leaves $e_C(0) = H'$.

Substituting for H' gives the expression for $e_C^*(0)$ for equilibrium (iv). Substituting the expression for $e_C^*(0)$ in the constraint that defines Case I gives $e_C^*(1)$. Finally, $e_{D'}^*(2)$ is obtained by noting that $e_{D'}(2) = L'$ for all points in the intersection of Σ and BR for $e_C(0) < H$. Thus, $e_{D'}^*(2) = L'$.

The only strategy left to be specified is $e_{D'}(1)$, which is no longer necessarily 1 as it was when $e_C(0) > H'$. With $e_C(0) = H'$, D' may mix at $\Omega_{D'}(1)$. To obtain $e_{D'}^*(1)$, note that because C mixes at $\Omega_C(0)$ and $\Omega_C(1)$ and $e_D(1) = 0$,

$$q_C = w_C - \varepsilon_{D'} e_{D'}^*(1)[w_C - [\delta d_C + (1 - \delta)s_C]]$$

Solving this for $e_{D'}^*(1)$ gives the expression for $e_{D'}^*(1)$ for equilibrium (iv).

Combining Bayes' rule and the expressions for the states' strategies gives the beliefs reported earlier. The constraint that $1 \geq H' = e_C^*(0)$ yields the restriction on $\varepsilon_{C'}$. Constraining the expression for $e_{D'}^*(1)$ to be less than 1 gives the restriction on $\varepsilon_{D'}$.

Now suppose $e_C^*(0) = 1$; then (i) results. Generically, $H < 1$, so the relation $H' \leq e_C(0) = 1 < H$ implies $e_D^*(1) = 0$, $e_{D'}^*(1) = 1$, $e_{D'}^*(2) = L'$, and

$$e_C^*(1) = [\varepsilon_{C'}/(1 - \varepsilon_{C'})][B_{D'}(2)/(1 - B_{D'}(2))]$$

Beliefs are given by Bayes' rule and by substituting the expressions for the states' strategies. Because $H' \leq e_C^*(0) < H$ and $e_C^*(0) = 1$, then $H > 1$, and, generically, $H' < 1$. Ensuring $H > 1$ yields the lower bound on $\varepsilon_{C'}$, and requiring H' to be less than 1 gives the upper bound. Because $e_C^*(0) = 1$, the expected payoff to exploiting the situation must be at least equal to the payoff to not exploiting the situation. This gives the restriction on $\varepsilon_{D'}$ for equilibrium (i).

Case II: $e_C(1)e_C(0) > [\varepsilon_{C'}/(1 - \varepsilon_{C'})][B_{D'}(2)/(1 - B_{D'}(2))]$

This case gives equilibrium (ii). The best-reply correspondence for $e_{D'}(2)$ implies $e_{D'}^*(2) = 1$. This leaves $e_C^*(0)$, $e_C^*(1)$, $e_D^*(1)$, and $e_{D'}^*(1)$ to be specified.

The specification begins with two observations. First, because the resolve of D' is strictly greater than that of D, it would seem intuitively that if $e_D^*(1) > 0$, then $e_{D'}^*(1) = 1$. Algebra shows that any value of $\beta_D(1)$ that sustains $e_D(1) > 0$ is strictly greater than the minimal value of $\beta_{D'}(1)$ that sustains $e_{D'}(1) = 1$. But $\beta_D^*(1) = \beta_{D'}^*(1)$; so if $e_D^*(1) > 0$, then $e_{D'}^*(1) = 1$.

The second remark is that in a crisis equilibrium it must be that $e_D^*(1) > 0$. Suppose the contrary: $e_D^*(1) = 0$. In a crisis equilibrium there must be some chance of resistance; so $e_{D'}^*(1) > 0$. But given these strategies, resistance unambiguously signals that the challenged state is resolute, and with $e_{D'}^*(2) = 1$, C's best reply is $e_C(1) = 0$. This, however, contradicts the inequality defining Case II. Thus, $e_D^*(1) > 0$. These remarks imply that $e_D^*(1) > 0$ and $e_{D'}^*(1) = 1$.

Now consider the problem facing C at $\Omega_C(1)$. Let $B_C(1)$ be the value of $\beta_C(1)$ that leaves C indifferent to escalating and to submitting. Then

$$B_C(1) = [1 - (1 - 2\delta)(1 - 3\delta)][1 - R_C]/[(1 - 2\delta)[(1 - 3\delta)R_C + 3\delta]]$$

Thus, C's best response at $\Omega_C(1)$ is $e_C(1) = 1$ if $\beta_C(1) > B_C(1)$, $e_C(1) \in [0, 1]$ if $\beta_C(1) = B_C(1)$, and $e_C(1) = 0$ if $\beta_C(1) < B_C(1)$. Applying Bayes' rule and substituting for $\beta_C(1)$ implies that C's best-reply correspondence can be written as

$$e_C(1) = 1 \qquad \text{if } e_D(1) > [\varepsilon_{D'}/(1 - \varepsilon_{D'})][B_C(1)/(1 - B_C(1))]$$
$$e_C(1) \in [0, 1] \quad \text{if } e_D(1) = [\varepsilon_{D'}/(1 - \varepsilon_{D'})][B_C(1)/(1 - B_C(1))]$$
$$e_C(1) = 0 \qquad \text{if } e_D(1) < [\varepsilon_{D'}/(1 - \varepsilon_{D'})][B_C(1)/(1 - B_C(1))]$$

To specify $e_D^*(1)$, begin by noting that the inequality defining Case II implies $e_C(1) > 0$. It will now be shown that $e_C(1) < 1$. Assume that $e_C(1) = 1$. Then the best-reply correspondence for C at $\Omega_C(1)$ gives

$$e_D(1) \geq \varepsilon_{D'}B_C(1)/[(1 - \varepsilon_{D'})(1 - B_C(1))]$$

If, moreover, $e_C(1) = 1$, then because $e_{C'}^*(1) = 1$, D will submit at $\Omega_D(1)$, for there is no chance of its prevailing. But if $e_D(1) = 0$, then

$$e_D(1) < \varepsilon_{D'}B_C(1)/[(1 - \varepsilon_{D'})(1 - B_C(1))]$$

a contradiction. This contradiction leaves $e_C^*(1) < 1$. The fact that $0 < e_C^*(1) < 1$ and the best-reply correspondence for C at $\Omega_C(1)$ yield

$$e_D^*(1) = \varepsilon_{D'}B_C(1)/[(1 - \varepsilon_{D'})(1 - B_C(1))]$$

The strategies left to be specified are $e_C^*(0)$ and $e_C^*(1)$, and this begins by obtaining a relation between them. For there to be an equilibrium,

$$0 \leq e_D^*(1) = \varepsilon_{D'}B_C(1)/[(1 - \varepsilon_{D'})(1 - B_C(1))] \leq 1$$

Because $0 < B_C(1) < 1$, $e_D^*(1) > 0$. Generically,

$$\varepsilon_{D'}B_C(1)/[(1 - \varepsilon_{D'})(1 - B_C(1))]$$

is less than 1; so $e_D^*(1)$ must also be generically less than 1. With $0 < e_D^*(1) < 1$, D is indifferent to escalating and submitting at $\Omega_D(1)$. So

$$s_D = \beta_D(1)[\delta d_D + (1 - \delta)[(1 - e_C^*(1))w_D + e_C^*(1)[2\delta d_D + (1 - 2\delta)s_D]]]$$
$$+ (1 - \beta_D(1))[\delta d_D + (1 - \delta)[2\delta d_D + (1 - 2\delta)s_D]]$$

Substituting for $\beta_D(1)$ yields

$$e_C^*(1) = 1 - \left[1 + \left(\frac{\varepsilon_{C'}}{1 - \varepsilon_{C'}}\right)\frac{1}{e_C(0)}\right]\left[\frac{[1 - (1 - \delta)(1 - 2\delta)][1 - R_D]}{(1 - \delta)[(1 - 2\delta)R_D + 2\delta]}\right]$$

This relation is the same as the relation between $e_C(0)$ and $\hat{e}_C(1)$ that was derived in Case I. Accordingly, the sequential equilibria in Case II must lie along $\hat{e}_C(1)$ in Figure A3.1 above the constraint Z. This implies $0 < e_C^*(1) < 1$.

C's best-response correspondence at $\Omega_C(0)$ will now be determined. Note that because C randomizes at $\Omega_C(1)$, C's expected payoff if the game reaches this information set is s_C. Then, letting Q_C be the value of the status quo at which C will be indifferent to exploiting the situation and accepting the status quo gives

$$Q_C = (1 - \varepsilon_{D'})[(1 - e_D^*(1))w_C + e_D^*(1)[\delta d_C + (1 - \delta)s_C]] \\ + \varepsilon_{D'}[(1 - e_{D'}^*(1))w_C + e_{D'}^*(1)[\delta d_C + (1 - \delta)s_C]]$$

Substituting the expressions for $e_D^*(1)$ and $e_{D'}^*(1)$ produces

$$Q_C = [((1 - \varepsilon_{D'}) - \varepsilon_{D'}B_C(1))/(1 - B_C(1))] \\ \times [(w_C - s_C) + \delta(w_C - d_C)] + \delta d_C + (1 - \delta)s_C$$

The best-reply correspondence for C at $\Omega_C(0)$ is therefore $e_C(0) = 1$ if $q_C < Q_C$, $e_C(0) \in [0, 1]$ if $q_C = Q_C$, and $e_C(0) = 0$ if $q_C > Q_C$.

The final step in determining $e_C^*(0)$ and $e_C^*(1)$ is to note that if there is to be a sequential crisis equilibrium, then $q_C \leq Q_C$. Otherwise, C will never challenge the status quo. A challenge will then unambiguously signal that the challenger is resolute. This challenger escalates with probability 1 for all $m \leq M_{C'}$; so there will be no resistance and no crisis. Hence, $q_C \leq Q_C$.

Disregarding the event $q_C = Q_C$, which has measure zero, the equilibrium strategies $e_C^*(0)$ and $e_C^*(1)$ may now be specified. If $q_C < Q_C$, then $e_C^*(0) = 1$, and $e_C^*(1)$ is the value of $\hat{e}_C(1)$ evaluated at $e_C(0) = 1$, which is the expression reported earlier for $e_C^*(1)$ in this equilibrium.

Expressions for the relevant beliefs are obtained with Bayes' rule and by substituting the expressions for the states' strategies.

Several conditions are needed to ensure the existence of the sequential crisis equilibrium in Case II. First, $\hat{e}_C(1)$ must be above the constraint Z at $e_C(0) = 1$. This is equivalent to assuming $H < 1$, which when solved for $\varepsilon_{C'}$ gives the restriction stated earlier. The second condition is that $q_C < Q_C$, which means that

$$\varepsilon_{D'} < [(1 - B_C(1))(w_C - q_C)]/[(w_C - d_C)[(1 - \delta)R_C + \delta]]$$

This also ensures that $1 - \varepsilon_{D'} > B_C(1)$, so that $e_D^*(1) < 1$. ∎

CHAPTER 4

Stability and longer brinkmanship crises

The preceding chapter examined the effects of various changes on the escalatory dynamics of brinkmanship crises. Such examinations are always bound by the limits of the model used in the investigation. One limitation of the model developed in Chapter 3 was that in order to simplify the analysis, the maximum length of a crisis in the model was fixed exogenously and was, moreover, assumed to be very short. In the longest possible crisis, the challenger would dispute the status quo, and both the defender and challenger would take two steps toward the brink, after which the defender would submit. These simplifications reduced the complexity of the analysis, but they made it impossible to study crucial aspects of the approach to deterrence based on the array of risk. One could not, for example, compare the effects on stability of being able to take smaller, less dangerous steps toward the brink and the effects of being able to take only larger and more dangerous steps.

This chapter begins to examine the dynamics of longer brinkmanship crises. In the model to be developed here, there is no exogenous restriction on the number of steps that the states can take. In these longer crises, states generally become less and less likely to escalate as the crisis unfolds. Each also becomes more and more confident that its adversary is resolute. If, therefore, two irresolute states are actually facing each other, misperception will grow worse throughout the crisis. The effects of changes in the states' levels of resolve, in the challenger's stake in the status quo, and in the degree of initial misperception in longer crises parallel those in shorter crises. The greater an adversary's resolve, for example, the more likely a state may be to escalate, and the greater the potential challenger's stake in the status quo, the less likely the defender will generally be to resist a challenge. Finally, the model makes it possible to examine the effects of having to approach the brink by taking steps of different sizes. An increase in the size of the incremental risk of losing collective control that each step toward the brink entails (i.e., an increase in δ) turns out to have two effects. First, it makes both the challenger and defender less likely to escalate at every stage of the crisis. It is as if they compensate for the greater level of autonomous risk by being less willing to create it. Second, the potential challenger becomes more likely to dispute the status quo. It is as if the smaller chance of escalation affords a greater opportunity to dispute the status quo.

The model

This analysis of longer brinkmanship crises is based on the formalization developed in Chapter 3. Two features of brinkmanship – that there is a series of decisions, and that the states escalate by generating an autonomous risk of disaster – are modeled here as they were previously. Indeed, the underlying complete-information game illustrated in Figure 3.2 is the same. The confrontation begins with a potential challenger's having to decide to attack, to exploit the situation, or to accept the status quo. If it challenges the status quo, the onus of escalation shifts to the defender. The defender then has three options: quitting, launching a massive nuclear attack, or escalating by taking a step toward the brink. If the defender escalates and the states do not lose collective control of events at that point, the onus of escalation shifts back to the challenger. The challenger must decide to quit, launch a massive nuclear attack, or escalate. The crisis continues, with the onus of escalation shifting back and forth with each step, raising the risk of losing collective control by an increment δ, until the crisis ends in a general nuclear exchange or until one of the states quits.

The third essential of brinkmanship, which is that the states lack complete information, is modeled somewhat differently than before. As in the previous model, a state, say C, is unsure whether it is facing a resolute defender D' or an irresolute defender D. Previously, the resolute defender was assumed to be able to quit, attack, or escalate, just as its irresolute counterpart could. To simplify matters, now suppose that the resolute defender D' is wedded to a strategy of always escalating.[1] That is, if the challenger escalates, then D' is certain to escalate.[2] This is illustrated in Figure 4.1, where the only alternative D' has at each of its decision nodes is to escalate.

Although incomplete information is formalized in this way in part to

[1] The earlier analysis was more complicated, because if D' could quit, attack, or escalate, then the game had to be solved for the equilibrium strategy of D' as well as those of C and D. In the present formulation in which D' and, as will also be assumed, C' can only escalate, the game need only be solved for the equilibrium strategies of C and D. Assuming that C' and D' always escalate also simplifies the analysis in another way. This assumption ensures that all information sets are reached with positive probability in equilibrium, and this avoids the difficult problem of deciding what are "reasonable" beliefs to hold off the equilibrium path. For further discussion of this latter issue, see the Appendix after Chapter 8.

[2] Modeling incomplete information in this way by assuming that the actors are wedded to a fixed strategy is based on the method used by Kreps et al. (1982) in their study of the effects of incomplete information on cooperation in a finitely repeated prisoner's dilemma.

Figure 4.1. Longer brinkmanship crises.

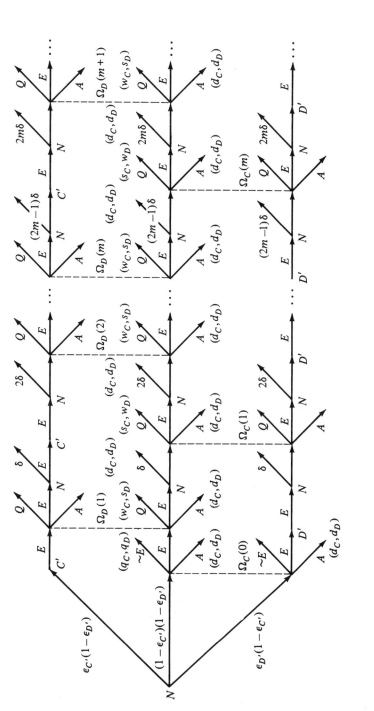

ease the analysis, this representation also addresses two substantive issues. First, because the game ends as soon as one state stops escalating, D' is, in effect, wedded to playing a strategy of tit for tat. In tit for tat, a state always does what its adversary just did, and, as in tit for tat, D' escalates if C has just escalated. Of course, if C quits, then D', following its strategy of always escalating, will still escalate if it has the opportunity. D', therefore, is not strictly following tit for tat. This difference, however, is unimportant and does not influence the outcome of the game, for if C quits, the game ends before D' has another opportunity to escalate. Effectively, then, D' is wedded to playing tit for tat. Thus, in deciding what to do, C is uncertain whether or not its adversary will play a strategy of tit for tat.[3]

The second issue is based on the observation that D' is in some sense irrational. Because it is wedded to a strategy of always escalating, D' will escalate even if this entails creating a certainty of disaster. That is, D' will escalate even if doing so requires it to trigger a disaster with probability 1. As will be seen, what drives escalation in this model is a state's attempt to derive the benefits of having a reputation for being resolute. D, for example, wants to have a reputation for behaving like D'. That is, it is rational for D to seem to be irrational like D'. D, in essence, is employing what has been called the strategy of the rationality of the irrational (Kahn 1965, pp. 57–8; Maxwell 1968), in that D rationally tries to appear to be, at least to some extent, irrational. Modeling incomplete information by assuming that the resolute state is wedded to a strategy of always escalating may illuminate the roles of both tit for tat and the strategy of the rationality of the irrational in brinkmanship bargaining.

Information is incomplete on both sides. D will also be assumed to be uncertain of the type of its adversary. D does not know if it is facing C or C', where the resolute challenger, C', is also wedded to a strategy of always escalating. The prior probability of facing the resolute defender D' is $\varepsilon_{D'}$, and the prior probability of facing the resolute challenger C' is $\varepsilon_{C'}$, and both of these probabilities are common knowledge.

Incomplete information is the force driving escalation in the model. If, for example, there were complete information, $M_C > M_D$, and C were facing D, then Proposition 3.1 would imply that C would challenge the status quo, and D would not resist. If, however, C were facing D', it would not escalate. But with incomplete information, C is unsure whether it is facing the resolute defender D' or the irresolute defender D. This gives an irresolute defender an incentive to develop and maintain a reputation for being resolute. A state's struggle to determine if its adversary is actually resolute

---

[3] See Kreps et al. (1982) for a game-theoretic analysis of tit for tat and Axelrod (1981, 1984) for a discussion of tit for tat as a bargaining strategy based on the results of computer simulations.

and its adversary's struggle to maintain a reputation for being resolute and derive the benefits of it are the seeds of escalation.

As in the previous model of brinkmanship, the information set at which C must decide whether or not to escalate for the mth time is denoted by $\Omega_C(m)$; $\beta_C(m)$ is the conditional probability that C is facing the irresolute defender D at $\Omega_C(m)$; $\Omega_D(m)$ and $\beta_D(m)$ are defined similarly. To describe the states' behavioral strategies, take $e_C(m)$ and $a_C(m)$ to denote, respectively, the probabilities that C will escalate or attack at $\Omega_C(m)$. Then the probability that C will submit is $1 - e_C(m) - a_C(m)$. The probabilities that D will escalate or attack at $\Omega_D(m)$ are, respectively, $e_D(m)$ and $a_D(m)$.

The family of sequential crisis equilibria

There may be gains to be had from having a reputation for being resolute. But there are also costs, for an irresolute defender generally must be willing to escalate and accept some risk of disaster. The game's sequential crisis equilibria formally balance these costs and benefits and describe the resulting dynamics. Proposition 4.1 specifies the complete set of sequential crisis equilibria for the incomplete-information game of brinkmanship.[4]

> **Proposition 4.1:** If $\varepsilon_{D'} > \bar{\varepsilon}_{D'} = (w_C - q_C)/[(w_C - d_C)((1 - \delta)R_C + \delta)]$
> then, generically, there are no sequential crisis equilibria, because C does not challenge the status quo. If $\varepsilon_{D'} < \bar{\varepsilon}_{D'}$, but $\varepsilon_{C'} > \bar{\varepsilon}_{C'} = (R_D - \delta)/[(1 - \delta)[(1 - 2\delta)R_D + 2\delta]]$ there are again no sequential crisis equilibria, but this time D does not resist C's challenge. If $\varepsilon_{D'} < \bar{\varepsilon}_{D'}$ and $\varepsilon_{C'} < \bar{\varepsilon}_{C'}$, then there exists a generically unique family of sequential crisis equilibria. Each member of this family is indexed by $\bar{m} \geq 0$, and D's strategies for any $\bar{m}$ are given by
>
> $$e_D^*(1) = \left(\frac{1}{1 - \varepsilon_{D'}}\right)\left[\left(\frac{w_C - q_C}{w_C - d_C}\right)\frac{1}{(1 - \delta)R_C + \delta} - \varepsilon_{D'}\right] = \frac{\bar{\varepsilon}_{D'} - \varepsilon_{D'}}{1 - \varepsilon_{D'}} \quad (4.1)$$
>
> If $\bar{m} \geq 1$,
>
> $$e_D^*(2) = \frac{R_C - 2\delta}{(1 - 2\delta)[(1 - 3\delta)R_C + 3\delta]} - \left(\frac{\varepsilon_{D'}}{1 - \varepsilon_{D'}}\right)$$
> $$\times \left[\frac{[1 - (1 - 2\delta)(1 - 3\delta)](1 - R_C)}{(1 - 2\delta)[(1 - 3\delta)R_C + 3\delta]}\right]\frac{1}{\varepsilon_D^*(1)} \quad (4.2)$$

---

[4] As before, no state will ever launch a general nuclear attack deliberately: $a_C^*(m) = a_D^*(m) = 0$ for all m. This means that in order to describe the equilibrium strategies, only the probabilities of escalation $e_C^*(m)$ and $e_D^*(m)$ need be determined.

If $\bar{m} \geq 2$, then for $2 \leq m \leq \bar{m}$,

$e_D^*(m+1)$

$$= 1 - \left(\frac{1 - (1 - 2m\delta)(1 - (2m+1)\delta)}{1 - (1 - 2(m-1)\delta)(1 - (2m-1)\delta)} \right)$$

$$\times \left(\frac{R_C - 2(m-1)\delta}{(1 - 2m\delta)[1 - (1 - (2m+1)\delta)(1 - R_C)]} \right) \left(\frac{1 - e_D^*(m)}{e_D^*(m)} \right) \quad (4.3)$$

And for $m > \bar{m} + 1$,

$e_D^*(m) = 0$

C's equilibrium strategies are given by

$$e_C^*(0) = \frac{\varepsilon_{C'}}{1 - \varepsilon_{C'}} \left[\frac{[1 - (1 - \delta)(1 - 2\delta)](1 - R_D)}{R_D - \delta - e_C^*(1)(1 - \delta)[(1 - 2\delta)R_D + 2\delta]} \right] \quad (4.4)$$

For $1 \leq m \leq \bar{m}$,

$e_C^*(m)$

$$= \left[1 + (1 - e_C^*(m+1)) \left(\frac{1 - (1 - (2m-1)\delta)(1 - 2m\delta)}{1 - (1 - (2m+1)\delta)(1 - 2(m+1)\delta)} \right) \right.$$

$$\left. \times \left(\frac{(1 - (2m+1)\delta)[1 - (1 - 2(m+1)\delta)(1 - R_D)]}{R_D - (2m-1)\delta} \right) \right]^{-1} \quad (4.5)$$

And for $m > \bar{m}$,

$e_C^*(m) = 0$

Because all information sets are reached with positive probability, beliefs are simply given by Bayes' rule.

To complete the specification of the family, the range of $\bar{m}$ must be given. Use (4.1), (4.2), and (4.3) to generate a sequence of numbers, and let $\bar{M}$ be the first integer for which $e_D^*(m) > 0$ for $0 \leq m \leq \bar{M} + 1$ and $e_D^*(\bar{M} + 2) < 0$. Now let $\bar{N}$ be the maximum value of $\bar{n}$ such that $e_C^*(0)$ generated by (4.4), (4.5), and the initial condition $e_C^*(\bar{n} + 1) = 0$ is positive. Then the range of $\bar{m}$ is $0 \leq \bar{m} \leq \min \{\bar{M}, \bar{N}, M_D - 1, M_C\}$.

Proposition 4.1 is derived in Appendix 4.1. If the probability of facing the resolute defender $\varepsilon_{D'}$ is too large, there is no challenge. The potential challenger accepts the status quo. If the potential challenger is sufficiently confident that it is confronting the irresolute defender, there may be a

Figure 4.2. The sequential crisis equilibria.

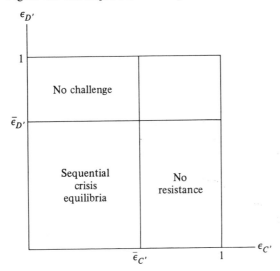

challenge, but still no crisis, for the defender may be sufficiently confident that the challenger is resolute (i.e., $\varepsilon_{C'}$ may be high enough) that a challenge will not be resisted. Only if both the challenger and the defender are sufficiently confident that their adversaries are irresolute will there be a crisis. Figure 4.2 illustrates the regions in which the sequential crisis equilibria exist.

Figure 4.3 illustrates the family of equilibrium strategies. After the defender has taken a first step toward the brink, the states become less and less likely to escalate as the confrontation continues. That is, as long as $e_C^*(m) > 0$, then $e_C^*(m)$ is decreasing in m for $m \geq 1$, and as long as $e_D^*(m) > 0$, then $e_D^*(m)$ is decreasing in m for $m \geq 2$.[5] The beginning of a crisis is, however, more complex. The potential challenger may be more or less likely to challenge the status quo than it is to escalate if its challenge is resisted. That is, $e_C^*(0)$ may be greater or less than $e_C^*(1)$. In the latter case, C would seem to be relatively reluctant to dispute the status quo. But if, however reluctantly, C does challenge the status quo, then C is relatively more likely to meet any initial resistance from the defender with further escalation. Similarly, the defender may be more or less likely to take a first step toward the brink than it is to take a second step.

The equilibrium strategies defined in the proposition describe the dynamics of escalation in longer brinkmanship crises. If there is a crisis, the confrontation begins with the potential challenger's believing that it is

[5] This is demonstrated in Appendix 4.1.

facing a resolute defender with probability $\varepsilon_{D'}$. If C is sufficiently confident that the defender is irresolute, it will challenge the status quo with probability $e_C^*(0)$. A challenge shifts the onus of escalation to irresolute defender D and forces it to update its assessment of the likelihood of its facing a resolute challenger from $\varepsilon_{C'}$ to $1 - \beta_D(1)$. After this reassessment, the defender is sufficiently confident that it is facing an irresolute challenger that it resists the challenge. D resists C's challenge by taking a step that "leaves something to chance" with probability $e_D^*(1)$. That is, D steps toward the brink and thereby generates some autonomous risk that the states will lose collective control of the crisis and that it will end in disaster. D's resistance shifts the onus of escalation back to C and forces it to revise its estimate of the probability that its adversary is resolute. C is still sufficiently confident that its adversary is irresolute that it will meet D's resistance by escalating with probability $e_C^*(1)$. C's escalation shifts the onus of escalation back to D. The crisis continues in this way, with the onus of escalation shifting back and forth until C or D quits or until the risk of disaster is realized and the crisis ends in the horror of a general nuclear exchange.

Figure 4.3. A family of brinkmanship equilibria.

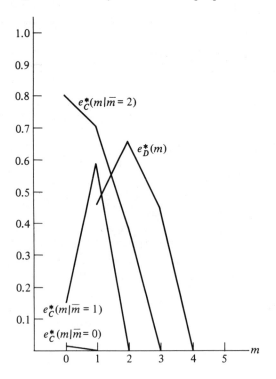

As the crisis unfolds and continued escalation entails generating larger and larger risks of disaster, each state becomes increasingly confident that it is facing a resolute adversary. Formally, the probabilities of facing a resolute adversary, $1 - \beta_C(m)$ and $1 - \beta_D(m)$, are increasing in m. This implies that each state's reputation for being resolute grows stronger as the crisis continues. Put another way, misperception becomes worse and worse as the crisis goes on, for although C becomes increasingly confident that it is facing D', and D becomes increasingly confident that it is facing C', C and D are actually facing each other.

The dynamics of escalation

The strategies defined in Proposition 4.1 describe the dynamics of escalation in longer brinkmanship crises and may be used to investigate how changes in the model's parameters affect escalation. The consequences of three changes will be considered here. First, what are the consequences of varying the states' levels of resolve? Recall that incomplete information is modeled somewhat more simply than in the preceding chapter. There, however, the states' levels of resolve were exogenously restricted in such a way that the number of times that the states might be willing to escalate was fixed and was small. It was assumed that $M_C = M_D = 1$, $M_{D'} = 2$, and $M_{C'} \geq 2$. That restriction forced the crisis to be very short. More important, it precluded examination of the effects of changes in the states' levels of resolve that would make them willing to escalate a different number of times. The simpler treatment of incomplete information here results in a more tractable extensive form that facilitates analysis of the game when the levels of resolve are arbitrary. The number of times that a state might escalate in a crisis becomes endogenous, and that permits investigation of the effects of changes in levels of resolve that will alter this number. The second set of consequences to be examined encompasses those due to changes in the value that the challenger places on the status quo. How do the equilibrium strategies change as q_C varies? Third, what are the effects of incomplete information on deterrence?

Before examining these consequences, the length of a crisis should be defined. Note that in the $\bar{m}$th equilibrium, that is, in the $\bar{m}$th member of the family of equilibria, C is willing to challenge the status quo and subsequently to escalate $\bar{m}$ times, and D is willing to escalate $\bar{m} + 1$ times. That is, $e_C^*(m) > 0$ for all $m \leq \bar{m}$, and $e_D^*(m) > 0$ for all $m \leq \bar{m} + 1$. Thus, the maximum number of times that a state might generate some risk of disaster in this crisis is $2\bar{m} + 1$. Accordingly, the length of a crisis associated with the $\bar{m}$th equilibrium is $2\bar{m} + 1$.

As noted earlier, critical-risk models (Snyder and Diesing 1977, pp. 48–52) suggest that the greater an adversary's resolve, the less likely a state will be to escalate, for the greater an adversary's resolve, the more likely it is to stand firm. That, in turn, would seem to make escalation more dangerous for the state. Shying away from this greater danger, the state is less likely to escalate the more resolute its adversary. As has already been shown, this does not hold for the short crises examined previously. It also fails to hold in longer crises.

Consider first the consequences of the defender being more resolute. In any existing member of the family of equilibria, an increase in the defender's resolve makes the challenger more likely, not less likely, to escalate throughout the crisis.[6] The challenger, however, may become less likely to challenge the status quo. Thus, an increase in the defender's resolve may affect the challenger differently at different stages of the confrontation. An increase in R_D may also add new members to the family of sequential crisis equilibria that will be longer than any of the previously existing crises.[7] Turning to the challenger's resolve, an increase in it may also make the defender more likely to escalate in an existing equilibrium, as well as make for longer crises by adding new members to the family of sequential crisis equilibria.

The effects of changing the levels of resolve are subtle, complicated, and difficult to explain intuitively. (Indeed, it is difficult to determine which, if any, of these effects are artifacts of the model and ought not to be explained untuitively.) As in the shorter crises, these complications seem to arise, at least in part, because of the interaction of the states' strategies and their beliefs about their adversaries' resolve. To illustrate this interaction, consider the decision confronting the defender at a given stage of the crisis, say at the information set $\Omega_D(m_0)$. Now suppose that the defender's resolve is increased. In the new equilibrium associated with this higher level of resolve, D still must be indifferent between escalating and submitting at $\Omega_D(m_0)$, because $0 < e_D^*(m_0) < 1$. But with greater resolve, D will strictly prefer to escalate at this stage of the crisis if C's strategies are unchanged from those of the original equilibrium. Thus, C's strategies must change in the new equilibrium so as to make D indifferent to escalating at $\Omega_D(m_0)$. Two types of changes are possible. C may be more likely to escalate in the future. That is, C may be more likely to escalate at $\Omega_C(m)$ for some $m \geq m_0$. This change does not affect the strength of D's belief that it is facing C at $\Omega_D(m_0)$: $\beta_D(m_0)$ is unaffected. This change does, however, increase the

---

[6] To show $\partial e_C^*(m)/\partial R_D > 0$ for $1 \leq m \leq \bar{m}$, differentiate (4.5) to show that for a fixed $e_C^*(m+1)$, $e_C^*(m)$ is increasing in R_D. Then, because $e_C^*(\bar{m}+1) = 0$, an increase in R_D raises $e_C^*(\bar{m})$. But an increase in R_D coupled with a larger $e_C^*(\bar{m})$ unambiguously raises $e_C^*(\bar{m}-1)$. Continuing in this way establishes the result.

[7] That is, $\bar{N}$ may increase, so that a larger $\bar{m}$ may satisfy the contraint that $\bar{m} \leq \min\{\bar{M}, \bar{N}\}$.

expected cost to D of escalating at $\Omega_D(m_0)$ by making C less likely to submit in the future. This tends to restore D's indifference. In the second type of change, C may have been less likely to escalate before the crisis reached $\Omega_D(m_0)$. Formally, $e_C^*(m)$ for some $m < m_0$ may be smaller in the new equilibrium than in the original. The effect of this is that D, when deciding what to do at $\Omega_D(m_0)$, is less confident that it is facing C and more confident that it is facing C'. This also reduces the expected value to D of escalation and tends to make D indifferent.

These two influences on $e_C^*(m)$ arise from considering just one of D's information sets, $\Omega_D(m_0)$. But D has several information sets, and this creates opposing pressures on $e_C^*(m)$. To make D less confident of facing C at D's information sets that follow, say, $\Omega_C(m_1)$, $e_C^*(m_1)$ will tend to fall. But to increase the expected return to D of escalating at its information sets that come before $\Omega_C(m_1)$, the challenger C will have to be more likely to escalate, and $e_C^*(m_1)$ will tend to rise. The model helps to identify the competing influences on $e_C^*(m)$ that are at work, and the precise balance struck between these opposing influences is specified in the equilibrium strategies described in Proposition 4.1.

The challenger's having a greater stake in the status quo will generally enhance stability, but not by making a challenge less likely. Rather, the defender will be less likely to escalate. More precisely, suppose that the challenger has a greater stake in the status quo. If a member of the family of sequential crisis equilibria exists after the increase in q_C, then the defender will be less likely to escalate throughout the crisis.[8]

Table 4.1 illustrates the effects of the challenger having different stakes in the status quo for some arbitrary but perhaps suggestive parameter values. The challenger's level of resolve is taken to be 0.105, so that the greatest risk of disaster that the challenger is willing to run in order to prevail is about 10 percent.[9] The defender's resolve is assumed to be 0.085, and the probability that the defender is facing the resolute challenger is 1 percent: $\varepsilon_{C'} = 0.01$. The number at the top of each cell is the length of the longest crisis in the family of crises associated with that cell. The number 5 in the cell for which the challenger's normalized stake in the status quo is zero ($q_C = 0$) and the probability of facing a resolute defender is 1 percent ($\varepsilon_{D'} = 0.01$) means that the maximum number of times that the states are willing to escalate by generating some risk of disaster in the longest crisis is five. There is some

---

[8] To see that $e_D^*(m)$ is decreasing in q_C, note that as q_C rises, $e_D^*(1)$ decreases. Then (4.2) shows that this decrease in $e_D^*(1)$ reduces $e_D^*(2)$. Finally, (4.3) implies that as $e_D^*(m)$ falls, $e_D^*(m+1)$ falls. Thus, the decrease in $e_D^*(2)$ reduces $e_D^*(3)$, which in turn reduces $e_D^*(4)$, which in turn reduces $e_D^*(5)$, and so on.

[9] The underlying values of prevailing, submitting, and suffering a disaster that produce this level of resolve are $w_C = 1$, $s_C = -1$, and $d_C = -18.048$.

Table 4.1. *The length of a crisis and the probability of war*

$\varepsilon_{D'}$	q_C				
	-0.8	-0.4	0	0.4	0.8
0.1	5 0.0455 0.00376	5 0.0446 0.00275	5 0.0427 0.00175	3 0.0298 0.00011	*
0.01	5 0.0479 0.00404	5 0.0478 0.00313	5 0.0477 0.00222	5 0.0474 0.00130	5 0.0457 0.00039
0.001	5 0.0481 0.00407	5 0.0481 0.00316	5 0.0481 0.00226	5 0.0480 0.00135	5 0.0479 0.00045
0.000001	5 0.0481 0.00407	5 0.0481 0.00317	5 0.0481 0.00226	5 0.0481 0.00136	5 0.0481 0.00045

* No sequential crisis equilibrium exists for these values.
Note: The length of the crisis and the probability of war are calculated for the case in which $R_D = 0.085$, $\varepsilon_{C'} = 0.01$, $\delta = 0.01$, $w_C = 1$, $s_C = -1$, and $d_C = -18.048$. The latter three values imply that $R_C = 0.105$.

chance that the challenger will escalate twice and the defender three times. The number in the center of the cell is the probability that this longest crisis will end in a general nuclear exchange. If, therefore, $q_C = 0$ and $\varepsilon_{D'} = 0.01$, the chances that the states will lose collective control, given that there has already been a resisted challenge, is 0.0477. Because the longest crisis in any family of equilibria is also the most dangerous, the probability that a crisis will end in war reported in any cell is therefore the probability that the most dangerous crisis in the family will end in disaster. Finally, recall the difference between situational stability and crisis stability. The former measures the probability that there will not be a general nuclear exchange from the point in the game tree at which C is deciding whether or not to dispute the status quo. The latter measures the probability that there will not be a war once there has been a resisted challenge.[10] The number at the bottom of the cell is the probability that the situation will end in disaster. So in the cell for which $q_C = 0$ and $\varepsilon_{D'} = 0.01$, the likelihood that the situation will end in disaster is 0.00222, or about two-tenths of 1 percent. Reading

[10] More formally, recall that situational stability is given by $1 - S_W$, and crisis stability is given by $1 - P_W$, where $S_W = e_C^*(0)e_D^*(1)P_W$ and $P_W = \delta + (1-\delta)e_C^*(1)[2\delta + (1-2\delta)e_D^*(2)[3\delta + \cdots]]$.

across the rows of Table 4.1 indicates that an increase in q_C enhances stability. But regardless of the values of q_C and $\varepsilon_{D'}$, the crisis and situation are remarkably stable. The probability of war given that there has been a resisted challenge never exceeds 5 percent, and the chance that a situation will end in disaster is much less, never more than one-half of 1 percent. The model seems quite stable.

Incomplete information plays an essential role in brinkmanship bargaining. Indeed, without it there would be no bargaining in the model: The state with the greatest effective resolve would escalate, and its adversary would submit. Incomplete information may, however, greatly enhance deterrence by reducing the likelihood of a challenge. For example, C's effective resolve in all of the equilibria summarized in Table 4.1 is greater than D's. With complete information, C would always dispute the status quo, and D would never resist. But with incomplete information, the probability of a challenge in any of these equilibria is never more than 0.11. Incomplete information about the resolve of the challenger in these examples does much to enhance deterrence. In other cases, however, incomplete information may not do much to improve deterrence. In the equilibrium associated with $\bar{m} = 2$ in Figure 4.3, the probability of a challenge falls to only 0.8. Incomplete information about the defender's resolve also affects the dynamics of escalation. The stronger the defender's initial reputation for being resolute (i.e., the larger $\varepsilon_{D'}$), the less likely D is to escalate throughout the crisis.[11]

Once again these effects seem to be due to the interaction between states' strategies and their beliefs about their adversaries. An increase in $\varepsilon_{D'}$ would initially make the challenger C more confident that it was facing the resolute defender when it was deciding whether or not to accept the status quo. That greater confidence would reduce the payoff to disputing the status quo and make a challenge less likely.[12] But that would mean that if there were a challenge, the defender would be more confident that the challenger was resolute. That, in turn, would reduce the payoff to escalating and leave the defender D less likely to resist a challenge.[13] But if resistance were less likely, the payoff to disputing the status quo would rise, and a

---

[11] To see that an increase in the strength of the challenger's belief that the defender is resolute leaves the defender less likely to escalate throughout the crisis, differentiate (4.1) with respect to $\varepsilon_{D'}$ to show that $\partial e_D^*(1)/\partial \varepsilon_{D'} < 0$. Inspection of (4.2) then demonstrates that $e_D^*(2)$ will have decreased with the increase in $\varepsilon_{D'}$. Finally, (4.3) implies that if $e_D^*(2)$ decreases, so will $e_D^*(3)$, and if $e_D^*(3)$ falls, so will $e_D^*(4)$, and so on. Thus, the larger $\varepsilon_{D'}$ and therefore the greater the defender's initial reputation for being resolute, the less likely the defender will be to escalate throughout the crises.

[12] More formally, if $\varepsilon_{D'}$ increases, then $e_C(0) = 0$ becomes C's best reply to D's original strategy.

[13] If $e_C(0) = 0$, then D is certain that it is facing C' at $\Omega_D(1)$; so $e_D(1) = 0$ is now D's best response.

challenge would be more likely.[14] That, of course, would leave the defender more confident that it was facing the irresolute challenger if there were a challenge, and so it goes. On balance, the greater the initial probability of facing the resolute defender in the model, the less likely the irresolute defender is to escalate.

The effects of incomplete information on the probability of war are mixed. The stronger the challenger's initial reputation for being resolute (i.e., the greater $\varepsilon_{C'}$), the greater $e_C^*(0)$, and the more likely C is to challenge the status quo. This tends to make the situation less stable. But the increase in $\varepsilon_{C'}$ has no effect on crisis stability, because the larger $\varepsilon_{C'}$ has no effect on the probability of a general nuclear exchange given that there has been a resisted challenge.[15] If, however, the defender has a stronger initial reputation for being resolute, D is, throughout the crisis, less likely to escalate, and this increases both situational stability and crisis stability. Table 4.1 illustrates the effects of increasing $\varepsilon_{D'}$ with some numerical examples. Although the probability that the situation and crisis will end in war falls as $\varepsilon_{D'}$ rises, the table suggests that once some uncertainty about the defender's resolve exists, variations in the degree of this uncertainty do not significantly affect the probability of war. In each column, the probability of the challenger facing a resolute defender, $\varepsilon_{D'}$, varies from one chance in ten to one in a million. Yet the probability of war hardly varies. Some aspects of deterrence may be quite sensitive to the beliefs and perceptions of each state about its adversary, but the model indicates that at least the probability of war is rather insensitive to a wide variation in beliefs about whether or not the defender is more resolute. Structural constraints, more than beliefs about the defender's resolve, seem to be more important determinants of the probability of war in the model.

The array of risk and the dynamics of escalation

In terms of the brinkmanship analogy, δ measures the size of the step that a state must take toward the brink if it decides to escalate. The larger δ, the larger the risk that a state must generate if it escalates. What are the consequences of an increase in δ for the dynamics of escalation and crisis stability? Does having to take a larger, more dangerous step make a state less willing to escalate? Does that, in turn, reduce the probability of war and enhance crisis stability? Or, if the states are less likely to escalate, does that create an opportunity for a potential challenger and make it more likely to dispute the status quo? And if a challenge to the status quo is more likely, does this raise the probability of war and reduce crisis stability? The model

---

[14] With $e_D(1) = 0$, C's best reply is to challenge the status quo: $e_C(0) = 1$.
[15] $e_C^*(m)$ for $m \geq 1$ is independent of ε_C.

may be used to explore these questions by examining the effects of changes in δ on the states' strategies.

Before investigating these effects, it will be useful to relate these issues to the array of risk. The array of risk conceptually bridges the gap between doing too much by launching a massive nuclear attack and doing too little by submitting. A state can pursue an intermediate course by exercising one of the limited options from the array of risk. This generates not a certainty but only a risk that the states will lose collective control and that the crisis will end in disaster. In a sense, then, δ measures the "grain" of the array of risk. That is, the smaller δ, the smaller the risk that escalation entails. The escalatory steps are closer together probabilistically. It is as if, in terms of Figure 2.2, the limited options that constitute the array of risk are closer together, in effect making the grain of the array of risk finer. Accordingly, questions about the effects of changes in δ may be rephrased in terms of the effects of changes in the grain of the array of risk. Studying the effects of increasing δ is, for example, akin to examining the consequences of coarsening the array of risk.[16]

The effect of increasing δ, and, in this sense, coarsening the array of risk, is to make both states less likely to escalate. That is, having to take larger risks with each step toward the abyss makes the defender less likely to step forward, and as long as the defender is not willing to run a risk of disaster that is greater than one chance in three (i.e., as long as $R_D \leq \frac{1}{3}$), then having to take riskier steps toward the brink also leaves the challenger less likely to escalate. The challenger, however, also becomes more likely to dispute the status quo. These influences pull the probability of war in opposite directions. The smaller likelihood of escalation tends to reduce the probability of war and enhance crisis stability. But the greater likelihood of a challenge and the fact that escalation now entails greater risks because δ is larger tend to increase the probability of war and reduce crisis stability. The net effect appears to be that increasing δ makes a general nuclear exchange more likely. Table 4.2 illustrates the effects for each member of a family of sequential crisis equilibria of variations in δ on the probability that the crisis and the situation will end in war. If, for example, $\delta = 0.020$, then the probability that the states will lose collective control, given that there has already been a resisted challenge in the equilibrium associated with $\bar{m} = 1$, is

---

[16] Although rephrasing questions in this way is suggestive, the two interpretations are not completely equivalent. As Figure 2.2 illustrates, the states may select various levels of risk. That is, a state may vary the size of the initial step toward the brink. After this first step, the confrontation continues, but this is left implicit in the formulation underlying Figure 2.2. The model, conversely, explicitly represents the continuing confrontation, but in order to simplify the game, the states are assumed to choose a single level of risk if they escalate. Each formulation leaves the opposite half of the problem implicit.

Table 4.2. *The grain of the array of risk and the probability of war*

δ	$\bar{m}$				
	0	1	2	3	4
0.005	0.005	0.0191	0.0333	0.0433	0.0483
	0.000004	0.000064	0.000337	0.00131	0.00504
0.010	0.010	0.0330	0.0477	0.0523	
	0.000017	0.000292	0.00222	0.0259	
0.015	0.015	0.0434	0.0542		
	0.000039	0.000822	0.0194		
0.020	0.020	0.0512			
	0.000071	0.00216			
0.025	0.025	0.0573			
	0.000115	0.00792			
0.030	0.030				
	0.000174				
0.035	0.035				
	0.000251				
0.040	0.040				
	0.000352				
0.045	0.045				
	0.000483				
0.050	0.050				
	0.000659				
0.055	0.055				
	0.000899				
0.060	0.060				
	0.001242				
0.065	0.065				
	0.001765				
0.070	0.070				
	0.002644				
0.075	0.075				
	0.004415				
0.080	0.080				
	0.009750				
0.085	—*				
	0.0*				

* No sequential crisis equilibrium exists for these values.
Note: The length of the crisis and the probability of war are calculated for the case in which $R_D = 0.085$, $\varepsilon_{C'} = \varepsilon_{D'} = 0.01$, $w_C = 1$, $s_C = -1$, and $d_C = -18.048$. The latter three values imply that $R_C = 0.105$.

0.0512. The chance of the situation ending in disaster is 0.00216. For any given equilibrium, an increase in δ generally increases the probability of an unlimited nuclear exchange and thereby reduces stability. Having to take larger, more dangerous steps generally makes the crisis and underlying situation more dangerous. But sometimes having to take a larger step may increase stability in the model. This seems to occur if a small increase in δ eliminates an equilibrium; then the remaining equilibria may be less dangerous than was the equilibrium that was eliminated by the increase in δ. Table 4.2 offers an example. The probability of war in the longest and therefore most dangerous crisis is 0.054 if $\delta = 0.015$. If δ increases to 0.020, then what was formerly the most dangerous crisis is eliminated, and the probability of war in the most dangerous of the remaining crises drops to 0.051.[17]

In sum, if each step toward the brink is more dangerous, both the defender and the challenger are less likely to escalate. But the challenger, knowing of this greater reluctance to escalate, is more inclined to take advantage of the situation by challenging the status quo. Although the states are less likely to escalate, this does not appear to be generally enough to offset the greater likelihood of a challenge and the greater risk that each

[17] To see more formally that having to take a more dangerous step makes the defender less likely to escalate, begin with equation (4.1). Inspection of this equation shows that $e_D^*(1)$ is decreasing in δ. Now, if C finds itself at $\Omega_C(1)$, it is less confident that it is facing D. Assuming that C continues to mix at $\Omega_C(1)$ in the new equilibrium associated with the larger δ, then the fact that C is less confident that it is facing the irresolute defender implies that $e_D^*(2)$ must fall in order to keep C indifferent. Thus, $e_D^*(2)$ is decreasing in δ, but this means that if C finds itself at $\Omega_C(2)$, it is again less confident that it is facing D. Applying the same argument shows that $e_D^*(3)$ is decreasing in δ. Continuing in this way demonstrates that $e_D^*(m)$ is decreasing in δ.

A more formal analysis also shows that as long as the defender's resolve is not too great (i.e., $R_D \leq \frac{1}{3}$), then the challenger C is less likely to escalate if steps toward the brink are more dangerous, but, second, it is less likely to dispute the status quo. To establish the first claim, recall that $e_C^*(\bar{m}+1) = 0$. Differentiating (4.5) with respect to δ at $m = \bar{m}$ then gives $\partial e_C^*(\bar{m})/\partial \delta < 0$ as long as $R_D \leq \frac{1}{3}$. (If $R_D > \frac{1}{3}$, the sign of $\partial e_C^*(\bar{m})/\partial \delta$ is ambiguous.) But equation (4.5) also implies that if δ is larger and $e_C^*(\bar{m})$ is smaller, then $e_C^*(\bar{m}-1)$ is smaller. Continuing in this way shows that $e_C^*(m)$ for $m \geq 1$ is decreasing in δ. To see that the challenger is more likely to dispute the status quo if the risk associated with each step is larger, consider D's decision at $\Omega_D(\bar{m}+1)$. Given that C will immediately submit if D escalates [i.e., $e_C^*(\bar{m}+1) = 0$], then the greater δ, the more confident D must be that it is facing C and not C' at $\Omega_D(\bar{m}+1)$ if D is to remain indifferent between escalating and submitting. That is, $\beta_D(\bar{m}+1)$ must be increasing in δ. But

$$\beta_D(\bar{m}+1) = (1-\varepsilon_{C'}) \prod_{i=0}^{\bar{m}} e_C^*(i) \bigg/ \left[\varepsilon_{C'} + (1-\varepsilon_{C'}) \prod_{i=0}^{\bar{m}} e_C^*(i) \right]$$

so if $\beta_D(\bar{m}+1)$ is to be increasing in δ, then $\prod_{i=0}^{\bar{m}} e_C^*(i)$ must also be increasing in δ. Yet, as was just shown, $e_C^*(m)$ for $1 \leq m \leq \bar{m}$ are decreasing in δ. Consequently, $e_C^*(0)$ must be increasing in δ.

step toward the brink entails. The probability of war rises as stepping toward the brink becomes more dangerous. Coarsening the array of risk generally seems to reduce stability.

This chapter and the preceding chapter have used formalizations of the brinkmanship analogy to provide insight into the approach to nuclear deterrence based on the strategy of leaving something to chance and the array of risk. The preceding chapter examined the effects on the dynamics of escalation of changes in the states' levels of resolve, the potential challenger's stake in the status quo, and the degree of misperception. The model illuminated the complicated interactions that may exist between a state's strategy and its adversary's beliefs about it and the effects of this interaction on crisis bargaining. In the model, the state with the greatest resolve might not prevail, and a state might be more, not less, likely to escalate the greater its adversary's resolve. A challenger's having a greater stake in the status quo did make a crisis less likely, but not necessarily because the potential challenger was less likely to dispute the status quo. Rather, the defender might be less likely to resist a challenge. Finally, it was seen that the effects of greater misperception could be both stabilizing and destabilizing.

The conclusions derived from the model in the preceding chapter were, however, limited because crises in that model were constrained to be short. The defender's level of resolve was assumed to be such that the defender would never take more than two steps toward the brink. This constraint made it impossible to examine the dynamics of longer brinkmanship crises. It also precluded an examination of some other crucial aspects of the approach to the credibility problem based on bridging the gap between doing too much and too little with an array of risk. The effects of being able to take small steps, which create small incremental risks of losing collective control, or of being able to take only large steps, which generate large risks, could not be studied within the confines of the restrictions placed on the model developed in the preceding chapter.

This chapter relaxed the constraint that required crises to be short, and that made it possible to examine the dynamics of longer brinkmanship crises. States in the model become increasingly confident that they are facing resolute adversaries and less and less likely to escalate the longer the confrontation lasts. When, therefore, two irresolute states are actually facing each other, misperceptions will be growing worse throughout the crisis. The crisis does not end because misperceptions have been reduced so that one state sees more accurately that its adversary is more resolute than it is. The effects of changes in the levels of resolve and the potential challenger's stake in the status quo are generally the same in both the models of longer and shorter crises. Finally, being able to take smaller, less risky steps toward the brink has two effects. The defender becomes more likely to escalate throughout the crisis. And as long as the defender's resolve is not too high, the challenger is also more likely to escalate but less likely to dispute the status quo. These two effects pull stability in opposite directions. The greater propensity to escalate tends to reduce stability, but the smaller chance of a challenge tends to improve it. On balance, stability seems to increase as steps toward the brink become less dangerous.

In the first approach that nuclear deterrence theory took to the credibility problem, the strategy that leaves something to chance related the use or threatened use of force to states' attempts to further their ends. That strategy explains how, at least in principle, states may attempt to coerce an adversary with a sanction that no state would ever deliberately be the first to impose. The assumption that there is no situation in which a deliberate, unlimited nuclear first strike would be imposed is crucial to the brinkmanship analogy and the formalizations of it. Indeed, this assumption does much to define the analogy. Nowhere along the curved slope leading to the abyss is it rational to push one's adversary into the chasm. There is no situation, no place along the slope, where the sanction might be imposed deliberately.

That defining assumption was quite restrictive. What if there were to exist a situation in which the sanction might be imposed deliberately? Is the approach based on the strategy that leaves something to chance and on the brinkmanship formalizations of it helpful in understanding the dynamics of escalation in these circumstances? Can anything be said about the likelihood that a crisis will escalate to an unlimited nuclear exchange when there is at least one situation in which a state might impose this sanction deliberately? The next two chapters examine the problem of stability when there are situations in which this unlimited sanction might be imposed deliberately.

Appendix 4.1

This appendix demonstrates Proposition 4.1. The demonstration is done in three steps. The first is to show that if a sequential crisis equilibrium exists, it must satisfy certain basic conditions. Then it will be shown that if a sequential crisis equilibrium satisfies these conditions, it must be of the form described in the proposition. Finally, $\varepsilon_{C'}$ and $\varepsilon_{D'}$ will be restricted to ensure that a sequential crisis equilibrium actually exists.

The first step is to establish that if a sequential crisis equilibrium exists, then two conditions must hold. First, C must be indifferent between escalating and submitting at $\Omega_C(m)$ and $e_C^*(m) > 0$ for $0 \leq m \leq \bar{m}$, where $\bar{m}$ is some integer. Second, $e_C^*(m) = 0$ for $m > \bar{m}$. To see this, let $\bar{m}$ be the maximum integer m such that $e_C^*(m) > 0$. Clearly such an $\bar{m}$ exists, for in a sequential crisis equilibrium, $e_C^*(0) > 0$. By construction, $e_C^*(m) = 0$ for $m > \bar{m}$; so it only remains to be shown that if a sequential crisis equilibrium exists, then it satisfies the first condition. To do this, assume the contrary. That is, for some $m' \leq \bar{m}$, C must strictly prefer to escalate at $\Omega_C(m')$, strictly prefer to submit, or be indifferent between them, but with $e_C^*(m') = 0$. In both of the latter cases, $e_C^*(m') = 0$, and this leads to a contradiction. To reach this contradiction, note that $e_C^*(m') = 0$ implies that the defender is certain that it is facing the resolute challenger C' at $\Omega_D(m' + 1)$: $\beta_D(m' + 1) = 0$. This means that $e_D^*(m' + 1) = 0$. But $e_D^*(m' + 1) = 0$ implies that $\beta_C(m' + 1) = 0$ and then that $e_C^*(m' + 1) = 0$. Continuing in this way leaves $e_D^*(m) = 0$ for $m \geq m'$. In particular, $e_D^*(\bar{m}) = 0$, because $\bar{m} \geq m'$, and this is a contradiction.

Assuming that C strictly prefers to escalate at $\Omega_C(m')$ also leads to a contradiction. Without loss of generality, let m' be the largest integer for which C strictly prefers to escalate at $\Omega_C(m')$; then

$$s_C < \beta_C^*(m')[2m'\delta d_C + (1 - 2m'\delta)[(1 - e_D^*(m' + 1))w_C + e_D^*(m' + 1)$$
$$\times [(2m' + 1)\delta d_C + (1 - (2m' + 1)\delta)s_C]]]$$
$$+ (1 - \beta_C^*(m'))[2m'\delta d_C + (1 - 2m'\delta)$$
$$\times [(2m' + 1)\delta d_C + (1 - (2m' + 1)\delta)s_C]]$$

Satisfying this inequality requires that $e_D^*(m' + 1) < 1$ and therefore implies that D's expected payoff at $\Omega_D(m' + 1)$ is s_D. This and the fact that $e_C^*(m') = 1$ means that escalation at $\Omega_D(m')$ brings

$$(2m' - 1)\delta d_D + (1 - (2m' - 1)\delta)[2m'\delta d_D + (1 - 2m'\delta)s_D]$$

This, however, is less than s_D, which is what D can have if it submits at $\Omega_D(m')$. Thus, D's best reply at $\Omega_D(m')$ is $e_D^*(m') = 0$. But if $e_D^*(m') = 0$, then $\beta_C^*(m') = 0$, and C's best reply is $e_C^*(m') = 0$. This, however, contradicts the assumption that C strictly prefers to escalate at $\Omega_C(m')$.

In sum, if a sequential crisis equilibrium exists, then C is indifferent between escalating and submitting at $\Omega_C(m)$ and $e_C^*(m) > 0$ for $m \leq \bar{m} \leq M_C$. If, moreover, $m > \bar{m}$, then $e_C^*(m) = 0$.

The second step is to demonstrate that if a sequential crisis equilibrium exists, then its strategies are defined by the expressions reported in Proposition 4.1. Suppose that C is indifferent to escalating or submitting at $\Omega_C(m)$ and $e_C^*(m) > 0$ for $m \leq \bar{m}$; then, for $1 \leq m \leq \bar{m}$,

$$s_C = \beta_C^*(m)(2m\delta d_C + (1 - 2m\delta)((1 - e_D^*(m + 1))w_C$$
$$+ e_D^*(m + 1)[(2m + 1)\delta d_C + (1 - (2m + 1)\delta)s_C]))$$
$$+ (1 - \beta_C^*(m))[2m\delta d_C + (1 - 2m\delta)$$
$$\times [(2m + 1)\delta d_C + (1 - (2m + 1)\delta)s_C]] \quad (A4.1)$$

Simplifying and substituting R_C for $(w_C - s_C)/(w_C - d_C)$ give

$$\frac{1}{\beta_C^*(m)} = (1 - 2m\delta)(1 - e_D^*(m + 1))$$

$$\times \left[\frac{R_C + (2m + 1)\delta(1 - R_C)}{[1 - (1 - 2m\delta)(1 - (2m + 1)\delta)](1 - R_C)} \right] \tag{A4.2}$$

But

$$\beta_C(m) = (1 - \varepsilon_D) \left[\prod_{i=1}^{m} e_D(i) \right] \left[\varepsilon_{D'} + (1 - \varepsilon_{D'}) \prod_{i=1}^{m} e_D(i) \right]^{-1}$$

Substituting this expression into (A4.2) yields

$$\prod_{i=1}^{m} e_D^*(i) = \left(\frac{\varepsilon_{D'}}{1 - \varepsilon_{D'}} \right)$$

$$\times \left(\frac{[1 - (1 - 2m\delta)(1 - (2m + 1)\delta)](1 - R_C)}{R_C - 2m\delta - e_D^*(m + 1)(1 - 2m\delta)[(2m + 1)\delta + (1 - (2m + 1)\delta)R_C]} \right) \tag{A4.3}$$

Reindexing this gives an expression for $\prod_{i=1}^{m-1} e_D^*(i)$ that holds for $2 \le m \le \bar{m} + 1$. Then, dividing this into $\prod_{i=1}^{m} e_D^*(i)$ and solving for $e_D^*(m + 1)$ gives

$$e_D^*(m + 1) = 1 - \left(\frac{1 - (1 - 2m\delta)(1 - (2m + 1)\delta)}{1 - (1 - 2(m - 1)\delta)(1 - (2m - 1)\delta)} \right)$$

$$\times \left(\frac{R_C - 2(m - 1)\delta}{(1 - 2m\delta)[1 - (1 - (2m + 1)\delta)(1 - R_C)]} \right) \frac{1 - e_D^*(m)}{e_D^*(m)} \tag{A4.4}$$

for $2 \le m \le \bar{m}$. (Generically, $e_D^*(\bar{m} + 1) \ne 0$, but $e_D^*(M_D + 1)$ must be zero. Thus to avoid a contradiction, $\bar{m} < M_D$.)

C's indifference at $\Omega_C(0)$ also implies $q_C = (1 - \varepsilon_{D'})[(1 - e_D(1))w_C + e_D(1) \times [\delta d_C + (1 - \delta)s_C]] + \varepsilon_{D'}[\delta d_C + (1 - \delta)s_C]$. This leaves

$$e_D^*(1) = \left(\frac{1}{1 - \varepsilon_{D'}} \right) \left[\left(\frac{w_C - q_C}{w_C - d_C} \right) \frac{1}{(1 - \delta)R_C + \delta} - \varepsilon_{D'} \right] \tag{A4.5}$$

Equation (A4.5) defines $e_D^*(1)$, and (A4.4) links $e_D^*(2), ..., e_D^*(\bar{m} + 1)$ recursively. Thus, all that is needed to complete the specification of D's strategies is to provide an initial condition for the recursive relation. Evaluating (A4.3) for $m = 1$ does this by defining $e_D^*(2)$ as a function of $e_D^*(1)$, leaving

$$e_D^*(2) = \frac{R_C - 2\delta}{(1 - 2\delta)[(1 - 3\delta)R_C + 3\delta]} - \left(\frac{\varepsilon_{D'}}{1 - \varepsilon_{D'}} \right)$$

$$\times \left[\frac{[1 - (1 - 2\delta)(1 - 3\delta)](1 - R_C)}{(1 - 2\delta)[(1 - 3\delta)R_C + 3\delta]} \right] \frac{1}{e_D^*(1)} \tag{A4.6}$$

In sum, (A4.5) defines $e_D^*(1)$, (A4.6) then gives $e_D^*(2)$, and (A4.4) determines $e_D^*(3), \ldots, e_D^*(\bar{m}+1)$. For $m > \bar{m}+1$, $e_D^*(m) = 0$.

To determine C's strategies, recall that $e_C^*(0) = 0$ for $m > \bar{m}$. The expressions for $e_D^*(m)$ show that generically, $1 > e_D^*(m) > 0$ for $1 \leq m \leq \bar{m}+1$. Hence, D is indifferent between escalating and submitting at $\Omega_D(m)$ for $1 \leq m \leq \bar{m}+1$. This implies

$$s_D = \beta_D^*(m)((2m-1)\delta d_D + (1-(2m-1)\delta)((1-e_C^*(m))w_D$$
$$+ e_C^*(m)[2m\delta d_D + (1-2m\delta)s_D]))$$
$$+ (1-\beta_D^*(m))[(2m-1)\delta d_D + (1-(2m-1)\delta)$$
$$\times [2m\delta d_D + (1-2m\delta)s_D]] \quad \text{(A4.7)}$$

for $1 \leq m \leq \bar{m}+1$. Letting $m = 1$ gives

$$e_C^*(0) = \frac{\varepsilon_{C'}}{1-\varepsilon_{C'}}\left[\frac{[1-(1-\delta)(1-2\delta)](1-R_D)}{R_D - \delta - e_C^*(1)(1-\delta)[(1-2\delta)R_D + 2\delta]}\right] \quad \text{(A4.8)}$$

Solving (A4.7) for $1 \leq m \leq \bar{m} \leq M_C$ in the same way that (A4.1) was solved gives the following recursive relation for $e_C^*(1), \ldots, e_C^*(\bar{m}+1)$:

$$e_C^*(m) = \left[1 + (1-e_C^*(m+1))\left(\frac{1-(1-(2m-1)\delta)(1-2m\delta)}{1-(1-(2m+1)\delta)(1-2(m+1)\delta)}\right)\right.$$
$$\left.\times \left(\frac{(1-(2m+1)\delta)[1-(1-2(m+1)\delta)(1-R_D)]}{R_D - (2m-1)\delta}\right)\right]^{-1}$$

$$\text{(A4.9)}$$

But $e_C^*(\bar{m}+1) = 0$. This, in turn, provides the needed initial condition so that (A4.9) now defines $e_C^*(1), \ldots, e_C^*(\bar{m})$ and then determines $e_C^*(0)$ through (A4.8). This completes the derivation of the challenger's and defender's strategies.

All that remains to be done is to restrict $\varepsilon_{D'}$ and $\varepsilon_{C'}$ to ensure that a sequential crisis equilibrium actually exists. This amounts to choosing these probabilities in a way that guarantees that the states' strategies are feasible in that the expressions for these strategies cannot require a state to escalate with a negative probability. Once the strategies have been shown to be feasible, then they will define the generically unique family of sequential crisis equilibria.

To obtain the restrictions on $\varepsilon_{D'}$, solve (A4.5) for $\varepsilon_{D'}$ subject to the condition that $0 < e_D^*(1) < 1$. Only the first inequality is binding, and it implies that

$$\varepsilon_{D'} < \bar{\varepsilon}_{D'} = \left(\frac{w_C - q_C}{w_C - d_C}\right)\frac{1}{(1-\delta)R_C + \delta}$$

There is also a second restriction on $\varepsilon_{D'}$. To specify it, solve (A4.5) for $\varepsilon_{D'}/[(1 - \varepsilon_{D'})e_D^*(1)]$ and substitute this into (A4.6). Then solve for $\varepsilon_{D'}$ subject to the constraint that $0 < e_D^*(2) < 1$. Again, only the first inequality is binding, and satisfying it requires

$$\varepsilon_{D'} < \bar{\bar{\varepsilon}}_{D'} = \bar{\varepsilon}_{D'}\left[\frac{R_C - 2\delta}{[1 - (1 - 2\delta)(1 - 3\delta)](1 - R_C)}\right]$$

Note, moreover, that $\bar{\bar{\varepsilon}}_{D'} < \bar{\varepsilon}_{D'}$.

To ensure that $e_D^*(m)$ is feasible for $m > 2$, assume $\varepsilon_{D'} < \bar{\bar{\varepsilon}}_{D'}$. [If $\varepsilon_{D'} > \bar{\bar{\varepsilon}}_{D'}$, then $e_D^*(2)$ is not feasible, and so the feasibility of $e_D^*(m)$ for $m > 2$ is no longer of any interest.] Suppose further that it can be established that $e_D^*(m)$ is decreasing in m as long as $m \geq 2$. Then let $\bar{M}$ be the largest integer m for which $e_D^*(m + 1) > 0$. Generically, $e_D^*(\bar{M} + 2)$ will be less than zero and thus infeasible. If $\bar{M} = 0$, then $e_D^*(2) < 0$, and the feasibility of $e_D^*(m)$ for $m > 2$ is not of any interest. If, however, $\bar{M} > 0$, then $e_D^*(m)$ for $2 \leq m \leq \bar{M} + 1$ are feasible for

$$e_D^*(2) > e_D^*(3) > \cdots > e_D^*(\bar{M} + 1) > 0 > e_D^*(\bar{M} + 2)$$

In sum, if $\varepsilon_{D'} < \bar{\bar{\varepsilon}}_{D'}$ and $e_D^*(m)$ is decreasing in m for $m \geq 2$, then the $e_D^*(m + 1)$ are feasible for $1 < m \leq \bar{M}_* < M_D$.

To see that $e_D^*(m)$ for $m \geq 2$ is actually decreasing in m as long as $e_D^*(m) > 0$, solve (A4.4) for $e_D^*(m)$ in terms of $e_D^*(m + 1)$, substitute this expression for $e_D^*(m)$ in $e_D^*(m) > e_D^*(m + 1)$, and solve this inequality for $e_D^*(m + 1)$. The result is that $e_D^*(m)$ is decreasing in m if $e_D^*(m + 1) < U_D(m)$ and $e_D^*(m + 1) > 0$, where

$$U_D(m) = \left(\frac{1 - (1 - 2m\delta)(1 - (2m + 1)\delta)}{1 - (1 - 2(m - 1)\delta)(1 - (2m - 1)\delta)}\right)$$

$$\times \left(\frac{R_C - 2(m - 1)\delta}{(1 - 2m\delta)[1 - (1 - (2m + 1)\delta)(1 - R_C)]}\right)$$

Now calculate $\bar{e}_D^*(m)$, where $\bar{e}_D^*(m)$ is the value of $e_D^*(m)$ defined by (A4.4) and the initial condition

$$\bar{e}_D^*(2) = (R_C - 2\delta)/[(1 - 2\delta)[(1 - 3\delta)R_C + 3\delta]]$$

This gives

$$\bar{e}_D^*(m + 1) = \frac{R_C - 2m\delta}{(1 - 2m\delta)[1 - (1 - (2m + 1)\delta)(1 - R_C)]}$$

Comparing $\bar{e}_D^*(m + 1)$ and $U_D(m)$ gives $\bar{e}_D^*(m + 1) < U_D(m)$. But $\bar{e}_D^*(2)$ is the least upper bound for $e_D^*(2)$, which is obtained by letting $\varepsilon_{D'} = 0$ in (A4.5). The facts that $\bar{e}_D^*(2) > e_D^*(2)$ and, by (A4.4), $\partial e_D^*(m + 1)/\partial e_D^*(m) > 0$ now imply that $\bar{e}_D^*(3) > e_D^*(3)$. This then means that $\bar{e}_D^*(4) > e_D^*(4)$, and, in general,

$\bar{e}_D^*(m+1) > e_D^*(m+1)$. Accordingly, $e_D^*(m+1) < \bar{e}_D^*(m+1) < U_D(m)$, and therefore $e_D^*(m)$ is decreasing in m.

In sum, if $\varepsilon_{D'} > \bar{\varepsilon}_{D'}$, there are no sequential crisis equilibria. In this case, $\varepsilon_{D'}$ is too large, and the payoff to not challenging the status quo at $\Omega_C(0)$ is always greater than the payoff to disputing the status quo. The probability that C is facing a resolute defender is too great, and there is no challenge. If $\bar{\varepsilon}_{D'} < \varepsilon_{D'} < \bar{\varepsilon}_{D'}$, then, assuming C's strategies to be feasible, $e_D^*(1)$ is given by (A4.5), and $e_D^*(m) = 0$ for $m > 1$. If $\varepsilon_{D'} < \bar{\varepsilon}_{D'}$, then (A4.5) defines $e_D^*(1)$, (A4.6) gives $e_D^*(2)$, and (A4.4) yields $e_D^*(3)$, ..., $e_D^*(\bar{m}+1)$, where $\bar{m} \leq \bar{M} < M_D$.

To find the restrictions on $\varepsilon_{C'}$ that will ensure that C's strategies are feasible, let $e_C^*(\bar{n}+1) = 0$ be the initial condition, and use (A4.8) and (A4.9) to determine $e_C^*(0), \ldots, e_C^*(\bar{n})$. Inspection of (A4.9) shows that $1 > e_C^*(m) > 0$ for $1 \leq m \leq \bar{n} \leq M_C$. Thus, only the feasibility of $e_C^*(0)$ is at issue. Constraining (A4.8) to be between 0 and 1, and then solving for $e_C^*(1)$, gives

$$e_C^*(1)_{\bar{n}} < \frac{R_D - \delta - \varepsilon_{C'}(1-\delta)[(1-2\delta)R_D + 2\delta]}{(1-\varepsilon_{C'})(1-\delta)[(1-2\delta)R_D + 2\delta]} \tag{A4.10}$$

where the subscript $\bar{n}$ on $e_C^*(1)$ indicates that $e_C^*(1)$ was obtained from the initial condition $e_C^*(\bar{n}+1) = 0$. Now assume that (A4.10) is satisfied for some $\bar{n}$. Then it will also be satisfied by $e_C^*(1)_{\bar{n}'}$, where $\bar{n}' < \bar{n}$. This follows from the observation that (A4.9) implies $\partial e_C^*(m)/\partial e_C^*(m+1) > 0$. Then, because $e_C^*(\bar{n}'+1)_{\bar{n}} > 0$ and $e_C^*(\bar{n}'+1)_{\bar{n}'} = 0$, $e_C^*(\bar{n}')_{\bar{n}} > e_C^*(\bar{n}')_{\bar{n}'}$. This, in turn, gives $e_C^*(\bar{n}'-1)_{\bar{n}} > e_C^*(\bar{n}'-1)_{\bar{n}'}$, and, in general, $e_C^*(m)_{\bar{n}} > e_C^*(m)_{\bar{n}'}$. Letting $m = 1$ shows that $e_C^*(1)_{\bar{n}'}$ satisfies (A4.10). Now let $\bar{N}$ be the maximum value of $\bar{n}$ for which $e_C^*(1)_{\bar{n}}$ satisfies (A4.10). Then, if $\bar{m} \leq \bar{N}$, all of C's strategies are feasible. Indeed, if $\bar{m} \leq \min\{\bar{M}, \bar{N}, M_D - 1, M_C\}$, then both C's and D's strategies are feasible.

To ensure that at least one sequential crisis equilibrium exists, $\bar{M}$ and $\bar{N}$ must be greater than or equal to zero. Taking $\varepsilon_{D'} < \bar{\varepsilon}_{D'}$ makes $\bar{M} \geq 0$. To make sure that $\bar{N} \geq 0$, $e_C^*(1)_{\bar{n}=0}$ must satisfy (A4.10). But the definition of $\bar{n}$ implies $e_C^*(\bar{n}+1) = 0$. So if $\bar{n} = 0$, $e_C^*(1) = 0$ must satisfy (A4.10). Letting $e_C^*(1)_{\bar{n}} = 0$ and solving (A4.10) for $\varepsilon_{C'}$ gives

$$\varepsilon_{C'} < \bar{\varepsilon}_{C'} = (R_D - \delta)/[(1-\delta)[(1-2\delta)R_D + 2\delta]]$$

If, therefore, $\varepsilon_{D'} < \bar{\varepsilon}_{D'}$ and $\varepsilon_{C'} < \bar{\varepsilon}_{C'}$, a family of sequential crisis equilibria exists, the members of which are indexed by $\bar{m}$, where $0 \leq \bar{m} \leq \min\{\bar{M}, \bar{N}, M_D - 1, M_C\}$. ∎

Although the demonstration of Proposition 4.1 is now complete, it will be useful to show that $e_C^*(m)$ is also decreasing in m for $1 \leq m \leq \bar{m}$. Use (A4.9) to substitute for $e_C^*(m)$ in $e_C^*(m) > e_C^*(m+1)$, and solve for $e_C^*(m+1)$. The result is

$$e_C^*(m+1) < U_C(m) = \left(\frac{R_D - (2m-1)\delta}{1 - (1-(2m-1)\delta)(1-2m\delta)} \right)$$

$$\times \left(\frac{1 - (1-(2m+1)\delta)(1-2(m+1)\delta)}{(1-(2m+1)\delta)[(1-2(m+1)\delta)R_D + 2(m+1)\delta]} \right)$$

That is, as long as $e_C^*(m) > 0$, $e_C^*(m+1) > 0$, and $U_C(m) > 0$, then $e_C^*(m) > e_C^*(m+1)$ if and only if $e_C^*(m+1) < U_C(m)$. Note, moreover, that if, as will be assumed, $R_C < 1 - 2\delta$, then as long as $U_C(m) > 0$, $U_C(m)$ is decreasing in m. This means that if $e_C^*(\bar{k}+1) < U_C(\bar{k})$ for some $\bar{k}$, then $e_C^*(\bar{k}) < U_C(\bar{k}-1)$. This follows assuming the contrary: $e_C^*(\bar{k}) \geq U_C(\bar{k}-1)$. This implies $e_C^*(\bar{k}+1) \geq e_C^*(\bar{k})$. This and the fact that $U_C(m)$ is decreasing then give $e_C^*(\bar{k}+1) \geq e_C^*(\bar{k}) \geq U_C(\bar{k}-1) > U_C(\bar{k})$. This contradicts the assumption that $e_C^*(\bar{k}+1) < U_C(\bar{k})$. Thus, $e_C^*(\bar{k}) < U_C(\bar{k}-1)$. Generalizing, $e_C^*(m+1) < U_C(m)$ for $m \leq \bar{k}$. This, then, gives $e_C^*(m) > e_C^*(m+1)$ for $1 \leq m \leq \bar{k}$. That is, $e_C^*(m)$ is decreasing from $e_C^*(1)$ to $e_C^*(\bar{k}+1)$. To show that $e_C^*(m)$ is decreasing in m for $1 \leq m \leq \bar{m}+1$, it will suffice to show that $e_C^*(\bar{m}+1) < U_C(\bar{m})$. But the definition of $\bar{m}$ implies $e_C^*(\bar{m}+1) = 0$. It need only be shown that $U_C(\bar{m}) > 0$. The definition of $U_C(m)$ shows $0 < e_C^*(\bar{m}) = U_C(\bar{m})/[1 + U_C(\bar{m})]$. Hence, $e_C^*(m)$ is decreasing in m from $e_C^*(1)$ to $e_C^*(\bar{m}+1)$.

CHAPTER 5

Crisis stability in the nuclear age

Nuclear deterrence theory has generally tried to relate the use of threatened use of force to states' efforts to secure their interests through the strategy that leaves something to chance or the strategy of limited retaliation. At a high level of generality, these strategies approach the relation between force and states' political objectives in fundamentally the same way: Each uses an array of limited options to bridge the gap between doing too much and doing too little. But at a somewhat lower level of generality, these strategies focus on different concerns. The strategy of leaving something to chance begins with the assumption that the sanction is such that it will never be imposed deliberately. That assumption defines the conceptual problem confronting this approach to the credibility problem: to explain how a state might use the threat of such a sanction to further its ends. Schelling's threats that leave something to chance solve this problem, at least in principle, by assuming that the states do not have complete collective control of events (Schelling 1960, pp. 187–203; 1966, pp. 99–105).

But the defining assumption that there is no situation in which the sanction will be imposed deliberately may be very limiting. Do the strategy that leaves something to chance and brinkmanship offer any insight into the dynamics of escalation in which there is at least one situation in which the sanction will be imposed deliberately? Or, put another way, what are the consequences of relaxing the assumption that there are no situations in which the sanction will be imposed deliberately and of reducing the corresponding dependence on there being some risk that the states may lose collective control?

Chapter 7 will take a large step away from this assumption by examining the strategy of limited retaliation, in which the sanctions are both imposed deliberately and are limited. This chapter and the next take an intermediate step, albeit one that leads to a reconsideration of an old and important problem in nuclear deterrence theory: the problem of first-strike advantages and crisis stability. These chapters continue to focus on the brinkmanship sanction of an unlimited nuclear first strike, but they relax the assumption that the sanction will never be imposed deliberately by assuming instead that there is at least one situation in which this unlimited sanction will be imposed deliberately. This means that the sanction no

110

longer has to be imposed autonomously as it must in brinkmanship. The states no longer have to be able to lose collective control. Events now may be fully under control in the first sense. It is enough that events are not fully under control in the second sense, in that no state can control the actions and reactions of another, for the unlimited sanction will be imposed deliberately if the interaction of the states' actions puts one of them in the situation in which it will deliberately use the sanction. What, then, are the dynamics of a crisis in which states try to use the unlimited sanction of a general nuclear attack coercively and in which there is at least one situation in which a state will launch this attack deliberately? In particular, can anything be said about the likelihood that a crisis will escalate to an unlimited nuclear exchange when there is at least one situation in which a state will deliberately impose the sanction of launching this attack? This chapter and the next address this question.

This question has been motivated by an attempt to begin to relax and move away from one of the most demanding assumptions underlying the strategy that leaves something to chance and the analogy of brinkmanship.[1] There are, however, two other motivations for this question. The first is related to an old problem in nuclear deterrence theory and policy. Suppose that, however slight, there is some advantage to striking first rather than second if there is to be a general exchange. A first-strike advantage does not imply that a state, by striking first, can avoid horrible destruction. Indeed, the only fate worse than striking first may be being struck first. A first-strike advantage means only that if there is to be a general exchange, it is better to strike first rather than second. The effect of a first-strike advantage, however modest it may be, is to create a situation in which a state will launch a first strike deliberately. If a state becomes sufficiently confident that its adversary is going to attack, then attacking in the hope of preempting an adversary's attack will become the best of a set of bad alternatives. The problem of crisis stability, then, is to understand the effects of first-strike advantages on the dynamics of escalation. The general conclusion, which may be called the conventional logic of crisis stability, is that the greater the first-strike advantage, the easier it is for a state to find

[1] Although the desire to relax confining assumptions may be seen as primarily a theoretical concern, there is, at least in this case, an important parallel policy concern. Relying on brinkmanship to relate force to political objectives means that a state is ultimately relying on the risk of losing collective control to deter an adversary from challenging its vital interests. This would seem a rather unsatisfactory foundation for policy. Lawrence Freedman, although not distinguishing between the two interpretations of events not being fully under control, put the matter clearly: "To rely on leaving things to chance, however realistic in terms of the actual fears and perceptions of political leaders and the difficulty of controlling the process of escalation once it was under way, seemed like the abandonment of strategy" (1986, p. 773).

itself in a situation in which attacking first is the best of a bad set of choices, and therefore the more likely a general exchange and the less stable the crisis.[2]

The emphases in these two ways of motivating this question about the dynamics of escalation differ. If an adversary's fear of suffering the sanction of an unlimited nuclear attack is to be used by a state to protect its interests, and if such a strategy is not ultimately to depend on this sanction's being imposed autonomously, then there must be at least one situation in which it will be rational to launch a first strike deliberately. Accordingly, this situation would seem to require the existence of a first-strike advantage, for otherwise it is difficult to conceive of a situation in which this sanction would be imposed deliberately. The emphasis here is on the necessity of a first-strike advantage. The emphasis in the problem of crisis stability is not on the necessity of a first-strike advantage and, in this sense, on its desirability, but on its undesirability, for it is the source of instability. A first-strike advantage makes it more likely that a crisis will escalate to an unlimited nuclear exchange. But despite their different emphases, these two motivations lead to the same question: What are the dynamics of crises in which there is an advantage to striking first?

The third motivation for this question is more general. The preceding analysis of brinkmanship focused on specific models and demonstrated that in those models there was some chance that the crisis would end in a general nuclear exchange. But how sensitive is this result to the particular properties of those models? Can any general conditions be identified that will either ensure that there is some chance of a crisis ending in a general exchange or guarantee that a crisis cannot end in that way? Again, this question leads to a consideration of the dynamics of crises in which there are advantages to striking first.

The three motivations reflect three different concerns. The first of these is to relax one of the most demanding assumptions of brinkmanship. The second is to study the relation between stability and first-strike advantages. The third is a concern for determining those general conditions under which a crisis can end in an unlimited nuclear exchange. But, as has been seen, a single question binds these concerns together. In this sense, these concerns are different facets of a single problem.

This chapter and the next examine the escalatory dynamics of crises in which there are first-strike advantages by reconsidering the problem of crisis stability. This chapter focuses on a simple game in which there are significant first-strike advantages. The conventional logic of crisis stability

---

[2] See Schelling (1960, pp. 209–29) and Jervis (1978) for a discussion of crisis stability that is referred to here as "the conventional logic of crisis stability" in order to distinguish it from the analysis in this chapter and the next.

would seem to imply that because of these advantages, there should be some chance that the game will end in a general nuclear exchange. The game, however, is completely stable. This game is used to illustrate a set of conditions that turn out to ensure stability even in the presence of first-strike advantages. The next chapter extends the analysis to a more general game-theoretic setting and shows that this stability is not peculiar to this simple game. Any game satisfying these conditions will be stable. The next chapter also examines the consequences of loosening the general conditions needed to ensure stability.

Stability with first-strike advantages

Once again, Schelling provides a point of departure. In his study of crisis stability in the nuclear age, Schelling (1960, pp. 207–29) focused on a highly stylized description of this age that seemed to capture the essence of the problem of crisis stability and preemption. Because the description was highly stylized, it was analytically tractable. Because the description seemed to capture the essence of the problem, its analysis held the promise of shedding light on the nature of crisis stability.

Three features characterize Schelling's stylization. First, there is "no fundamental basis for war" (Schelling 1960, p. 207). That is, a general nuclear war would be so horrible that if a state had to choose between the certainty of war, even a war in which it was sure of having the first strike, and the certainty of peace, albeit a peace secured by submitting to its adversary, then the state would choose to avoid a general nuclear war. But second, if there is going to be a war, if war is inevitable, it is better to strike first rather than second. There is an advantage to striking first. These first two characteristics of the stylization relax the defining assumption of brinkmanship, which is that there is no advantage to striking first. A general nuclear war is so terrible that the only fate worse than striking first is being struck first, but it is still better to strike first instead of second. The third characteristic is that both states fully appreciate the situation in which they find themselves (Schelling 1960, pp. 207–8).

This section presents a game-theoretic model of a situation that is consistent with this stylization. Thus, the conventional logic of crisis stability implies that because there are first-strike advantages in this situation, there should be some risk of preemption. But, as will be seen, there is no risk. The game is completely stable, even though there is an advantage to striking first.

The game is illustrated in Figure 5.1. Nature, N, begins by making a random move: Nature will take the left branch with probability p and the right branch with probability $1 - p$. Beginning the game with a random move is a modeling technique that, as will be seen, formally creates the fundamental uncertainty that is the essence of the problem of preemption and crisis stability.

If Nature plays left, state I is the first state in the game to move. I must decide between two options. It can quit and thereby end the game by playing Q. Ending the game at this point avoids an unlimited nuclear exchange, but it also brings I the loser's payoff L_I. II receives the payoff to prevailing of P_{II}. Or I may decide to launch an unlimited nuclear attack, A. If I attacks, II must then choose between two options. Because I has already attacked, I is certain in the game to achieve a first strike. Nevertheless, II is not indifferent to its two options. Given that I has attacked, II can obtain a higher payoff by attacking rather than quitting. One interpretation of this is that a prompt second strike, which may be thought of as II playing A, given that I has attacked, is better than a slow second strike, which is represented by Q. Because II prefers A to Q, $S_{II} > W_{II}$, where S_{II} is the payoff to II of attacking immediately with its second strike, and W_{II} is the payoff to not attacking and, in effect, waiting until later to launch a second strike. I, moreover, is not indifferent to II's decision. I prefers that II quit and thereby be able to launch only a less effective second strike. That is, $F_I > f_I$.

Figure 5.1. A game of preemption.

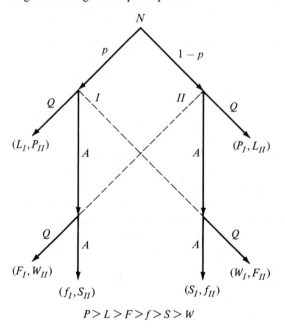

$P > L > F > f > S > W$

If Nature plays right, II is the first state to move in the game, and it must choose between Q and A. Now, however, when II is making its decision, I has not already committed itself to attacking. If II quits by playing Q, the game ends without there having been an unlimited nuclear exchange. II receives the loser's payoff of L_{II}, and I obtains the payoff to prevailing of P_I. If II attacks, it achieves a first strike, and I must then decide what to do. Given that it has been attacked, I prefers attacking to quitting: $S_I > W_I$. Conversely, II would prefer that I did not attack: $F_{II} > f_{II}$.

To complete the specification of the relation among the payoffs, recall that in the stylization of the problem of preemption and crisis stability there is no fundamental basis for war. That is, although prevailing is better than losing, losing and thereby avoiding an unlimited nuclear exchange is better than the payoff to even a successful first strike (Schelling 1960, p. 208). In terms of payoffs, this means that $P > L > F$, where the subscripts have been dropped because the relation applies to both I and II. There are, however, first-strike advantages: $f > S$. Combining these gives the following relation among the payoffs: $P > L > F > f > S > W$. That is, prevailing, P, is better than avoiding a nuclear exchange by submitting, L, which is better than achieving the most successful first strike but nevertheless having to absorb a second strike, F, which is better than launching a first strike but having to absorb a more effective second strike, f, which is preferred to being attacked first but retaliating with a more effective second strike, S, which, finally, is better than being attacked first and retaliating with a less effective second strike W.

The final step in describing the preemption game in Figure 5.1 is to discuss its information structure. Both of I's decision nodes are in the same information set. Similarly, both of II's decision nodes are in the same information set. A state's information set represents what the state knows when it must make a given decision. More specifically, a state knows whether or not it is in a particular information set, but a state cannot determine where it is in a given information set. A state must therefore form beliefs about where it is in an information set, and these beliefs are in turn shaped by the other state's strategy. In the preemption game, I does not know if it is at the upper-left decision node, in which case it is the first to move in the game, or if it is at the lower-right node, in which case it is the second state to move. Similarly, II does not know if it is at the upper-right decision node, in which case it has the first move in the game, or if it is at the lower-left node, in which case it has the second move.

The game's information structure and the relation among the payoffs formally create the same dilemma as that posed by the problem of preemption. Viewing the game from I's perspective, suppose that when it had to choose between Q and A, I was certain that it was at the lower-right decision node. At that node, war is inevitable. *II* has already committed itself to attacking, and regardless of whether *I* chooses *Q* or *A*, *I* cannot avoid an unlimited nuclear exchange. In the stylization of the problem of preemption, a state will attack if it believes that war is unavoidable. The same is true of the game in Figure 5.1: *I* attacks if it is certain that war is inevitable, that is, if it is certain that it is at the lower-right node, because $S_I > W_I$. Now suppose that when it has to choose between *Q* and *A*, *I* is certain that it is at its decision node at the upper left. Here, war is not inevitable. Indeed, *I* can avoid an unlimited exchange by quitting. In the stylization in which there is "no fundamental basis for war" (Schelling 1960, p. 209), a state will submit if it is certain of being able to avoid an unlimited nuclear exchange by accepting the limited losses of submitting. The preemption game also captures this aspect of the stylization. If *I* is certain that it is at the upper-left node, then *I* will quit. Quitting brings L_I, and the best that attacking can bring is F_I. But $L_I > F_I$; so *I* prefers to quit.

The dilemma posed in the game, as in the logic of crisis stability, is that *I* is not sure that war is inevitable. *I* does not know if it is at the upper-left node, in which case war is avoidable, or if it is at the node at the lower right, in which case war is inevitable and attacking is the best strategy. The more confident that *I* is that war is inevitable (i.e., the higher the probability *I* ascribes to being at the lower-right node), the higher the expected payoff to attacking, and the lower the expected payoff to not attacking. At some threshold probability, *I* becomes sufficiently confident that war is inevitable that the expected payoff to attacking is greater than the expected payoff to not attacking, and *I* attacks.

To help make the preemption game more concrete, suppose that state *I*'s early warning systems suddenly indicate that *II* has launched a massive attack. This may be a false alarm. A practice tape simulating an enemy attack may, for example, have been accidentally loaded onto the on-line system.[3] If the warning is actually a false alarm, *I* is, in effect, at its upper-left decision node in Figure 5.1, in that if *I* decides to attack on the basis of this warning, it will be launching a first strike. It will be starting an exchange that was otherwise avoidable. But the warning may not be a false alarm: *II* may have launched an attack. If so, then *I* is at its lower-right node, and war is inevitable. *I*'s best strategy is to attack. The difficulty is that the warning is the only information that *I* has. It cannot distinguish between the possibility of a false alarm and a real attack, and this is formalized in the game by including *I*'s two decision nodes in the same information set.

---

[3] A practice tape simulating a massive Soviet attack actually was accidentally loaded onto the on-line system in 1979. An alert was called, and ten air interceptors were scrambled before the mistake was discovered and corrected; see Carter (1987, p. 629) and Sagan (1989a, 1989b).

Figure 5.2. The normal form of the preemption game.

II

	A	Q
A	$pf_I + (1-p)S_I \quad (1-p)f_{II} + pS_{II}$	$pF_I + (1-p)P_I \quad (1-p)L_{II} + pW_{II}$
Q	$pL_I + (1-p)W_I \quad (1-p)F_{II} + pP_{II}$	$pL_I + (1-p)P_I \quad (1-p)L_{II} + pP_{II}$

(I labels the rows)

$$P > L > F > f > S > W$$

Given what it knows, which is that its warning systems indicate that II has launched an attack, I must decide how likely II is to have launched an attack and on the basis of that evaluation decide whether or not to attack. This is the dilemma posed by the preemption game.[4]

The essence of the conventional logic of crisis stability is that when there are first-strike advantages, then there is some chance that the threshold of inevitability needed to justify launching an attack will be crossed. There is some risk that one or both states will attack because it seems sufficiently likely that war is inevitable. But is this correct? More formally, is there any chance that, in an equilibrium of the game in Figure 5.1, one of the states will attack? The answer to this question is no. With one further restriction on the states' payoffs, the probability that I or II will attack in equilibrium is zero. The situation is completely stable even though there is a first-strike advantage.

To show this, it will be useful to transform the extensive game of Figure 5.1 into its normal form. Each state in the game tree has a single decision to make, whether to quit or attack, and this decision is made in ignorance of what the other state does. Accordingly, this situation can be represented by the normal-form game in Figure 5.2.

---

[4] In an actual crisis, a state might decide not to attack immediately, but rather to try to verify the alarm. The preemption game is too simple to allow for this, but a more complicated model could. More complicated games are considered in the next chapter. The point here is merely that the issue of false alarms can be examined, albeit in a very simple context, with the preemption game in Figure 5.1, and viewing the game from this perspective helps to clarify what is at issue.

The payoffs in the matrix in Figure 5.2 are derived from the tree in Figure 5.1. Suppose, for example, that both states adopt the strategy Q. If Nature happens to play left, which it will do with probability p, then I moves first in the game. At this point, I, according to its strategy, quits by playing Q. The game ends with payoffs (L_I, P_{II}). If Nature happens to play right, then II moves first. II then quits, and the game ends with payoffs (P_I, L_{II}). Thus, the expected payoff to I if both states play Q is $pL_I + (1-p)P_I$. This is the payoff reported for I in the (Q, Q) cell of the payoff matrix in Figure 5.2. The other payoffs are calculated similarly.

In some circumstances the probability of an attack is zero, and the situation is completely stable, despite the existence of first-strike advantages. To identify these circumstances, compare I's strategy of attacking, which is represented by the top row of Figure 5.2, to I's strategy of quitting, which is in the bottom row. Suppose that I is certain that II will play Q. Then I's payoff to quitting is $pL_I + (1-p)P_I$ and to attacking is $pF_I + (1-p)P_I$. Because $L_I > F_I$, I's payoff to quitting is greater than its payoff to attacking. If, therefore, I believes that II is playing Q, I will certainly not attack, for it is sure to do better by quitting. Similarly, if II is completely confident that I will play Q, II's best strategy will also be to play Q.

Now assume $L - F > S - W$ for both I and II. A justification for this assumption will be discussed later. At this point, note that this assumption implies that for at least one of the states the payoff to playing Q is higher than the payoff to playing A regardless of what the other state does. Q is a strictly dominant strategy for I or II.[5] Suppose that it is I that prefers to quit regardless of what II does. Then I will play Q. But given that I is doing this, Q also offers II its highest payoff. In equilibrium, neither state attacks. If, alternatively, II prefers to quit regardless of what I does, then II will quit. Q, in turn, will maximize I's payoff. Again, neither state attacks in equilibrium. The situation is completely stable even though there are first-strike advantages.

The crucial stabilizing assumption that $L - F > S - W$ is a mathematical

---

[5] To see this, suppose that $p \geq \frac{1}{2}$. Then quitting strictly dominates attacking for I. As shown earlier, I strictly prefers to quit if II quits; so all that remains to be shown is that I strictly prefers to quit even if II attacks. To do this, note that the assumption that $L - F > S - W$ ensures that $(L_I - f_I)/(S_I - W_I) > 1$, for with $F > f$, then $L - f > L - F$, and consequently $L - f > S - W$, or $(L - f)/(S - W) > 1$. I, moreover, will strictly prefer to quit given that II is attacking only if the payoff to quitting is greater than the payoff to attacking, i.e., only if $pL_I + (1-p)W_I > pf_I + (1-p)S_I$. This inequality implies $(L_I - f_I)/(S_I - W_I) > (1-p)/p$. But if $p \geq \frac{1}{2}$, then $(1-p)/p \leq 1$. This leaves $(L_I - f_I)/(S_I - W_I) > 1 \geq (1-p)/p$. Thus, I strictly prefers quitting to attacking even if II attacks, and therefore Q strictly dominates A for I. A similar argument shows that if $p \leq \frac{1}{2}$, II strictly prefers quitting to attacking regardless of what I does.

formalism. But considering two less formal, more intuitive, and more general aspects of this assumption will help to make it more concrete and meaningful. One aspect of this assumption will be discussed here. The second aspect will be addressed later in the context of the discussion of why the conventional logic of crisis stability is misleading in the preemption game. Each of the expressions $L - F$ and $S - W$ has an intuitive interpretation. The former is the difference between the payoff to the most successful first strike (which with large, robust, and relatively survivable strategic forces still means having to endure a terribly destructive second strike in retaliation) and the payoff to quitting. This difference is the net cost of attacking and then suffering a devastating second strike, whereas by quitting a state would have avoided an unlimited nuclear exchange. Similarly, the latter expression is the net cost to a state of waiting to attack and thereby reducing the effectiveness of its second strike, whereas by attacking immediately a state would have achieved a more effective second strike. The assumption $L - F > S - W$ requires that the former be greater than the latter. The net loss of striking first and thereby triggering a nuclear exchange that could have been avoided is larger than the net loss of launching a less effective rather than more effective second strike.

The game-theoretic model developed earlier is clearly too simple to be accepted as a model of a crisis. There are, for example, too few choices in the game, and its information structure is much too simple. A set of richer, more elaborate models will be considered in the next chapter. For now, the important point is that despite its simplicity, the game satisfies the three stylized conditions that describe the environment that poses the problem of crisis stability and preemption. First, there is an advantage to striking first in the game. But, second, because even a successful first strike cannot protect a state from a terribly costly retaliatory second strike, the only fate worse than striking first is being struck first. There is no fundamental basis for war. And, finally, the states fully appreciate their situation. Thus, the conventional logic of crisis stability, if applied to this game, would seem to imply that because there are first-strike advantages, there will also be some risk of a state becoming sufficiently confident that war is inevitable that it will attack. Yet, as has been shown, no state ever attacks. Apparently, no state ever becomes sufficiently confident that war is inevitable to justify attacking. The conventional logic of crisis stability in this model is misleading. This raises two questions: First, why is this logic misleading? Second, how general is this result? Is there something special about this particular game that makes it stable despite the conventional logic of crisis stability, or are there more general conditions that ensure stability? The next section takes up the first question by examining the conventional logic in more detail.

The conventional logic of crisis stability

The conventional logic of crisis stability is that first-strike advantages are destabilizing and that the greater the first-strike advantage, the less stable the crisis. This logic is easily formalized, and doing so will help to explain why it is misleading. If a state attacks preemptively, its payoff in this formulation is F. If a state does not attack, one of two outcomes is possible. If a state's adversary attacks, then that state, by not attacking, condemns itself to suffering a first strike and retaliating with a second strike. Let S be the payoff to this outcome. If, however, neither the state nor its adversary attacks, then the states avoid a nuclear exchange and receive some compromise payoff. Let C denote this payoff. In the stylization of the problem of preemption in the nuclear age there is a first-strike advantage. So the payoff to striking first is greater than the payoff to striking second: $F > S$. But also in keeping with the stylization, even a successful first strike cannot protect a state from suffering a horribly costly retaliatory second strike. In terms of payoffs, this means that $C > F$. Now let τ be a state's subjective probability that war is inevitable. That is, the state believes that the probability that its adversary is attacking is τ. Then the expected payoff of not preempting is $\tau S + (1 - \tau)C$.

Attacking preemptively is rational if its payoff is greater than the payoff to not preempting. Attacking is optimal if $F > \tau S + (1 - \tau)C$. Solving for τ gives $\tau > (C - F)/(C - S)$. Defining the threshold τ^* to be $(C - F)/(C - S)$, then attacking becomes the best of a set of bad alternatives if a state believes that the probability that war is inevitable is greater than τ^*. Attacking is rational if $\tau > \tau^*$. Conversely, waiting and not preempting is optimal if a state's level of confidence is less than this threshold.

The essence of the conventional logic of crisis stability is captured in the relation between the threshold τ^* and the size of the advantage to striking first, $F - S$. To see this, rewrite the expression for τ^* to obtain $\tau^* = 1 - (F - S)/(C - S)$. Now note that as long as there is an advantage to striking first (i.e., as long as $F - S > 0$), the threshold τ^* is less than 1. As long as there is an advantage to striking first, there is some probability that will make attacking the best of a set of bad alternatives. Moreover, the higher the payoff to striking first, or the lower the payoff to being struck first, the greater the first-strike advantage, and the lower the threshold.[6] And the lower the threshold, then presumably the easier it is to cross, and consequently the less stable the crisis. Finally, suppose that, as in the strictest interpretation of mutually assured destruction, there is no advantage to striking first, so that $F = S$. Then the value of the threshold τ^*

---

[6] That is, $\partial \tau^*/\partial F < 0$ and $\partial \tau^*/\partial S > 0$.

is 1, and the threshold can never be crossed. Crises in this strictest interpretation of mutually assured are very stable.

The formalization of the conventional logic of crisis stability reveals a peculiar aspect of this logic, and this is the source of the conventional logic's misleading conclusions. First-strike advantages mean that τ^* is less than 1, and this creates instabilities by making it possible for τ to be greater than τ^*. But note that the conventional analysis treats τ and τ^* quite differently: τ^* is a function of the parameters C, F, and S that describe the structure of the crisis, and, therefore, the threshold τ^* is endogenously determined by the structure of the crisis. But τ is not an explicit function of any parameter that describes the crisis; τ is formally exogenous.

Treating the strength of a state's belief that war is inevitable as formally exogenous is problematic, for this treatment is at odds with the notion of a crisis as a bargaining process. A crisis is generally seen as a bargaining process in which each state attempts to shape its adversary's beliefs. One tries to alter an adversary's assessment about the relative costs and benefits of continuing the confrontation in the hope that the adversary will eventually back down. In a condition of mutually assured destruction, for example, each superpower knows that the other is capable of inflicting catastrophic damage on it. A crisis is less about what one can do than about what one is willing to do. Each state attempts to further its ends by influencing its adversary's beliefs about what it is willing to do. Inherent in the notion of a crisis as a bargaining process is the presumption that a state's beliefs are affected by its adversary's actions. That is, beliefs are endogenous. Yet in the conventional logic of crisis stability, beliefs are not related to the crisis formally.[7]

The formally exogenous treatment of beliefs raises questions that reflect on the problem of stability. Can structural features of a crisis constrain a state's belief that war is unavoidable? Can such constraints keep this belief from becoming strong enough to justify attacking? For example, can the fact that even a successful first strike cannot protect a state from a terribly costly second strike keep τ below τ^*? If so, then the crisis will be stable despite the existence of first-strike advantages.

As shown earlier, the preemption game in Figure 5.1 is completely stable. The reason for this is that the model allows the states' beliefs to be treated endogenously. This makes beliefs, like strategies, interdependent. What one state believes affects what it does, and those actions in turn affect what the

---

[7] In treating beliefs exogenously, what has become the conventional logic of crisis stability, although perhaps simpler, fails to capture much of the subtlety and insight of Schelling's original analysis of the problem (1960, pp. 207–29). An essential element of his treatment was the endogeneity of beliefs.

other state believes. This interdependence means that neither state can become sufficiently confident that war is inevitable to justify its attacking.

It takes two steps to show this. The first determines a strict lower bound, τ^*_{min}, on the threshold of inevitability needed to justify attacking. Because τ^*_{min} is a strict lower bound, $\tau^*_{min} < \tau^*$. The second step demonstrates that the probability that war is inevitable never exceeds this lower bound: $\tau \leq \tau^*_{min}$. These two inequalities imply $\tau < \tau^*$ and that no state attacks. The crisis is stable even with first-strike advantages.

The crucial assumption $L - F > S - W$ defines this lower bound, and this is the second aspect of this assumption that helps to explain why it is needed to stabilize the crisis. This assumption implies that no state will attack unless the probability that war is inevitable is greater than $\frac{1}{2}$. Or, equivalently, τ^* is always greater than $\frac{1}{2}$, which means that $\tau^*_{min} = \frac{1}{2}$ is a strict lower bound of τ^*.

To see that the assumption that $L - F > S - W$ implies that no state will attack unless it believes that the probability that war is inevitable is greater than $\frac{1}{2}$, suppose that I believes that the chance that war is avoidable is $\frac{1}{2}$. If I quits while actually at its upper-left node in Figure 5.1, where war is avoidable, it receives L_I. If war is actually inevitable (i.e., I is at its lower-right node), then the payoff to quitting is W_I. The expected payoff to quitting, given that the probability that war is inevitable is $\frac{1}{2}$, is therefore $\frac{1}{2}L_I + \frac{1}{2}W_I$. To calculate the expected cost of attacking in these circumstances, note that if I attacks when war can be avoided, the best it can do is to obtain the payoff to the most successful first strike, F_I. If I attacks when war is inevitable, its payoff is S_I. If, therefore, I believes that the chance that war is inevitable is $\frac{1}{2}$, the best it can expect to do by attacking is $\frac{1}{2}F_I + \frac{1}{2}S_I$. Thus, I will certainly not attack when it believes the probability that war is inevitable is $\frac{1}{2}$ if the payoff to quitting is greater than the payoff to attacking, that is, if $\frac{1}{2}L_I + \frac{1}{2}W_I > \frac{1}{2}F_I + \frac{1}{2}S_I$, or, equivalently, if $L_I - F_I > S_I - W_I$. But this is precisely what the stabilizing assumption says, and in this way it ensures that I will not attack if the probability that war is inevitable is $\frac{1}{2}$. This, in turn, means that the threshold of inevitability needed to justify attacking is still higher; so $\frac{1}{2} < \tau^*$. Thus, $\frac{1}{2}$ is a strict lower bound for this threshold: $\tau^*_{min} = \frac{1}{2}$.

To establish that the game is stable when beliefs and strategies are interdependent, it will now suffice to show that the probability representing the strength of a state's belief that war is inevitable can never exceed $\frac{1}{2}$. If, that is, $\tau^*_{min} = \frac{1}{2}$ and $\tau^*_{min} < \tau^*$, then showing that τ is always less than or equal to $\frac{1}{2}$ will ensure stability. At first it appears that it should be easy for beliefs to cross this lower bound of $\frac{1}{2}$. If the probability that I will move first, which is p, is high, and if I is very likely to attack, then it would seem that II should be very confident that war is inevitable (i.e., that II is at its lower-left node in Figure 5.1) and that attacking is rational. This is essentially the conventional logic of crisis stability. The difficulty with this logic is that the probability that I will move first and the probability that it will attack are not independent. They are interdependent. Loosely, the higher the value of p, the more confident I is that it is at its upper-left node and that war is avoidable. This makes I less likely to attack. These two factors oppose each other. The higher p tends to make II more confident that war is inevitable, but the smaller chance that I will attack tends to make II less confident that war is inevitable. On balance, the effect of these opposing influences is that the probability that war is inevitable never exceeds $\frac{1}{2}$.[8] Neither state ever becomes sufficiently confident that war is inevitable that it attacks.

This result contrasts sharply with the flavor of the conventional logic. If, in that logic, the first-strike advantage is small (i.e., if $F - S$ is small), then the threshold τ^* is close to 1 and presumably is difficult to cross. The crisis, even in the conventional logic, is relatively stable. But the threshold needed to ensure stability in the preemption game is much less than 1 and much less than that suggested by the conventional logic. Indeed, a first-strike advantage that lowers the threshold to what, by the conventional logic, would seem to be a quite unstable level (e.g., $\tau^* = 0.6$) still leaves the threshold greater than $\frac{1}{2}$ and thus still high enough to ensure stability in the model.

In sum, the conventional logic of crisis stability is misleading if applied to the preemption game in Figure 5.1, because that logic ignores the structural features of a crisis that may constrain the states' beliefs that war is inevitable. When these features are taken into account, at least in the context of the specific model examined earlier, these beliefs are constrained to be below the threshold at which attacking becomes rational. Despite the implications of the conventional logic, there is no risk of crossing this threshold. There are first-strike advantages, but the situation is completely stable.

[8] To see this, suppose that this probability does exceed $\frac{1}{2}$. For this to be possible, p must be greater than $\frac{1}{2}$, for if p were less than or equal to $\frac{1}{2}$, then even if I were certain to attack, the probability that II would be at its lower-left node and that war would be inevitable would be less than $\frac{1}{2}$. So $p > \frac{1}{2}$. Note, however, that the probability that war appears inevitable to I, which is the probability of its being at its lower-right node, is less than or equal to $1 - p$. If, therefore, $p > \frac{1}{2}$, then $1 - p < \frac{1}{2}$, and I believes that the probability that war is inevitable is less than $\frac{1}{2}$. All of this means that if there is some chance that II is at its lower-left node and, consequently, that there is some chance that war is inevitable when $p > \frac{1}{2}$, then I must have attacked when the probability that war was inevitable was less than or equal to $\frac{1}{2}$. But that cannot be, for the assumption $L - F > S - W$ implies that no state will attack as long as it believes that the probability that war is inevitable is less than or equal to $\frac{1}{2}$. Thus, the probability measuring the strength of II's belief that war is unavoidable cannot exceed $\frac{1}{2}$. A similar argument shows that the same holds for I. In the preemption game in Figure 5.1, no state can come to believe that the probability that war is inevitable is greater than $\frac{1}{2}$.

The general conditions of stability and potential sources of instability

The stability of the preemption game in Figure 5.1 raises two questions. The first is why the conventional logic is misleading in this example, and that is attributed to its failure to treat beliefs as formally endogenous. The second question asks if there is something peculiar about the preemption game that ensures stability or if some more general conditions are responsible for stability. The next chapter formally identifies a set of conditions that do ensure stability and then tries to examine some of the consequences of relaxing them. This section discusses the four most significant conditions needed to ensure stability somewhat less formally.

Identifying the conditions needed to ensure stability contributes to a better understanding of the problem of preemption and crisis stability and, more generally, the escalatory dynamics of crises in which there are situations in which a state might deliberately launch a general nuclear attack. Indeed, identifying general conditions that are sufficient to ensure stability also serves to identify the potential sources of instability, for if a set of conditions ensures stability, then at least one of these conditions must be violated if there is to be any instability. The more refined understanding of these problems that emerges from elaborating and clarifying the relation among the factors needed to ensure stability indicates that the conventional logic focuses attention too narrowly on the size of any first-strike advantage. Instability results from a more subtle interaction of several factors, of which the size of any first-strike advantage is only one. By itself, the existence of an advantage to striking first is not enough to create instability.

Four major conditions assure stability.[9] If these conditions are satisfied, then even though there is an advantage to striking first, the probability that there will be an exchange in equilibrium is zero. The first condition is that states always retain collective control: An attack cannot happen unless a state orders it. There is no risk of a purely accidental general nuclear attack. In the preemption game, for example, Nature cannot launch an attack directly by playing A. Only the states can attack.

Precluding a purely accidental general nuclear attack, however, does not preclude the possibility of other types of accidents. Only one narrowly defined type of accident has been excluded. A general nuclear attack cannot result directly from an accident. Such an attack cannot be triggered automatically by a false alarm caused by, for example, a rising moon, a flock of geese, failure of a computer chip (Bracken 1983, pp. 48–9), or the loading of a practice tape simulating a Soviet attack onto the on-line system

---

[9] Several technical conditions are also needed. These are described in the next chapter.

(Carter 1987, p. 629; Sagan 1989a, 1989b). The exclusion of a purely accidental general nuclear attack, however, does not imply that there can be no accidents or false alarms. To the contrary, the model, as indicated earlier, may be seen as a model of a false alarm. Excluding purely accidental general nuclear exchanges implies only that an accident or false alarm can lead to such an attack only indirectly by creating a situation in which the national command authority accepts the risk that it may be acting on the basis of a false alarm and nevertheless decides to attack deliberately. Events are not fully under control, but only in the second sense in that no state controls another.

It is important to emphasize that excluding the possibility that the states can lose collective control does not, at least in principle, eliminate the possibility of an inadvertent general nuclear exchange. Because events are not fully under control in the second sense, this outcome remains a possibility. If, for example, $L - f < S - W$ in Figure 5.1, then there exist equilibria in which the states will deliberately launch an unlimited attack. It is, moreover, the risk that this outcome will occur because events, although fully under control in the first sense, are not fully under control in the second sense that is the essence of the problem of preemption and of the conventional logic of crisis stability. This is clear from the emphasis in the conventional logic on the threshold at which attacking becomes rational and the risk of crossing this threshold. The problem in the conventional logic is that events are not fully under control in the second sense.[10]

The second assumption needed to ensure stability is that whenever a state has the option of attacking, it also has the option of trying to submit to its adversary. If, moreover, a state tries to submit before its adversary has committed itself to attacking, then the crisis will end with the state's submission and without there being an unlimited nuclear exchange.

The preemption game in Figure 5.1 satisfies this condition. Whenever a state has the option of attacking, it also has the option of trying to submit by playing Q. If, moreover, a state plays Q when war is still avoidable (i.e., I plays Q at its upper-left node or II plays Q at its upper-right node), then the game will end, and there will not be a general exchange.

The option of being able to attempt to submit and thereby avoid a nuclear exchange if one's adversary has not already attacked is a structural aspect of the game used to model a crisis. This structural feature helps to prevent a nuclear exchange by constraining the beliefs that would justify an attack. But this option is a theoretical construct in an abstract game. It is an

---

[10] Nevertheless, assuming that the states always remain in collective control remains a strong assumption. The next chapter relaxes this assumption by reintroducing some autonomous risk. This will show that there is a subtle relation between stability and the two senses in which events are not fully under control.

assumption about a model and may or may not be a sensible assumption to make about an actual crisis. Indeed, the stabilizing effects of such an option can be appreciated without asserting that such an option exists in any particular crisis. As noted earlier, the most important function of identifying the conditions that are sufficient to ensure stability may be that doing so also serves to identify potential sources of instability, especially those sources that have not been identified previously.

Nevertheless, it is useful to ask if this theoretical construct might have any empirical referents in actual crises. For what, in other words, is this construct an apt analogy? The essence of having this option is not, as the preemption game in Figure 5.1 may have suggested, that the game must end immediately if a state tries to submit and its adversary has not already attacked. The essence of having the ability of being able to submit if one's adversary has not already attacked is rather that each state has an option that has two properties. First, the exercise of this option must be evident to one's adversary, or, more formally, its exercise must be common knowledge. Second, if an adversary observes that this option has been exercised, then attacking is not in the adversary's best interest. If an actual option is to be an empirical referent corresponding to the theoretical construct, it should satisfy these two criteria.

Whether or not any real options meet these criteria depends very much on the actual capabilities of the superpowers' strategic arsenals and their command and control systems. But suppose, for example, that to launch an effective first strike, a state's strategic forces must be brought to a higher state of readiness than is normally maintained: A state must "generate" its strategic forces before being able to launch an effective first strike. Assume further that each state is able to monitor the other's alert status and will know if its adversary is generating its strategic forces. Now suppose that in the midst of a crisis an adversary either does not increase the readiness of its strategic arsenal or reduces it, and a state observes its adversary's failure to generate its forces. The state then reasons that such a step makes no sense if its adversary is planning to attack. But the only justification for this state to attack would be that it expects its adversary to attack. Accordingly, this state will not attack, although it may maintain the pressure on its adversary by not reducing its alert status or through other means. Given the suppositions that the alert status of the states can be monitored and that an effective first strike requires that forces be brought to a high state of readiness, an empirical referent corresponding to the theoretical construct of being able to attempt to resign and thereby avoid a nuclear exchange if one's adversary has not already attacked would seem to be the ability to maintain an alert status that will ensure that a devastating second strike can still be launched but that an effective first strike cannot be.

In this light, it is interesting to observe that during the Cuban missile crisis the Soviet Union apparently did not put its strategic forces on alert.[11] As U.S. Air Force General David Burchinal described Krushchev's position in the crisis, "We put a gun to his head and he didn't move a muscle."[12] The Soviets, it would seem, not only had but also exercised an actual option that corresponded to the theoretical construct. Indeed, in many crises in the nuclear era, including the most severe crises over Berlin and, later, over missiles in Cuba, American leaders, at least, were not significantly concerned by the prospect of the Soviets attempting to launch a first strike, and there was little reciprocal fear (Betts 1987, p. 164).

Finally, it should be emphasized that although escalation may not mean risking that the reciprocal fear of surprise attack or some other process will lead to a general nuclear exchange, escalation may still do other things. It may, for example, indicate a willingness to inflict and endure severe but limited punishment in order to have one's way. Escalation may also enhance one's military position and thereby improve the prospects of prevailing in a limited contest of military strength. These effects may convince an adversary to come to terms. Escalation may still be an important means of exerting coercive pressure, although perhaps not for the reasons commonly assumed.

The third condition is that the net cost of launching a first strike and thereby having to absorb a second strike, when by coming to terms a general nuclear exchange could have been avoided, is larger than the net cost of launching a less effective rather than a more effective second strike. This condition is a generalization of the assumption that $L - F > S - W$, which is what was used to stabilize the preemption game in Figure 5.1. When this third condition is combined with the second condition, which assumes that states have the option of attempting to quit, they imply that no state will attack in equilibrium unless it believes that the probability that war is inevitable is greater than $\frac{1}{2}$.[13]

Two points should be underscored. First, the size of any first-strike advantage is still relevant to stability. If the advantage to striking first is so large that a state will attack even if it believes that the probability that war is inevitable is less than $\frac{1}{2}$, then there may be an unlimited exchange, even if all of the other conditions needed to ensure stability are satisfied. If, as noted earlier, $L - f < W - S$ in the preemption game, then the threshold needed to justifying attacking is less than $\frac{1}{2}$, and there are equilibria in which I and II

[11] Trachtenberg (1985, pp. 156–61). See, however, the discussion of Soviet submarines in the Caribbean during the crisis (Sagan 1985, pp. 112–18).

[12] Quoted in Trachtenberg (1985, p. 161). Also see Burchinal's comments on the Cuban missile crisis in Kohn and Harahan (1988, pp. 92–5).

[13] Lemma 6.1 demonstrates that these two conditions do imply this.

will attack. It is surprising, however, that the threshold needed to ensure stability can be so low. As long as the threshold exceeds the lower bound of $\frac{1}{2}$, the crisis will be completely stable. In particular, there will be no risk of a general nuclear exchange if the threshold of inevitability at which it becomes rational to attack is, say, 60 percent. But viewed from the perspective of the conventional logic, a crisis in which the threshold is this low will be likely to be described as highly unstable.

The second point to be emphasized is that the size of the lower bound on the threshold needed to justify attacking if the crisis is to be stable is related to the number of nuclear superpowers. If there are two superpowers in the international system, this lower bound is $\frac{1}{2}$. But if there are M nuclear superpowers, then as is shown in the next chapter, the stabilizing lower bound for the threshold is $(M-1)/M$. To ensure stability, the payoffs and first-strike advantages must be such that no state will attack unless the probability that war is unavoidable is greater than $(M-1)/M$. Note that as the number of nuclear superpowers increases, the lower bound needed to ensure stability rises. Thresholds that were above this lower bound for some M and therefore ensured stability may no longer exceed the lower bound as M increases. If, for example, there are two nuclear superpowers, and the threshold needed to justify attacking is 0.6, then the game is stable, because $(M-1)/M = 0.5$, and this is less than the threshold of 0.6. If, however, the threshold remains 0.6, but there are instead three nuclear superpowers, the crisis may no longer be stable, because $(M-1)/M = \frac{2}{3}$, and this is less than 0.6. In this sense, then, stability decreases as the number of nuclear superpowers increases.[14]

The fourth condition needed to ensure stability is the formalization of the third feature that characterized Schelling's stylization. He assumed that the states fully appreciated their situation. More formally, the fourth condition is that the first three conditions are common knowledge. That is, every player knows that the first three conditions are met and that the other players know that they are met and that all the other players know that all of the other players know that the conditions are met, and so forth. The first three conditions describe an objective situation. But, as has been pointed out many times (Jervis 1982–3), deterrence depends on beliefs about a situation rather than on the actual situation. The same is true in game-theoretic analyses of deterrence. If, for example, the actual payoffs satisfy $L - F > S - W$, but the states believe that this condition has not been met, then the game used to model this situation may not satisfy the first three

---

[14] This conclusion is suggestive of Waltz's conclusion (1979) that a bipolar system is more stable and less prone to war than is a multipolar system. And although nuclear weapons play no part in Waltz's argument, the greater uncertainty associated with a greater number of superpowers is the key to both his argument and that developed here.

conditions, and there may be some chance of an exchange in this game. The common-knowledge assumption is crucial because it links the states' beliefs about the situation to the situation.[15] The states are assumed to understand fully the objective situation described by the first three conditions.

A final qualification about limited options is in order. Any option satisfying the third assumption in a game that satisfies the other assumptions will not be played in equilibrium. Of course, in games that are more complicated than the preemption game in Figure 5.1 there may be many more options than A, and these other alternatives need not satisfy the third assumption. In addition to the possibility of launching an unlimited attack by playing A, there may, for example, also be an option A' that corresponds to launching a limited attack. Depending on the underlying payoffs, it might well be that, unlike A, a state would launch A' even if it were confident its adversary was not launching a limited attack. If so, then A' would no longer satisfy the third assumption, and a state might play A' in equilibrium (although it remains the case that A would not be played). The set of games that satisfy the stabilizing conditions includes games in which there are limited options. But, unfortunately, the preceding analysis is silent on the question of the effects of first-strike advantages on the likelihood of limited attacks. Whether these effects can be analyzed only in the context of specific games or whether there are any more general results remains an open question. Accordingly, it is important to remember that crisis stability is interpreted narrowly here, as elsewhere (Schelling 1960, 1966; Jervis 1978; Brams 1985; Brams and Kilgour 1987; O'Neill 1987; Powell 1987, 1988, 1989a, 1989c), as relating to the probability of a general or unlimited exchange.

The strategy that leaves something to chance and brinkmanship have attempted to solve the credibility problem by linking the use or threatened use of force to states' efforts to further their ends with a sanction that it is assumed will not be imposed deliberately. This chapter has begun to move away from this demanding assumption and its associated emphasis on the risk of losing collective control by supposing instead that there is at least one situation in which a state will deliberately be the first to impose the brinkmanship sanction of a general nuclear attack. Assuming there to be some advantage to striking first created this situation and led directly to reconsidering the problem of crisis stability and preemption.

This reexamination identified four conditions that ensure that crises will

---

[15] More precisely, the common-knowledge assumption ensures that the extensive game used to model the crisis and especially the states' uncertainty satisfies the first three assumptions. Theorem 6.1 in the next chapter shows that any game satisfying these three assumptions is completely stable.

be stable despite there being an advantage to striking first. Because these conditions are sufficient to ensure stability, their explication also identifies the potential sources of instability, for if there is to be any instability, at least one of the sufficient conditions must be violated. The first condition is that a general nuclear attack may be the inadvertent consequence of escalation, but it cannot be purely accidental. States always remain in collective control. Second, whenever a state can attack, it can also attempt to end the crisis by submitting to its adversary. If, moreover, its adversary has not already committed itself to launching a general nuclear attack, the crisis will end with the state's submission, and there will not be a general nuclear exchange. Third, if there are two nuclear superpowers in the international system, then it must be that neither state will launch a general nuclear attack unless it believes that the probability that a general nuclear war is inevitable is greater than $\frac{1}{2}$. If there are M nuclear superpowers in the system, then it must be that no state will launch a general nuclear attack unless it believes that the probability that a general nuclear war is inevitable is greater than $(M-1)/M$. Because $(M-1)/M$, which is a lower bound on the threshold of inevitability needed to ensure stability, rises as the number of nuclear superpowers in the system increases, a bipolar system may in this sense be said to be more stable than a multipolar system. The final condition needed for stability is that the states fully appreciate their situation, in that the first three conditions are common knowledge.

The conventional logic of crisis stability holds that if there are first-strike advantages, then there is some chance of an unlimited exchange. The larger the advantage to striking first, moreover, the greater the chance of an exchange. Yet the game examined here is completely stable even though there are first-strike advantages in it. The conventional logic of crisis stability focuses too narrowly on first-strike advantages. Stability results from a more subtle interaction of several factors, of which the size of any first-strike advantage is only one.

This chapter has presented a simple model of a crisis that is completely stable despite the existence of first-strike advantages and has asserted that four conditions ensure stability not only in this simple example but also in any model satisfying these conditions. The first task in the next chapter is to demonstrate that this assertion holds. The second task is to examine some of the consequences of relaxing the four conditions and, especially, to examine the effects on stability of relaxing the first condition and thereby allowing for the possibility that the states may lose collective control. This yields a result that is very close in spirit to the conclusions of the conventional logic of crisis stability.

CHAPTER 6

Stability and the lack of control

The strategy that leaves something to chance and brinkmanship appeal to a sanction that, it is assumed, would not be imposed deliberately. The problem, then, is to explain how threats that ultimately rely on such a sanction can be related to states' attempts to protect their interests. The preceding chapter began to move away from this assumption by discussing the dynamics of escalation when there is one situation in which the sanction will be imposed deliberately. This chapter describes the game-theoretic foundations underlying that discussion. This is done in two steps. The first is to define a large class of games. The games in this class are then shown to be completely stable, even though there are significant first-strike advantages. The probability of there being a general nuclear exchange in any game satisfying the conditions defining the class is zero. These conditions are sufficient to ensure stability.

Once sufficient conditions of this kind have been identified, it is natural to try to investigate the consequences of relaxing them. The first assumption to be relaxed will be the assumption that there are only two nuclear superpowers. Here it will be shown that if there are M superpowers, and if the threshold of inevitability needed to justify launching a first strike is larger than $(M-1)/M$, then the crisis will be completely stable. Therefore, $(M-1)/M$ forms a lower bound on the threshold of inevitability such that the crisis will be stable as long as all of the states' thresholds exceed this lower bound.

The other assumption to be relaxed is that there is no autonomous risk of an unlimited attack. There will, instead, be some risk that the states may lose collective control. When this risk is reintroduced, it is no longer possible to ensure that a crisis will be completely stable. It is, however, possible to demonstrate that the probability that a first strike will be launched deliberately, which will be denoted by $\mathscr{F}_D$, is related to the probability that a first strike will be launched because the states lose collective control, $\mathscr{F}_N$, according to

$$\mathscr{F}_D < \mathscr{F}_N \left(\frac{1}{M(1-T^*)} - 1 \right)^{-1} \tag{6.1}$$

131

where M is still the number of nuclear superpowers, and T^* is the threshold of inevitability needed to justify a deliberate first strike.

The possibility that a confrontation may end in a deliberate attack exists because events are not fully under control, in the sense that no state controls the actions and reactions of another. Accordingly, $\mathscr{F}_D$ is akin to the probability that the confrontation will end in a general nuclear exchange because events are not fully under control in this sense. Similarly, $\mathscr{F}_N$ is the probability that the confrontation will end in a general nuclear exchange because of a collective loss of control. In this way, (6.1) establishes a formal relation between the two senses in which events may not be fully under control that were described in Chapter 2.

The expression on the right side of (6.1) is an upper bound on the probability that there will be a deliberate first strike. This upper bound is an increasing function of the probability that the states will lose collective control. As the autonomous risk of a first strike rises, the upper bound rises, and in this sense the crisis becomes less stable. This suggests that the more likely states are to lose collective control, the more likely the crisis may be to end in a deliberate exchange because events are not fully under control in the second sense.

The upper bound for the probability of a deliberate first strike is also decreasing in the threshold of inevitability needed to justify launching a deliberate first strike. As the threshold of inevitability rises, that is, as a state must be increasingly confident that war is inevitable before it is willing to attack, the upper bound falls. The crisis, in this sense, becomes more stable as the threshold of inevitability rises.

There is, finally, a still simpler upper bound on this probability, one that is very much in keeping with the conclusion of the conventional logic of crisis stability. The probability of a deliberate first strike plus the probability of a first strike resulting from a collective loss of control must be less than or equal to 1: $\mathscr{F}_D + \mathscr{F}_N \leq 1$. Using this to eliminate $\mathscr{F}_N$ in (6.1) gives $\mathscr{F}_D < M(1-T^*)$. As the threshold of inevitability approaches 1, the probability that a state will become sufficiently confident to launch a first strike deliberately approaches zero. The conventional logic reached the same conclusion: As the size of the first-strike advantage approached zero, the threshold of inevitability needed to justify attacking deliberately, τ^*, approached 1, and that, it was presumed, reduced the chances of crossing the threshold. The difference between the analysis that follows and the conventional logic has less to do with their respective conclusions; these are quite similar, although the former illuminates the importance of there being some risk of a collective loss of control in ways that the latter does not. The difference has more to do with the nature of the argument. The conventional logic treats beliefs as being formally exogenous. The discussion that follows brings them into the analysis by making them endogenous, albeit in a stylized way.

The class of games

Before formalizing the conditions that define the class of games and ensure stability, it will be useful to state them less formally:

i The states always retain collective control over whether or not there is a general nuclear exchange. There is no autonomous risk of a state launching a first strike. An unlimited nuclear attack can happen only if a state orders it. An accident may be responsible for a false alarm, but that cannot trigger an attack directly. If the false alarm is to lead to an attack, it can do so only indirectly by leading a state to attack on the basis of it. Between any accident and an unrestricted attack, there must be a decision to attack. Events are not fully under control, but only in the second sense.

ii A state can launch an unlimited attack only once. Moreover, as long as a state has the option of attacking, it can also attempt to terminate the crisis by accepting its adversary's terms. If the adversary has not already attacked, accepting the adversary's terms will end the confrontation.

iii It is better to strike first than second. But even a successful first strike cannot protect a state from such a devastating second strike that the state would have preferred to have accepted its adversary's terms rather than suffer the second strike. Moreover, this devastating second strike is sure to come, because it is also assumed that an adversary will have the capability to launch a retaliatory second strike if it is struck first and will believe doing so to be in its interest.

iv Assumptions (i), (ii), and (iii) are common knowledge. That is, each state knows them, knows that the other states know them, knows that the other states know that the other states know them, and so forth.

Assumptions (iii) and (iv) ensure that the games in this class satisfy the three stylized conditions that describe the problem of preemption. The other assumptions are additional restrictions that are needed to ensure stability.

To formalize the class of games, denote this class by Γ, and let $G \in \Gamma$ be a finite game in extensive form with perfect recall. There are $m + 1$ players, m states $S_1, S_2, \ldots, S_m$, and Nature. To allow for the possibility of incomplete information in G, there are also t_k types of states S_k, where S_k^i for $i = 1, 2, \ldots, t_k$ denotes the ith type of state k.

Of the states, only two, S_1 and S_2, are superpowers. That is, only these states can launch an unlimited, society-destroying attack. More formally, let A denote the alternative of a massive nuclear attack in the game. Then the only decision nodes in the tree at which A may be played belong to S_1 or S_2.

A first strike and second strike may be defined in the following way. Let Z be the set of terminal nodes in $G \in \Gamma$. S_1 will be said to have struck first if the game ends at $z \in Z$ and S_1 was the first state to take A along the path to z. S_2 will be said to have struck second if the game ends at $z \in Z$ and S_1 struck first along the path to z. Thus, S_2 may be said to have struck second in the game in one of two ways: First, S_2 may explicitly have attacked by playing A after S_1 played A. Second, S_2 may be assumed implicitly to have attacked after S_1 played A. In this case, the payoffs incorporate the implicit assumption that S_2 has launched a second strike. (This second, implicit way of modeling a second strike is used in the preemption game in Figure 5.1, where the payoff to playing Q after one's adversary has played A is assumed to correspond to launching a slow second strike. Allowing second strikes to be modeled in this way makes it possible to study simpler games, like that in Figure 5.1, in which only the decision to launch a first strike is modeled explicitly.)

The first restriction on the members of Γ is that there is no autonomous risk that a state will launch a general nuclear attack. This can be formalized by assuming that Nature cannot attack. That is, the alternative A is not present at any node belonging to Nature. This, however, is the only type of accident that is prohibited. All other accidents (i.e., all other acts of Nature) are allowed.

Turning to the second assumption, a state can attack only once. That is, a state can play A only once along any path through the tree. Now consider any information set h at which a superpower, say S_1, can attack. Because S_1 still has the option of attacking, it must be that it has not previously attacked. Accordingly, S_1 may try to terminate the crisis by accepting S_2's terms. If S_2 has not already attacked, S_1's acceptance of S_2's terms will end the crisis. More formally, let y be any node in h. Then at y, S_1 may select an alternative Q that represents S_1's attempt to quit the crisis. If S_2 has not already attacked somewhere along the path to y, then the game will end if S_1 chooses Q at y.

Some further notation will facilitate the statement of the third restriction. Let h be an information set belonging to a superpower, say S_1, at which S_1 has the alternative of attacking, A. Then, by assumption (ii), S_1 has not already attacked, and therefore it also has the alternative of attempting to terminate the crisis by playing Q.

The nodes of h can be partitioned into two types. In the first, S_1 has not already been attacked. Letting $\phi(h)$ denote this set, $\phi(h)$ is the set of nodes in h at which S_1 will be launching a first strike if it attacks. More formally, $y \in \phi(h)$ if $y \in h$ and S_2 has not played A along the path to y. Now let $\sigma(h)$ be the set of nodes at which S_1 will be launching a second strike if it attacks: If $y \in \sigma(h)$, then S_2 has launched an attack against S_1 somewhere along the path to y. Then, $\sigma(h) = h - \phi(h)$.

Now let (μ, π) be any perfect Bayesian equilibrium of any $G \in \Gamma$, where μ is a system of beliefs, and π is a profile of the states' strategies.[1] $EU_S(A|y, (\mu, \pi))$ is the expected payoff to S starting from y and assuming S plays A at y and that play thereafter follows the strategies given by (μ, π). $EU_S(Q|y, (\mu, \pi))$ is defined similarly, except that S quits at y. Because the game ends if S plays Q at any $y \in \phi(h)$, $EU_S(Q|y, (\mu, \pi)) = U_S(Q|y)$ for any $y \in \phi(h)$.

The formal restriction on the states' payoffs may now be stated. Let h be any information set such that h is reached with positive probability and there is some possibility that the owner of h could launch a first strike at h. More formally, assume $P(h|(\mu, \pi)) > 0$ and $\phi(h) \neq \varnothing$. Then the restriction on the payoffs that formally defines assumption (iii) is

$$\min_{y \in \phi(h)} \{ U_S(Q|y) - EU_S(A|y, (\mu, \pi)) \}$$
$$> \max_{y \in \sigma(h)} \{ EU_S(A|y, (\mu, \pi)) - EU_S(Q|y, (\mu, \pi)) \} \geq 0 \quad (6.2)$$

where (μ, π) is any perfect Bayesian equilibrium, and, if $\sigma(h)$ is empty, the maximum over $y \in \sigma(h)$ is defined to be zero. Note further that although it simplifies some of the discussion, the game need not end if a state plays Q at $y \in \phi(h)$. All that is required is that (6.2) be rewritten as

$$\min_{y \in \phi(h)} \{ EU_S(Q|y, (\mu, \pi)) - EU_S(A|y, (\mu, \pi)) \}$$
$$> \max_{y \in \sigma(h)} \{ EU_S(A|y, (\mu, \pi)) - EU_S(Q|y, (\mu, \pi)) \} \geq 0$$

and be assumed to hold for all perfect Bayesian equilibria.

This formalization requires some discussion. To see that (6.2) may be a reasonable formalization of a technological state of affairs in which there are first-strike advantages but even a successful first strike is certain to bring a terribly costly second strike, consider the term on the left side of the first inequality in (6.2). Because $y \in \phi(h)$, S has not already been attacked if play has reached y. Thus, if S attempts to terminate the crisis by choosing Q,

---

[1] The weakest notion of a perfect Bayesian equilibrium is used here: It is a sequentially rational assessment in which the only condition required of beliefs is that they satisfy Bayes' rule where this rule applies. (See the Appendix following Chapter 8 for a discussion of this type of equilibrium.)

the crisis will end, because neither state has launched an unlimited nuclear attack. The payoff to this outcome is $U_S(Q|y)$. If, however, S attacks at y, then S will have struck first when the game ends. The payoff to this is $EU_S(A|y,(\mu,\pi))$. Assuming that S's first strike ensures that it will have to endure its adversary's second strike in any perfect Bayesian equilibrium, then $U_S(Q|y) - EU_S(A|y,(\mu,\pi))$ is the difference between the payoff to accepting an adversary's terms, and in so doing avoiding an unrestricted nuclear war, and the payoff to suffering an unlimited second strike. If the nuclear era is such that it is better to strike first than second, but even a second strike is certain to bring a devastating reply, then $U_S(Q|y) - EU_S(A|y,(\mu,\pi))$ would seem to be large for all $y \in \phi(h)$. Accordingly, the minimum of these differences over $\phi(h)$ should also be large.

Turning to the term on the right side of the first inequality in (6.2), S's adversary has already initiated a first strike because $y \in \sigma(h)$. Regardless of what S does, it will suffer an unlimited first strike. Thus, $EU_S(A|y, (\mu,\pi)) - EU_S(Q|y,(\mu,\pi))$ is the difference between the payoff to a more effective second strike and the payoff to a less effective second strike. With large, relatively survivable strategic arsenals and no effective strategic defenses, this difference would seem to be small for all $y \in \sigma(h)$.

This analysis focuses on general conditions needed to ensure stability, not on whether or not particular games are stable. If, however, the stability of a particular game were at issue, then there would be little point in trying to see if the game satisfies condition (6.2). Determining this would entail finding or at least characterizing that game's perfect Bayesian equilibria. But if one already had the game's equilibria, one could simply look at them to see if there were any chance of a general nuclear exchange. In evaluating the stability of a particular game, it may be more useful to have a condition that, although more demanding than (6.2), is easier to verify and, moreover, does not depend on obtaining a game's equilibrium strategies first. To this end, let $Z_Q(\phi(h))$ be the set of terminal nodes that follow the nodes in $\phi(h)$, given that the owner of h plays Q at h. Similarly, let $Z_Q(\sigma(h))$ be the set of terminal nodes that follow the nodes in $\sigma(h)$, given that the owner of h plays Q at h. Finally, take $Z_A(\phi(h))$ and $Z_A(\sigma(h))$ to be the sets of terminal nodes that follow, respectively, $\phi(h)$ and $\sigma(h)$, given that the owner of h plays A at h. Then suppose that the payoffs satisfy the following condition, which, because it depends only on comparing the payoffs at terminal nodes, not on deriving equilibrium strategies, is easier to verify than the relation defined in (6.2): For all h such that $\phi(h) \neq \varnothing$,

$$\min_{y \in \phi(h)} \{\min\{U_S(z): z \in Z_Q(\phi(h(y)))\} - \max\{U_S(z): z \in Z_A(\phi(h(y)))\}\}$$
$$> \max_{y \in \sigma(h)} \{\max\{U_S(z): z \in Z_A(\sigma(h(y)))\} - \min\{U_S(z): z \in Z_Q(\sigma(h(y)))\}\} \geq 0$$

If this inequality holds, then the relation described in (6.2) also holds, and assumption (iii) is satisfied.

In terms of the game in Figure 5.1, this inequality requires $L - F > S - W$, for

$$\min_{y \in \phi(h)} \left\{ \min \left\{ U_S(z): z \in Z_Q(\phi(h(y))) \right\} - \max \left\{ U_S(z): z \in Z_A(\phi(h(y))) \right\} \right\}$$

$$= \min_{y \in \phi(h)} \left\{ \min \left\{ L \right\} - \max \left\{ F, f \right\} \right\}$$

$$= L - F$$

$$> \max_{y \in \sigma(h)} \left\{ \max \left\{ U_S(z): z \in Z_A(\sigma(h(y))) \right\} - \min \left\{ U_S(z): z \in Z_Q(\sigma(h(y))) \right\} \right\}$$

$$= \max_{y \in \sigma(h)} \left\{ \max \left\{ S \right\} - \min \left\{ W \right\} \right\}$$

$$= S - W$$

This, moreover, ensured the stability of this game.

The formalization of the final assumption is simply that assumptions (i), (ii), and (iii) are common knowledge. In effect, this has already been done implicitly by assuming that the game representing the situation satisfies (i), (ii), and (iii).[2]

An impossibility theorem

Theorem 6.1 shows that in equilibrium, no state will ever launch an unlimited attack. In particular, then, no state will ever launch such an attack preemptively. No process, neither the reciprocal fear of surprise attack nor any other, would make it rational for a state to launch such an attack.

> **Theorem 6.1:** *The probability of an unlimited nuclear exchange in any perfect Bayesian equilibrium of any $G \in \Gamma$ is zero.*

The intuition underlying the proof of this theorem is straightforward. The argument proceeds by contradiction. Assume that there exists an equilibrium in which there is some chance of a deliberate first strike. Then the assumption that the threshold of inevitability needed to justify

---

[2] The interesting games in Γ are those, like that in Figure 5.1, in which there are overlapping information sets because of the states' uncertainty about the order in which they move. In such games, the problem of what are reasonable beliefs to hold off the equilibrium path may be especially difficult. For example, the conjecture in sequential equilibria that if an information set with probability zero is reached, then there will be no further deviations from the equilibrium strategies may be incompatible with beliefs being structurally consistent. See Kreps and Ramey (1987) for a discussion of this.

attacking deliberately is greater than $\frac{1}{2}$ implies that the probability that S_1 will strike first, given that there will be a first strike, is less than $\frac{1}{2}$. Similarly, the probability that S_2 will be the first to strike, given that there will be a first strike, is less than $\frac{1}{2}$. This, however, immediately leads to a contradiction. If the probability that S_1 will strike first, given that there will be a first strike, is less than $\frac{1}{2}$ and the probability that S_2 will strike first, given that there will be a first strike, is also less than $\frac{1}{2}$, then the sum of these probabilities, which is the probability that S_1 or S_2 will strike first, given that one of the states will strike first, is less than 1. But this is a contradiction, for if only these two states can attack, then the probability that one of them has struck first, given that there has been a first strike, must be 1. This contradiction implies that there cannot be an equilibrium in which there is some chance of a deliberate first strike.

Before proving the theorem, it will be helpful to establish a lemma. To state the lemma, let (μ, π) be any perfect Bayesian equilibrium of $G \in \Gamma$, and let h be any information set of G. Define $a(h|(\mu, \pi))$ to be the probability specified by (μ, π) that the owner of h will attack at h. Then if the probability of reaching h is positive [i.e., if $P(h|(\mu, \pi)) > 0$], then $\frac{1}{2}$ is a strict lower bound on the threshold of inevitability needed to justify attacking. That is, a state can attack at h only if it believes that the probability that war is inevitable is greater than $\frac{1}{2}$. More formally:

> **Lemma 6.1:** *If $P(h|(\mu, \sigma)) > 0$ and $a(h|(\mu, \pi)) > 0$, then $P(\sigma(h)|(\mu, \pi))$ $> P(\phi(h)|(\mu, \pi))$, or, equivalently, $P(\sigma(h)|(\mu, \pi))/P(h|(\mu, \pi)) > \frac{1}{2}$.*

Proof: Let S be the owner of h. For S to be able to attack at h, A must be an alternative at h. By assumption (ii), if A is an alternative at h, so is Q. Now, S may have many options at h other than A and Q. But if $a(h|(\mu, \pi)) > 0$ in equilibrium, then the expected value of selecting A must be at least as great as that of choosing Q. That is,

$$\sum_{y \in h} [EU_S(A|y, (\mu, \pi)) \cdot \mu_h(y)] \geq \sum_{y \in h} [EU_S(Q|y, (\mu, \pi)) \cdot \mu_h(y)]$$

where $\mu_h(y)$ is S's belief that it is at y conditioned on being in h. Because $P(h|(\mu, \pi)) > 0$, Bayes' rule applies at h, and $\mu_h(y) = P(y|(\mu, \pi))/P(h|(\mu, \pi))$. Substituting for $\mu_h(y)$ and recalling that $\phi(h)$ and $\sigma(h)$ partition h, the preceding inequality may be rewritten to give

$$\sum_{y \in \sigma(h)} [EU_S(A|y, (\mu, \pi)) - EU_S(Q|y, (\mu, \pi))] \cdot P(y|(\mu, \pi))$$

$$\geq \sum_{y \in \phi(h)} [EU_S(Q|y, (\mu, \pi)) - EU_S(A|y, (\mu, \pi))] \cdot P(y|(\mu, \pi))$$

Thus,

$$\left[\max_{y \in \sigma(h)} \{ EU_S(A \mid y, (\mu, \pi)) - EU_S(Q \mid y, (\mu, \pi)) \} \right] \cdot P(\sigma(h) \mid (\mu, \pi))$$

$$\geq \left[\min_{y \in \phi(h)} \{ EU_S(Q \mid y, (\mu, \pi)) - EU_S(A \mid y, (\mu, \pi)) \} \right] \cdot P(\phi(h) \mid (\mu, \pi))$$

Now note that if $P(\sigma(h) \mid (\mu, \pi)) = 0$, then this inequality cannot be satisfied. The left side equals zero, and (6.2) and the assumption that $P(h \mid (\mu, \pi))$ > 0 mean that the right side is positive. Thus, if $a(h \mid (\mu, \pi)) > 0$, then $P(\sigma(h) \mid (\mu, \pi)) > 0$.

But assumption (iii) also ensures that the minimum on the right of the inequality is greater than the maximum on the left. Hence, $P(\sigma(h) \mid (\mu, \pi)) >$ $P(\phi(h) \mid (\mu, \pi))$. Because $P(\sigma(h) \mid (\mu, \pi)) + P(\phi(h) \mid (\mu, \pi)) = P(h \mid (\mu, \pi))$ and $P(\sigma(h) \mid (\mu, \pi)) > P(\phi(h) \mid (\mu, \pi))$, then $P(\sigma(h) \mid (\mu, \pi)) / P(h \mid (\mu, \pi)) > \frac{1}{2}$. That is, a state will attack at h only if the probability that war seems unavoidable at h, $P(\sigma(h) \mid (\mu, \pi)) / P(h \mid (\mu, \pi))$, is greater than $\frac{1}{2}$. ∎

Proof of Theorem 6.1: The proof of the theorem proceeds by contradiction. Suppose, that is, that there exists some $G \in \Gamma$ and some perfect Bayesian equilibrium of G, (μ, π), in which there is a positive probability of a nuclear exchange. This will be shown to lead to a contradiction.

Let ∇ be the set of nodes that are reached with positive probability and at which a state will launch a first strike with a positive probability. That is, $\nabla = \{y : P(y) > 0, y \in \phi(h) \text{ for some } h, a(h) > 0\}$. By assumption, at least one state will attack with a positive probability in (μ, π); so $\nabla \neq \varnothing$. Moreover, ∇ can be partitioned into the sets of nodes belonging to each of the superpowers. That is, let ∇_1 and ∇_2 be the nodes in ∇ that belong to S_1 and S_2, respectively. Then ∇_1 and ∇_2 partition ∇.

The probability that S_k will attack first, which will be denoted by $\mathscr{F}_k$, is $\mathscr{F}_k = \sum_{y \in \nabla_k} a(h(y) \mid (\mu, \pi)) P(y \mid (\mu, \pi))$. In calculating $\mathscr{F}_k$, it will be convenient to sum over information sets rather than decision nodes. To do this, let H_k be the set of information sets at which there is some chance that S_k or, if there is incomplete information, one of the types of S_k will launch a first strike. Then $H_k = \{h : y \in h, y \in \nabla_k\}$ for $k = 1, 2$. $\mathscr{F}_k$ may be rewritten as

$$\mathscr{F}_k = \sum_{h \in H_k} \left[\sum_{y \in \phi(h)} a(h \mid (\mu, \pi)) P(y \mid (\mu, \pi)) \right]$$

$$= \sum_{h \in H_k} a(h \mid (\mu, \pi)) P(\phi(h) \mid (\mu, \pi)) \tag{6.3}$$

Then the probability that S_k will attack first, given that there will be an attack, is $\mathscr{F}_k / \mathscr{F}$, where $\mathscr{F} = \mathscr{F}_1 + \mathscr{F}_2$. Moreover, the probability that S_k will strike first, given that some state will strike first, is less than $\frac{1}{2}$: $\mathscr{F}_k/\mathscr{F} < \frac{1}{2}$. To see this, note that Lemma 6.1 gives $P(\sigma(h)|(\mu,\pi)) > P(\phi(h)|(\mu,\pi))$. This yields

$$\mathscr{F}_k = \sum_{h\in H_k} a(h|(\mu,\pi))P(\phi(h)|(\mu,\pi)) < \sum_{h\in H_k} a(h|(\mu,\pi))P(\sigma(h)|(\mu,\pi))$$

Now, without loss of generality, suppose $k=1$. Then

$$\mathscr{F}_1 < \sum_{h\in H_1} a(h|(\mu,\pi))P(\sigma(h)|(\mu,\pi))$$

The sum on the right is less than or equal to the probability that S_1 will launch a second strike. (It may be less, because H_1 does not contain sets at which $\phi(h) = \varnothing$ and $a(h) > 0$.) But the probability that S_1 will strike second is less than or equal to the probability that S_2 will strike first, because the only way to reach nodes at which S_1 strikes second is through nodes at which S_2 attacks first:

$$\mathscr{F}_1 < \sum_{h\in H_1} a(h|(\mu,\pi))P(\sigma(h)|(\mu,\pi)) \le \mathscr{F}_2 = \mathscr{F} - \mathscr{F}_1$$

Solving for $\mathscr{F}_1/\mathscr{F}$ leaves $\mathscr{F}_1/\mathscr{F} < \frac{1}{2}$. A similar argument gives $\mathscr{F}_2/\mathscr{F} < \frac{1}{2}$.

This leads immediately to a contradiction. $\mathscr{F}_k/\mathscr{F}$ is the conditional probability that S_k will be the first to attack, given that there will be a first strike. Thus, the sum of $\mathscr{F}_1/\mathscr{F}$ and $\mathscr{F}_2/\mathscr{F}$ must equal 1. But if $\mathscr{F}_1/\mathscr{F}$ and $\mathscr{Y}_2/\mathscr{F}$ are both less than $\frac{1}{2}$, then their sum must be less than 1. ∎

Theorem 6.1 shows that any game satisfying assumptions (i), (ii), and (iii) is completely stable. These conditions are almost necessary too. To see this, note that assumptions (ii) and (iii) enter the analysis only in the proof of the lemma. Accordingly, the conclusion of the lemma, which is that no state will attack at any h that is reached with positive probability in any perfect Bayesian equilibrium (μ,π) unless $P(\sigma(h)|(\mu,\pi))/P(h|(\mu,\pi)) > \frac{1}{2}$, can be substituted for assumptions (ii) and (iii), and the proof of Theorem 6.1 will still go through. Assumption (i) and the conclusion of the lemma are also necessary conditions in the loose sense that if either of them is violated, then there exists at least one game that satisfies the other condition and in which there is a positive probability of an attack. The preemption game in Figure 5.1 is an example of a game in which there is a positive probability of an attack if the assumption that a state will attack only if the probability of its launching a first strike is less than or equal to $\frac{1}{2}$ is violated. The brinkmanship model studied in Chapter 3 does not satisfy the first assumption (i.e., Nature can attack), but this model does satisfy the other assumption, for no state will ever launch a deliberate attack in this game. The brinkmanship model violates only the assumption that the states retain collective control; yet there is still some chance of a general nuclear exchange.

Figure 6.1 offers another example of a game that fails to satisfy the conditions needed to ensure stability and in which there is some chance of a general exchange. To see that the game actually is unstable, note that the combination of strategies in which both *I* and *II* attack and *II* believes that it is at its upper decision node is a perfect Bayesian equilibrium in which there is certain to be a general exchange. The source of this instability is twofold. First, the game does not satisfy assumption (ii). When *I* must decide what to do, it knows that *II* has not attacked. Formally, if *y* is *I*'s decision node and *h* is *I*'s information set, then $y \in \phi(h)$. *I*, however, cannot end the crisis by playing *Q* as is required by assumption (ii). The game fails to meet this condition. But as noted earlier, the assumption that the game must end immediately if *S* plays *Q* at $y \in \phi(h)$ can be relaxed by adopting a somewhat more general formulation of (6.2). Allowing for this, the game in Figure 6.1 now cannot meet the requirements of this more general formulation. This formulation demands that

$$\min_{y \in \phi(h)} \{EU_S(Q \mid y, (\mu, \pi)) - EU_S(A \mid y, (\mu, \pi))\}$$

$$> \max_{y \in \sigma(h)} \{EU_S(A \mid y, (\mu, \pi)) - EU_S(Q \mid y, (\mu, \pi))\} \geq 0$$

But in the equilibrium in which both states attack, the right side of the first inequality for *I* is $-10 - (-8) = -2$. The game also fails to satisfy the conclusion of Lemma 6.1, which, if satisfied and in combination with

Figure 6.1. An unstable game in which quitting is impossible.

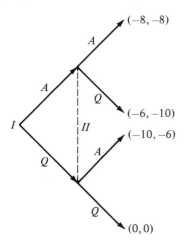

assumption (i), would be sufficient to ensure stability. Γ's $\sigma(h)$ is empty; so $P(\sigma(h)|(\mu, \pi))/P(h|(\mu, \pi)) = 0$. Thus, I attacks in the perfect Bayesian equilibrium that was just described, although $P(\sigma(h)|(\mu, \pi))/P(h|(\mu, \pi)) \leq \frac{1}{2}$. This contradicts the conclusion of Lemma 6.1.

Some extensions

The final task of this chapter is to examine some of the consequences of relaxing some of the assumptions that ensure stability and thereby define the set of games Γ. In particular, the effects of allowing there to be more than two superpowers and of reintroducing the possibility that the states may lose collective control will be considered. Suppose that there are M superpowers. Then it is easy to show that a game will still be stable if the threshold of inevitability needed to justify a first strike is greater than the lower bound $(M-1)/M$. As long as no superpower will launch a first strike unless it believes that the probability that war is inevitable is greater than $(M-1)/M$, the game will be completely stable. Because the lower bound needed to ensure stability increases as the number of nuclear superpowers in the system rises, stability in this sense may be said to decrease as the number of nuclear superpowers grows.

Before establishing that $(M-1)/M$ is a stabilizing lower bound, a number of definitional difficulties must be finessed. As soon as there are more than two nuclear superpowers, the question of who is attacking whom becomes relevant. With only two superpowers, when one state played A, it was implicit that this state was attacking the other nuclear superpower. But who is being attacked if a state plays A and there are more than two nuclear superpowers? One way to approach this would be to identify an attack in terms of both the attacking state and the attacked state. That, however, would be quite cumbersome. Another approach is not to focus on the probability of having already been attacked but to focus on the probability that no one has yet attacked. That is, regardless of the difficulties of interpreting $\sigma(h)$ when there are more than two nuclear superpowers, the meaning of $\phi(h)$ remains clear. Along the path to any node in $\phi(h)$, no state has launched an unlimited attack at any other state. Then, $P(\phi(h)|(\mu, \pi))/P(h|(\mu, \pi))$ is the probability that war is avoidable at h, and $P(\sigma(h)|(\mu, \pi))/P(h|(\mu, \pi))$ will simply be taken to be $1 - P(\phi(h)|(\mu, \pi))/P(h|(\mu, \pi))$.

Finally, it should be noted that with more than two nuclear superpowers, condition (ii) may be less appropriate. If there are more than two superpowers, it may be less reasonable to assume that a state can end the crisis if it attempts to do so before another state has attacked. With three or more nuclear superpowers, if one of them signals that it is not going to attack, then each of the others still must be convinced that none of the others will attack. Given these preliminaries, the following holds:

> **Theorem 6.2:** *Let Γ' be derived from Γ by dropping the assumption that there are only two superpowers. Then the probability of an unlimited nuclear exchange in any perfect Bayesian equilibrium of any $G' \in \Gamma'$ is zero if the threshold of inevitability needed to justify a deliberate first strike for every nuclear superpower is above the lower bound $(M-1)/M$.*

Proof: The proof of this theorem closely parallels that of Theorem 6.1. Again arguing by contradiction, suppose that there exists some $G' \in \Gamma'$ and some perfect Bayesian equilibrium of G', (μ', π'), in which there is some chance of an unlimited nuclear exchange. This will be shown to lead to a contradiction.

Let V be the set of nodes that are reached with positive probability and at which a state will launch a first strike with a positive probability. Then, $V = \{ y: P(y) > 0, y \in \phi(h) \text{ for some } h, a(h) > 0 \}$. By assumption, at least one state will attack with a positive probability in (μ', π'); so $V \neq \varnothing$. As before, V can be partitioned into the sets of nodes belonging to each of the superpowers. That is, let $V_1, \ldots, V_M$ be the nodes in V that belong to $S_1, \ldots, S_M$. Then $V_1, \ldots, V_M$ partition V.

The probability that S_k will attack first, which will be denoted by $\mathscr{F}_k$, is $\mathscr{F}_k = \sum_{y \in V_k} a(h(y) | (\mu', \pi')) P(y | (\mu', \pi'))$. In the calculation of $\mathscr{F}_k$ it will again be convenient to sum over information sets rather than decision nodes. As before, define H_k to be the set of information sets at which there is some chance that S_k will launch a first strike: $H_k = \{ h: y \in h, y \in V_k \}$, where $k = 1, \ldots, M$. $\mathscr{F}_k$ may be rewritten as

$$\mathscr{F}_k = \sum_{h \in H_k} \left[\sum_{y \in \phi(h)} a(h | (\mu', \pi')) P(y | (\mu', \pi')) \right]$$

$$= \sum_{h \in H_k} a(h | (\mu', \pi')) P(\phi(h) | (\mu', \pi')) \tag{6.4}$$

Then the probability that S_k will attack first, given that there will be an attack, is $\mathscr{F}_k / \mathscr{F}$, where $\mathscr{F} = \sum_{i=1}^{M} \mathscr{F}_i$.

By assumption, a state can attack at an information set h that is reached with positive probability only if

$$1 - P(\phi(h) | (\mu', \pi')) / P(h | (\mu', \pi'))$$
$$= P(\sigma(h) | (\mu', \pi')) / P(h | (\mu', \pi')) > (M-1)/M$$

This, in turn, implies that a state will attack only if the conditional probability of that state actually being the first to attack in the game is also less than $1/M$. That is, a state can attack only if $\mathcal{F}_k/\mathcal{F} < 1/M$. To see this, note that the previous relation gives $P(\sigma(h)|(\mu', \pi')) > (M-1)P(\phi(h)|(\mu', \pi'))$. This and (6.4) then yield

$$(M-1)\,\mathcal{F}_k = (M-1)\sum_{h \in H_k} a(h|(\mu', \pi'))P(\phi(h)|(\mu', \pi'))$$

$$< \sum_{h \in H_k} a(h|(\mu', \pi'))P(\sigma(h)|(\mu', \pi'))$$

Letting $k=1$, then $(M-1)\mathcal{F}_1 < \sum_{h \in H_1} a(h|(\mu', \pi'))P(\sigma(h)|(\mu', \pi'))$. The term on the right is less than or equal to the probability that S_1 will attack after some other state has already attacked. But the probability that S_1 will strike after some other state strikes is less than or equal to the probability that $S_2, \ldots, S_M$ will strike first. That is,

$$(M-1)\,\mathcal{F}_1 < \sum_{h \in H_1} a(h|(\mu', \pi'))P(\sigma(h)|(\mu', \pi')) \leq \mathcal{F}_2 + \cdots + \mathcal{F}_M = \mathcal{F} - \mathcal{F}_1$$

Solving for $\mathcal{F}_1/\mathcal{F}$ gives $\mathcal{F}_1/\mathcal{F} < 1/M$. A similar argument yields $\mathcal{F}_k/\mathcal{F} < 1/M$ for all k.

As before, this leads immediately to a contradiction. $\mathcal{F}_k/\mathcal{F}$ is the conditional probability that S_k will be the first to attack, given that there will be a first strike. Thus, $\sum_{k=1}^{M} \mathcal{F}_k/\mathcal{F} = 1$. But if $\mathcal{F}_k/\mathcal{F} < 1/M$ for all k, then their sum must be less than 1. ■

The problem of crisis stability focuses on the probability of a deliberate first strike. Given this focus, the assumption that there was no autonomous risk of a first strike and that states always retained collective control of whether or not there would be a general exchange was a useful point of departure for the analysis of this problem. But it is also important to attempt to determine the consequences of relaxing this assumption by reintroducing the possibility that the states will lose collective control.

The following establishes an upper bound for the probability of a deliberate first strike. This upper bound is a function of the autonomous risk of a first strike and of the threshold of inevitability needed to justify attacking. This upper bound defines a relation between the probability of the states losing collective control and the probability of a deliberate first strike.

Some preliminaries are needed in order to derive this upper bound. Let Γ'' be the set of games described earlier, except that games in Γ'' need not satisfy conditions (i) and (iii). That is, Nature may attack in $G'' \in \Gamma''$, and as yet nothing has been said about the threshold of inevitability required to justify a deliberate attack. In keeping with the notation employed, let $\mathcal{F}_1, \ldots, \mathcal{F}_M$, respectively, be the probabilities that $S_1, \ldots, S_M$ will launch a first strike deliberately. Also let $\mathscr{F}_N$ be the probability that a first strike will be launched because the states lose collective control. That is, $\mathscr{F}_N$ is the probability that Nature will strike first. Finally, take T* to be the threshold of inevitability needed in order to justify a first strike. That is, a state will attack at an information set that is reached with positive probability only if $P(\sigma(h)|(\mu'',\pi''))/P(h|(\mu'',\pi'')) > T^*$. Then:

> **Theorem 6.3:** Let (μ'',π'') be a perfect Bayesian equilibrium of $G'' \in \Gamma''$. If there are M nuclear superpowers and the threshold of inevitability needed to justify a deliberate first strike is T*, then
>
> $$\left(\frac{1}{M(1-T^*)} - 1\right)\mathscr{F}_D < \mathscr{F}_N$$
>
> where $\mathscr{F}_D = \sum_{i=1}^{M} \mathscr{F}_i$ is the probability of a deliberate first strike. If $M(1-T^*) < 1$, then
>
> $$\mathscr{F}_D < \mathscr{F}_N\left(\frac{1}{M(1-T^*)} - 1\right)^{-1} \tag{6.5}$$

Proof: The proof of this so closely parallels that of Theorems 6.1 and 6.2 that only a sketch is required. Although Nature can now attack, (6.3) still holds. That is, for $k = 1, \ldots, M$,

$$\mathscr{F}_k = \sum_{h \in H_k} a(h|(\mu'',\pi''))P(\phi(h)|(\mu'',\pi''))$$

Now, if $a(h|(\mu'',\pi'')) > 0$, then

$$P(\sigma(h)|(\mu'',\pi''))/P(h|(\mu'',\pi'')) > T^*$$

This gives

$$P(\sigma(h)|(\mu'',\pi'')) > (T^*/(1-T^*))P(\phi(h)|(\mu'',\pi''))$$

Substituting this into the expression for $\mathscr{F}_k$ and focusing for the moment on $k = 1$ leaves

$$(T^*/[1-T^*])\mathscr{F}_1 < \sum_{h \in H_1} a(h|(\mu'',\pi''))P(\sigma(h)|(\mu'',\pi''))$$

The term on the right is less than or equal to the probability that S_1 will launch a second strike. But the probability that S_1 will strike second is less than or equal to the probability that it has been attacked first, which is less than or equal to $\mathscr{F}_2 + \mathscr{F}_3 + \cdots + \mathscr{F}_M + \mathscr{F}_N$. That is, $(T^*/(1-T^*))\mathscr{F}_1 < \sum_{i=2}^{M} \mathscr{F}_i + \mathscr{F}_N$. A similar argument shows that $(T^*/(1-T^*))\mathscr{F}_j < \sum_{i \neq j}^{M} \mathscr{F}_i +$

$\mathscr{F}_N$ for all j. Summing these inequalities and collecting terms gives $(1/[M(1-\text{T*})]-1)\mathscr{F}_D < \mathscr{F}_N$. ∎

Theorem 6.3 is in some ways a generalization of Theorem 6.1. Let $M = 2$. Then (6.5) gives $[(2\text{T*}-1)/(1-\text{T*})](\mathscr{F}_1 + \mathscr{F}_2) < \mathscr{F}_N$. If, as is assumed in Theorem 6.1, there is no autonomous risk, then the probability that Nature will attack is zero: $\mathscr{F}_N = 0$. Then as long as $\text{T*} > \frac{1}{2}$, the inequality reduces to $\mathscr{F}_1 + \mathscr{F}_2 < 0$. But this is impossible, for $\mathscr{F}_1$ and $\mathscr{F}_2$ are probabilities and must be greater than or equal to zero. This contradiction implies that there is no equilibrium (μ'', π'') in which there is a positive probability of a general nuclear exchange. The game is completely stable, and this is precisely the conclusion of Theorem 6.1.

To assess the effects of changes in $\mathscr{F}_N$ and T* on the upper bound of the probability of a deliberate first strike, observe that the upper bound $[1/(M(1-\text{T*}))-1]^{-1}\mathscr{F}_N$ is increasing in $\mathscr{F}_N$.[3] As the probability of losing control increases, the upper bound of the probability of a deliberate first strike increases, and in this sense the crisis becomes less stable. It is also easy to see that the upper bound is decreasing in T*; that is, $\partial[1/(M(1-\text{T*}))-1]^{-1}\mathscr{F}_N/\partial\text{T*} < 0$. Thus, as the threshold of inevitability needed to justify attacking rises, the upper bound falls, and in this sense the crisis becomes more stable. This is quite similar to the conclusion of the conventional logic of crisis stability. Accordingly, Theorem 6.3 may be seen as providing some more secure game-theoretic foundations for this conclusion.

A final step makes this similarity still clearer. The probability that there will be a deliberate first strike or an accidental first strike must be less than or equal to 1: $\mathscr{F}_D + \mathscr{F}_N \leq 1$. Combining this inequality and (6.5) shows that the probability of a deliberate first strike is less than $M(1-\text{T*})$; that is, $\mathscr{F}_D < M(1-\text{T*})$. If, therefore, the threshold of inevitability needed to justify a deliberate first strike is so high that T* is close to 1, the probability of a deliberate first strike is small. This is essentially what the conventional logic implied. If the first-strike advantages in this logic were small, then the threshold τ^* would be close to 1. That is, $\tau^* = 1 - (F-S)/(C-S)$ would be near 1 when the size of the first-strike advantage, $F-S$, was close to zero. This presumably made the threshold difficult to cross and the chances of a deliberate first strike small.

The differences between the discussion here and the conventional logic have less to do with their conclusions and more to do with the support for

---

[3] Although the upper bound is increasing in $\mathscr{F}_N$, this must be interpreted carefully. It is unclear whether or not the actual game can be modified so that in equilibrium, $\mathscr{F}_N$ will be larger, nor is it clear whether or not that would actually increase the equilibrium probability of a deliberate general nuclear exchange.

them. The risk of losing collective control plays no explicit part in the conventional logic. But this discussion has shown that the risk of a deliberate first strike depends in an important way on there being some risk of losing collective control. If there is no risk, then crises, or at least the models of them, may be completely stable despite the existence of large first-strike advantages. This discussion, unlike the conventional logic, has also brought states' beliefs within the scope of analysis, albeit in a very simple and stylized way.

This chapter and the last have begun to move away from what in many ways is the defining assumption of the approach to the credibility problem based on the strategy that leaves something to chance and brinkmanship. This approach assumes that there is no situation in which the sanction will be imposed deliberately. These chapters have examined the dynamics of crises in which there is a first-strike advantage and consequently at least one situation in which the sanction will be imposed deliberately. When it is better to strike first than second, a state will attack if it becomes sufficiently confident that war is unavoidable. The question then becomes whether or not a state can become this confident. To address this, beliefs must be brought within the analysis.

The examination shows that in the models, the probability of a deliberate first strike and the probability of a first strike resulting from a collective loss of control are related. There is a connection between the risk that exists because events are not fully under control in the sense that no state can control the actions and reactions of another and the risk that arises because events are not fully under control in the sense that the states may lose collective control. As the risk of losing collective control rises, the upper bound on the risk of a deliberate attack rises, and the crisis in this sense becomes less stable.

The next chapter takes a larger step away from the assumption that the sanction will not be imposed deliberately. In the strategy of limited retaliation, the use or threatened use of force is linked to states' attempts to secure their ends through an array of punishment. In this second approach to linking force to states' political objectives, the sanctions are imposed deliberately, but more important, the sanctions themselves are limited. Because they are limited, they leave an adversary with something more to lose. An adversary remains vulnerable to further punishment, and the fear of still greater losses may bring it to terms. The next chapter examines the escalatory dynamics of the strategy of limited retaliation.

CHAPTER 7

The strategy of limited retaliation

Both the strategy that leaves something to chance and the strategy of limited retaliation attempt to relate force or the threat of it to states' efforts to further their ends in the same fundamental way. An array of limited options bridges the gap between doing too much and doing too little. What distinguishes these two approaches to the credibility problem is not their reliance on limited options but rather the way in which these options are differentiated. Each option in brinkmanship generates a different risk of losing collective control of events. Each option in the strategy of limited retaliation inflicts a different level of punishment.

The strategy that leaves something to chance and the analysis of the problem of crisis stability are direct conceptual descendants of the doctrine of massive retaliation. All of them ultimately appeal to the same sanction: a massive, unlimited nuclear attack. The strategy of limited retaliation, in contrast, relies on limited sanctions. The crucial difference between a limited sanction and an unlimited sanction is that if a state imposes the former on an adversary, the adversary still has something left to lose, and the fear of losing what is left may constrain its retaliation. Imposing an unlimited sanction, however, leaves an adversary with nothing more to lose and little, if any, incentive to restrain its retaliation. And it is the expectation that an unlimited attack will provoke an unlimited retaliation that makes the cost of deliberately imposing an unlimited sanction greater than the cost of not doing so. This, in turn, renders the threat to impose this sanction deliberately incredible and necessitates that there be some risk that the states will lose collective control over this sanction.

A state uses the array of punishment to exert coercive pressure on an adversary in the strategy of limited retaliation. By exercising a limited option that leaves an adversary with something more to lose, a state tries to make the threat of future punishment sufficiently credible that an adversary will conclude that the cost of continuing would be greater than the cost of submitting. Should this threat of future destruction prove insufficiently credible, then this state can exercise another limited option in order to make the prospect of still further destruction more credible. This chapter examines the dynamics of limited retaliation. What, for example, are the consequences of a finer array of punishment? Does having smaller, less destructive limited options make war more likely because a state is more likely to use them if challenged? Or do these options make war less likely because a potential challenger, recognizing that a challenge is more likely to be resisted, is less likely to mount one?

The complete-information model

The model of the strategy of limited retaliation, like the brinkmanship models, reflects an implicit judgment about what the essence of the problem is. Three features seem essential to this strategy. As with brinkmanship, there must be a series of decisions. A confrontation entails a sequence of decisions whether or not to escalate. Second, if a state escalates, it does so by inflicting a limited amount of punishment on its adversary. Finally, there is some source of uncertainty.

The first feature is formalized in the model by letting the potential challenger decide if it will accept or dispute the status quo. If it challenges the status quo, then the burden of decision shifts to the defender, who must choose to quit, to launch an unlimited attack, or to escalate by exercising a limited option. If the defender escalates, the challenger must then decide to quit, to launch a massive attack, or to escalate by exercising a limited option. The confrontation continues in this way, with the onus of escalation shifting back and forth.

The second feature is modeled by assuming that whenever a state escalates, it does so by destroying some part of its adversary. In this gruesome strategy, a state may, for example, destroy one of its adversary's cities to make the threat of future destruction more credible. As the confrontation continues, the damage done increases as each state destroys more and more parts of its adversary.

Incomplete information about an adversary is the source of uncertainty in the model. Neither state is certain of the type of its adversary. As in the model of longer brinkmanship crises, each state believes that there is some chance that it is facing an adversary that is wedded to a strategy of always meeting escalation with escalation.

The complete-information game is illustrated in Figure 7.1. There are two players, a challenger, C, and a defender, D. The challenger and defender

Figure 7.1. Limited retaliation with complete information.

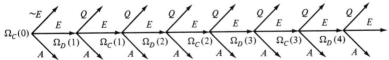

start with some initial level of resources, r_C and r_D, respectively. In the gruesome story underlying the strategy of limited retaliation and the model, r_C may be thought of as the number of the challenger's cities, and r_D as the number of the defender's cities.

The challenger begins play by choosing one of three alternatives. It can refrain from challenging the status quo by playing $\sim E$, in which case the game ends immediately. Or C can launch an unlimited nuclear attack against D by choosing A. This, too, ends the game: C's unlimited attack destroys D, and D is assumed to destroy C in retaliation. Finally, C may exploit the situation by challenging the status quo with E. This shifts the onus of escalation onto D.

A challenge forces the defender to decide which of three courses to follow. First, it can submit to the challenge by quitting the crisis with Q. Second, D can launch an unlimited attack against C by following A. As before, an unlimited attack ends the game in both states' utter destruction. Third, D can escalate, E, by launching a limited attack against C. That is, D can destroy part of what C values. Let p_D be the amount of punishment the defender inflicts on the challenger with a limited attack. Then, D's limited attack leaves $r_C - p_D$ of C intact.

The defender's limited attack shifts the onus of escalation back to the challenger. C must now decide among the three options that just confronted D. C can submit by playing Q and end the game. C can end the game by launching an unlimited attack against D. Or C can launch a limited attack against D with E. This attack destroys part of what D values and leaves D with $r_D - p_C$, where p_C is the amount of punishment C's limited attack inflicts.

The challenger's limited attack shifts the onus of escalation back to the defender. As before, D must decide if it will quit the crisis by submitting to C, launch an unlimited attack, or carry out a limited attack. A limited attack again destroys p_D of C. After D's second limited attack, C is left with $r_C - 2p_D$.

The game continues in this way, with the onus of escalation shifting back and forth. C's mth limited attack leaves $r_D - mp_C$ of D intact, and D's mth attack leaves $r_C - mp_D$ of C intact. Once it starts, escalation can end in only one of three ways. First, one of the states might end the crisis by submitting to its adversary. Second, at some point one of the states might end the game by launching an unlimited nuclear attack. Third, "a war of endurance might bleed both sides to death" (Schelling 1962b, p. 429). Each state might continue to launch limited attacks against its adversary until one of them was completely destroyed, albeit incrementally. Symbolically, the attacks might continue until $r_C - M_D p_D = 0$ or $r_D - M_C p_C = 0$, where M_D is the number of limited attacks that it takes D to leave C with nothing more to lose, and M_C is the number of limited attacks that it takes C to leave D with nothing left to lose. (To simplify matters, r_C and r_D are assumed to be evenly divisible by p_D and p_C, respectively.) Once one of the states, say C, is completely destroyed (i.e., once $m = M_D$, so that $r_C - mp_D = 0$), then it has nothing left to lose and is assumed to destroy D in retaliation. Thus, the game can continue only as long as both states have something more to lose. As soon as one of the states has nothing left to lose, it destroys its adversary, and the game ends. In terms of the game tree, this means that the last decision node in the tree is characterized by a choice between quitting and completely destroying an adversary. D's last decision node in Figure 7.1, for example, is the last decision node precisely because at this point all that remains intact of C is p_D, and D must choose between quitting and attacking. If D quits, the game ends with D's submission. If, however, D attacks, C is left with nothing more to lose and is assumed to retaliate against D with an unlimited attack. The game ends in the complete destruction of both C and D.

It will be convenient to use the following notation for the states' strategies and information sets, which, in the complete-information game, are individual decision nodes. Paralleling the notation used in the brinkmanship model, let $\Omega_D(m)$ be the information set at which the defender must carry out the mth limited attack on C if it is to escalate. Similarly, $\Omega_C(m)$ for $m \geq 1$ is the information set at which C must carry out the mth limited attack on D if it is to escalate. At $\Omega_C(0)$, C is deciding whether or not to dispute the status quo. C has to choose one of three alternatives at $\Omega_C(m)$. It can quit, escalate by launching a limited attack, or launch an unlimited attack. Consequently, C's behavioral strategy at $\Omega_C(m)$ can be described by the probability that C will escalate, $e_C(m)$, and the probability that C will launch an unlimited attack, $a_C(m)$. The probability that C will quit the crisis is given by $1 - e_C(m) - a_C(m)$. D's behavioral strategies are labeled similarly. At $\Omega_D(m)$, D will escalate with a limited attack with probability $e_D(m)$, will launch an unlimited attack with probability $a_D(m)$, and will quit with probability $1 - e_D(m) - a_D(m)$.

To complete the description of the game, the payoffs must be specified. This specification is necessarily somewhat arbitrary. There are no clear historical parallels to the situation underlying the strategy of limited retaliation that might be used to inform the specification of the payoffs, nor are there any widely accepted analogies in the existing work on limited retaliation that might help to specify the payoffs. Fortunately, the equilibrium outcomes of, at least, the complete-information game turn out to be quite insensitive to the precise specification of the payoffs.

Two considerations motivate the specification of the payoffs that will be assumed here. First, if the game ends after a state has suffered a given level of destruction, the payoff to this outcome should reflect the amount of punishment a state has endured. Second, the incremental value of prevailing or the incremental cost of quitting should fall as the amount of damage a state has suffered increases. The idea here is that the more destruction a state has endured, the less able it will be to exploit the fruits of its "victory."

To formalize these motivations, note that the game can end in one of three ways. The game might end with continuation of the status quo if C decides against making a challenge. Let the payoff to this be (r_C, r_D), where the first element in the ordered pair is the challenger's payoff. Alternatively, the two states might completely destroy each other, either because one of them launches an unlimited attack or because they bleed each other to death. Normalize the payoff to this outcome to be $(0, 0)$.

The third way that the game might end is that one of the states might submit. Suppose that the challenger prevails because the defender submits. In this outcome, the challenger's payoff should reflect the influences of, first, the loss due to the limited punishment that D may have wrought on C and, second, the gain due to prevailing. The precise payoff to the challenger if it prevails after suffering m limited attacks will be taken to be $(r_C - mp_D) + (1 - mp_D/r_C)w_C$. The first term reflects the first motivation, for $(r_C - mp_D)$ is what remains of the challenger after it has endured m limited strikes. The second term reflects the second motivation. It is the incremental gain due to prevailing after suffering m limited attacks, where w_C is the incremental gain the challenger receives if the defender does not resist the challenge. Note that the size of the gain depends on m. The greater m, that is, the more damage the challenger has suffered, the smaller the incremental gain of prevailing. In the extreme, if the defender bleeds the challenger to death (i.e., if $r_C - mp_D = 0$), then the incremental gain of prevailing will be zero: $(1 - m(p_D/r_C))w_C = 0$. Prevailing is worthless if in doing so one has been bled to death.

Similarly, the payoff to D of submitting after C has attacked m times is taken to be $(r_D - mp_C) - (1 - mp_C/r_D)s_D$, where s_D is the incremental loss that D will suffer if it does not resist C's initial challenge. That is, if D submits as soon as C challenges the status quo, its payoff will be $r_D - s_D$, and its incremental loss will be s_D. Again, the first term reflects how much of D has not been destroyed when the confrontation ends. The second term is the incremental loss of submitting.

Finally, suppose that the game ends because C submits to D. The payoff to D of prevailing after having endured m limited attacks is $(r_D - mp_C) + (1 - mp_C/r_D)w_D$, where w_D is the incremental gain that prevailing brings if D can do so by coercing C into submitting after it has challenged the status quo but before it has carried out a limited attack against D. As with C, the incremental gain that D derives from prevailing declines as D suffers more damage. The payoff to C of submitting after having been attacked m times is $(r_C - mp_D) - (1 - mp_D/r_C)s_C$.

It will also be assumed that the payoff to prevailing after having been attacked m times is greater than the payoff to submitting after having been attacked m times. This implies $w_C + s_C > 0$ and $w_D + s_D > 0$. And as long as a state has something left to lose, submitting will be assumed to be better than being completely destroyed. This leaves $r_C - s_C > 0$ and $r_D - s_D > 0$. Finally, it will also be convenient to assume that the difference between winning and losing is less than the absolute payoff to losing. That is, $r_C - s_C > w_C + s_C$ and $r_D - s_D > w_D + s_D$.

Thinking of the game as a rather unusual auction may help to clarify its basic structure. The challenger starts with r_C dollars, and the defender begins with r_D dollars. Initially the auctioneer asks the challenger if it wants to participate in the auction; the defender has no choice in the matter. If the challenger does not, then there is no auction, and the challenger and defender are left with r_C and r_D. If the challenger wants to participate, then the auction begins. The object of the auction is to coerce one's adversary into submitting, which in the auction is the equivalent of passing when it is one's turn to bid. The defender has the first bid. If it passes, the auction ends, and the challenger receives w_C and therefore ends the auction with $r_C + w_C$. The defender has to pay s_D and ends with $r_D - s_D$. If the defender decides to bid, then the auctioneer subtracts p_D from the challenger. The challenger is then left with $r_C - p_D$ and must decide whether or not to bid. If it passes, the game ends. The defender receives w_D and leaves the auction with $r_D + w_D$. The challenger pays an additional $(1 - (p_D/r_C))s_C$ for passing after the defender has bid once and is left with a total of $r_C - p_D - (1 - (p_D/r_C))s_C$. If, instead, the challenger bids, p_C is subtracted from the defender, leaving it with $r_D - p_C$. If the defender then passes, the game ends, and an additional $(1 - (p_C/r_D))s_D$ is subtracted from the defender, which leaves it with a total of $r_D - p_C - (1 - (p_C/r_D))s_D$. The challenger receives $(1 - (p_D/r_C))w_C$ for prevailing and ends the game with $r_C - p_D + (1 - (p_D/r_C))w_C$. If the defender bids a second time, then p_D will be subtracted from the challenger a second time, leaving it with $r_C - 2p_D$. It will then be the challenger's turn to bid. If the challenger passes, the defender receives $(1 - (p_C/r_D))w_D$, leaving it with $r_D - p_C + (1 - (p_C/r_D))w_D$, and the challenger loses $(1 - 2(p_D/r_C))s_C$, which gives it a total of $r_C - 2p_D - (1 - 2(p_D/r_C))s_C$. If the challenger bids for a second time, an additional p_C is subtracted from the defender, leaving it with $r_D - 2p_C$. The auction continues in this way until one of the states passes. If no state passes, then eventually one of the states runs out of money. At that point, the auctioneer ends the auction by subtracting from the other state whatever money it still has, and both states are left with nothing.

This auction differs in a subtle yet crucial way from the dollar auction that has been used to study escalation (Shubik 1971; O'Neill 1986). In the dollar auction, two players bid for a dollar. The bidding alternates back and forth until one of the players passes. At that point, the dollar is awarded to the player who did not pass. The important feature of this auction, however, is that regardless of which player wins the dollar, both players pay the auctioneer their bids. If, for example, one player has bid seventy-five cents and the other then passes after having previously bid fifty cents, the first player receives the dollar and pays seventy-five cents, for a gain of twenty-five cents, whereas the second player pays the value bid and loses fifty cents.

Shubik (1971) and O'Neill (1986) offered the dollar auction as a model of escalation and noted that, in practice, the bids often exceed a dollar. That is, individual players often end up paying more than the value of winning. Schelling explicitly appealed to a variant of the dollar auction as an analogy for the strategy of limited retaliation. "In early days, San Franciscans, it is said, conducted 'duels' by throwing gold coins one by one into the Bay until one or the other called it quits" (Schelling 1962a, pp. 243–4).

The dollar auction, however, is a problematic analogy for the strategy of limited retaliation. In this strategy, a state "bids" by attacking its adversary and destroying part of it. If a state bids, it does not pay the price of its bid; its adversary does. This is in keeping with the game and auction described earlier, but it does not accord well with the dollar auction. If a state bids in the dollar auction, it, not its adversary, pays the price of the bid. Accordingly, the auction described earlier would seem to provide a better analogy for the strategy of limited retaliation than would the dollar auction.

It is also interesting to compare brinkmanship and the strategy of limited retaliation as different kinds of auctions. A comparison of the brinkmanship model examined in Chapter 3 and the model of limited retaliation developed here shows them to be quite similar. At each stage in each model, the states must choose from the same set of alternatives. They can quit, escalate, or attack. The primary difference between these models is that in the brinkmanship model, escalation imposes a cost not only on an adversary but also, because the autonomous risk is shared, on the escalating state. As escalation continues in this model, the cost of making the next bid, that is, the autonomous risk of disaster, rises. The brinkmanship model, then, is like an auction in which bidding is costly to both participants and in which the cost of bidding rises as the bidding continues. Indeed, a state's resolve in this auction interpretation of brinkmanship is essentially a measure of the maximum cost a state is willing to pay in order to make the next bid, given that if it bids, its adversary will then submit. In sum, escalating in the dollar auction, in the strategy of limited retaliation, or in brinkmanship imposes direct costs on, respectively, the escalating state, the escalating state's adversary, or both states.

The complete-information equilibria

This section describes the sequential equilibria of the complete-information game.[1] The equilibria suggest that each state would like to have a large number of limited options, each of which would, if exercised, inflict relatively little punishment on an adversary. Moreover, each state would also like to have counterforce options capable of disrupting an enemy's attack. Surprisingly, counterforce options are still desirable even though a state cannot use them to limit the total amount of damage that an adversary can inflict.

The number of limited attacks that it takes for a state to leave its adversary with nothing left to lose is crucial to the analysis of the game's equilibria. Recall that M_C is the number of limited attacks that it takes C to leave D with nothing more to lose. Having nothing left to lose means $r_D - M_C p_C = 0$. This gives $M_C = r_D/p_C$, where, as noted earlier, r_D is assumed to be evenly divisible by p_C. Similarly, M_D is the number of limited attacks that it takes D to leave C with nothing left to lose, and $M_D = r_C/p_D$.

> **Proposition 7.1:** *The complete-information game has a unique sequential equilibrium. If $M_C \geq M_D$, C challenges the status quo in this equilibrium, and D submits immediately. If $M_D > M_C$, C does not challenge the status quo.*

Proof: This proposition is proved in two steps. The first is to determine which state owns the last decision node in the game tree. Once that has been done, the states' strategies will be obtained through backward programming. M_C and M_D determine which state owns the last decision node in the game. To see this, suppose $M_C \geq M_D$. Then, after each state has attacked $M_D - 1$ times, the challenger will have $r_C - (M_D - 1)p_D > 0$, and the defender will have $r_D - (M_D - 1)p_C > 0$. Substituting r_C/p_D for M_D shows that the challenger has p_D left. Note that because the defender is the first to carry out a limited attack in the game, the decision of what to do after each state has attacked $M_D - 1$ times belongs to the defender. But because the challenger has only p_D left to lose, the defender will leave the challenger with nothing left to be lost if it attacks. Thus, if the defender attacks for the M_Dth time, the challenger will be completely destroyed, and the game will end in both

---

[1]   Because the game has perfect information, the set of subgame perfect equilibria is the same
     as the set of sequential equilibria. See the Appendix following Chapter 8 for a discussion of
     the relation between subgame perfect equilibria and sequential equilibria.

states' complete destruction. The last decision node in the game belongs to the defender and is the node at which it must decide whether or not to attack for the M_Dth time if $M_C \geq M_D$. (In the game in Figure 7.1, $M_C \geq M_D = 4$.) A similar argument shows that the challenger owns the last decision node if $M_C < M_D$.

Backward programming then gives the states' strategies. With $M_C \geq M_D$, the last decision node in the tree belongs to D. That is, $\Omega_D(M_D)$ is the last decision node in the tree. If D attacks there, the game ends, and D's payoff will be zero. If D submits, its payoff to quitting will be positive. More precisely, D and C must have attacked each other $M_D - 1$ times for the game to have reached $\Omega_D(M_D)$. Hence, D's payoff will be $(r_D - (M_D - 1)p_C) \times (1 - (s_D/r_D)) > 0$. Submitting at $\Omega_D(M_D)$ is D's best response.

The node immediately preceding $\Omega_D(M_D)$, which is C's last decision node, is $\Omega_C(M_D - 1)$. If C launches an unlimited attack, it will receive zero. If C submits, it will do better, obtaining a positive payoff of $p_D(1 - (s_C/r_C)) > 0$. But if C attacks, then D will quit at $\Omega_D(M_D)$ without inflicting any more punishment on C. That will leave C with $p_D(1 + (w_C/r_C))$. Because $p_D(1 + (w_C/r_C)) > p_D(1 - (s_C/r_C))$, attacking at $\Omega_C(M_D - 1)$ will offer C the highest payoff.

The node immediately preceding $\Omega_C(M_D - 1)$ is $\Omega_D(M_D - 1)$. If D launches an unlimited attack there, its payoff will be zero. If D launches a limited attack, C will then retaliate with a limited attack at $\Omega_C(M_D - 1)$, after which D will submit at $\Omega_D(M_D)$. Because it is better to submit earlier rather than later after having endured more punishment, D will submit at $\Omega_D(M_D - 1)$.

Because D will submit at $\Omega_D(M_D - 1)$, C will escalate at $\Omega_C(M_D - 2)$, which is the node immediately preceding $\Omega_D(M_D - 1)$. Continuing in this way shows that C will escalate at every $\Omega_C(m)$ and that D will submit at every $\Omega_D(m)$. In particular, C will exploit the situation at the beginning of the game, and D will submit as soon as it is challenged.

A similar argument shows that if $M_D > M_C$, then C owns the last decision node, and therefore C will quit at every $\Omega_C(m)$, and D will escalate at every $\Omega_D(m)$. Hence, at the beginning of the game there is no challenge. ■

Before turning to the role of counterforce options and the consequences of having smaller, less destructive limited options, three remarks are in order. First, Proposition 7.1 may be stated more concisely. The state with the largest M prevails. (If $M_C = M_D$, then because D is the first to attack, C still prevails.) Second, just as no state would ever deliberately launch an unlimited attack in the brinkmanship model, no state ever launches an unlimited attack here. Although each state, throughout the confrontation, has the ability to destroy its adversary with an unlimited attack, it never resorts to that. Of course, this should be expected in a sequential equilibrium, for after the nuclear revolution the threat to launch this type of attack is inherently incredible. Finally, the equilibrium of the complete-information game is quite insensitive to the precise specification of the states' payoffs. Essentially, all that is required is that the payoffs satisfy two conditions. First, the payoff to escalating must be sufficiently high, and the cost one must pay to escalate must be sufficiently low, that a state will escalate if it is certain that its adversary will submit immediately thereafter. In this model, this holds because escalating by launching a limited attack is assumed to hurt an adversary, but not the attacking state. Interestingly, this formal condition is quite similar to one that Kahn takes to be characteristic of the general problem of escalation: "The value of victory is usually great enough so that it would be worth while for either side to raise its commitment enough to win the escalation *if it were certain that the other side would not counter the rise*" (Kahn 1965, p. 7; emphasis in the original). The second condition required of the payoffs is that the owner of the last decision node in the tree quit. This holds in the model, because if a state attacks at this node, it will leave its adversary with nothing left to lose, and the adversary is assumed to retaliate by completely destroying the other state. Given this outcome to attacking at the last decision node, the owner of this node will prefer quitting to attacking. With these two restrictions and complete information, then, regardless of the precise specification of the payoffs, the game unravels, just as it did in the proof of Proposition 7.1, and this leaves the unique sequential equilibrium defined in Proposition 7.1.

The evolution of American nuclear strategy has been characterized by a perennial call for limited options that will be more selective and will inflict less punishment on an adversary. There have also been frequent calls for counterforce options that could destroy an adversary's military capabilities or disrupt its ability to carry out well-coordinated attacks. Secretary of Defense McNamara wanted such options in 1962 as part of his effort to introduce more flexibility into the war plan or the Single Integrated Operational Plans (SIOP). These options were also at the center of the Schlesinger doctrine in the early 1970s and continued to play an important part in the countervailing strategy of the late 1970s and early 1980s (Davis 1976; Slocombe 1981; Ball 1982–3; Freedman 1986, 1989; Sagan 1989b).

In the model, each state would like to have a larger number of smaller, less destructive limited options, as well as better counterforce capabilities than its adversary. Because the state with the largest M prevails, a state is better off if its M is larger than its adversary's. M_C, which is the maximum number of limited attacks it takes the challenger to leave the defender with nothing more to lose, is equal to r_D/p_C. If $M_C \geq M_D$, the challenger prevails. But for any fixed M_D, M_C will be greater than or equal to M_D if the amount of punishment the challenger inflicts on the defender in a limited attack, p_C, is sufficiently small. In this sense, then, C is better off if it has smaller, less destructive limited options.

The challenger, it seems, would also like to have counterforce capabilities. Again, the challenger prevails if $M_C \geq M_D$, and counterforce capabilities may reduce M_D. With $M_D = r_C/p_D$, then M_D can be made less than any fixed M_C by taking the amount of punishment the defender inflicts on the challenger when the defender carries out a limited attack, p_D, to be sufficiently large. This suggests that the challenger would be better off if it had counterforce capabilities that could disrupt the defender's strategic forces so that the defender had to choose between backing down or launching larger, more destructive limited attacks. That is, the challenger would like to have counterforce capabilities capable of increasing p_D.

An extreme example will illustrate the logic underlying this. Suppose that the challenger launches a counterforce attack that leaves the defender with only the two options of submitting or launching a massive, unlimited attack against the challenger. In effect, the challenger has put the defender in the position of having to rely on the inherently incredible doctrine of massive retaliation. In this situation, the defender submits. In sum, counterforce capabilities are desirable in the model, but not for the purpose of limiting damage. Each state can always be destroyed in the model if its adversary decides to launch an unlimited attack. Counterforce capabilities are, at least in principle, desired for coercive bargaining purposes because they can be used to limit an adversary's options.

The American desire for nuclear counterforce capabilities in strategic doctrine and strategy has been attributed to "conventionalization," which "is the attempt to treat nuclear bombs as though they were conventional weapons, to apply the same ways of thinking to them that applied in the prenuclear era" (Jervis 1984, p. 56). Conventionalization, in essence, denies that there has been a nuclear revolution and asserts that the classical logic of war still applies. That is, the fact that both superpowers have secure second-strike forces has not fundamentally changed the relation between a state's political objectives and the use or threatened use of force that existed before the nuclear revolution. The desire for counterforce capabilities that has characterized American strategic doctrine may actually be due to conventionalization. But the model suggests that the conclusion that the nuclear revolution has deprived counterforce capabilities of any role is problematic. In the game, each state is completely vulnerable to its adversary throughout the confrontation. The nuclear revolution is implicit in the model. Yet, surprisingly, counterforce capabilities continue to have a role.

Although the equilibrium of the complete-information game has some interesting and suggestive properties, it lacks any dynamics. In equilibrium, there are no crises. Either the challenger accepts the status quo or, if the challenger disputes the status quo, the challenge is not resisted. There is never a resisted challenge, and so there are no crises. To make the model dynamic, the third feature of limited retaliation, which is that there is some source of uncertainty, will be introduced into the model. Each state will be assumed to lack complete information about its adversary.

Incomplete information

Incomplete information will be modeled in the same way that it was modeled when longer brinkmanship crises were examined. The challenger is unsure whether it is facing a resolute defender D' or an irresolute defender D. As in the brinkmanship model, what distinguishes D from D' is that the resolute defender D' is wedded to the strategy of always escalating. If the challenger disputes the status quo or launches a limited attack against D', D' will always retaliate by launching a limited attack against the challenger.

As before, the resolute defender may be interpreted in two ways. First, it is, in effect, playing a strategy of tit for tat. As long as the game continues, the resolute defender does what the challenger just did. Thus, in deciding what to do, the challenger is uncertain whether or not its adversary will play a strategy of tit for tat. Second, note that the resolute defender may act irrationally. Even if attacking the challenger will leave it with nothing more to lose, the resolute defender, being wedded to a strategy of always attacking, will attack even though the challenger will then launch an unlimited attack that will completely destroy the defender. As the equilibrium strategies will show, the irresolute defender is playing on the challenger's fear that it is facing a resolute defender that may act irrationally. In this sense, then, the irresolute defender is pursuing the strategy of the rationality of the irrational.

Information is incomplete on both sides, and the game is illustrated in Figure 7.2. The defender is also unsure whether it is facing an irresolute challenger, C, or a resolute challenger, C', where C', like D', is wedded to a strategy of always escalating. The prior probability that the challenger is facing the resolute defender is $\varepsilon_{D'}$, and the prior probability that the defender is confronting the resolute challenger is $\varepsilon_{C'}$, where these probabilities are common knowledge.

Incomplete information drives escalation in the strategy of limited retaliation just as it did in brinkmanship. If there were complete information and the challenger was sure that it was facing the irresolute defender, with $M_C \geq M_D$, then Proposition 7.1 would imply that the challenger would dispute the status quo, and D would immediately submit. If, however, the challenger were certain that it was facing the resolute

Figure 7.2. Limited retaliation with incomplete information on both sides.

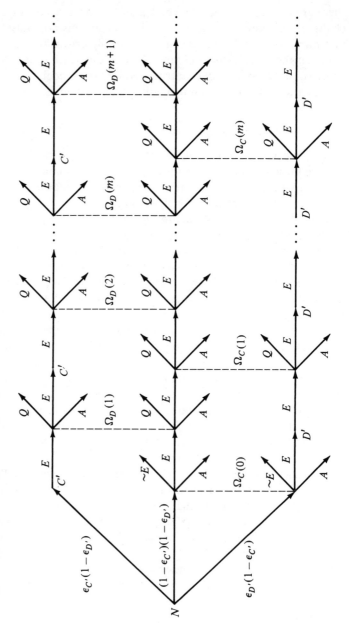

defender D', there would be no challenge. But with incomplete information, the challenger is unsure whether it is facing a resolute defender or an irresolute defender. This makes having a reputation for being resolute valuable. But these benefits come at some cost, for an irresolute defender must, to some extent, be willing to escalate if challenged. In the model, it is this willingness that drives escalation and creates crises. Proposition 7.2 formally describes the dynamics.

Proposition 7.2: *If $\varepsilon_{D'} > \bar{\varepsilon}_{D'} = M_D w_C / [r_C - s_C + M_D(w_C + s_C)]$, there are no sequential crisis equilibria, because C does not challenge the status quo. If $\varepsilon_{D'} < \bar{\varepsilon}_{D'}$ but $M_D = 1$ or $\varepsilon_{C'} > \bar{\varepsilon}_{C'} = [r_D - s_D + M_C(w_D + s_D)] / [2(r_D - s_D) + M_C(w_D + s_D)]$, there still are no sequential crisis equilibria, but now because D does not resist C's challenge. If $M_D \geq 2$, $\varepsilon_{D'} < \bar{\varepsilon}_{D'}$, and $\varepsilon_{C'} < \bar{\varepsilon}_{C'}$, then there exists a generically unique family of sequential crisis equilibria. Each member of this family is indexed by $\bar{m} \geq 0$, and D's strategies for any $\bar{m}$ are*

$$e_D^*(1) = 1 - \frac{r_C - s_C + M_D s_C}{(1 - \varepsilon_{D'})[r_C - s_C + M_D(w_C + s_C)]} \tag{7.1}$$

If $\bar{m} \geq 1$,

$$e_D^*(2) = 1 - \frac{r_C - s_C}{r_C - s_C + (M_D - 1)(w_C + s_C)}$$
$$\times \left[\frac{M_D w_C}{M_D w_C - \varepsilon_{D'}[r_C - s_C + M_D(w_C + s_C)]} \right] \tag{7.2}$$

If $\bar{m} \geq 2$, then for $2 \leq m \leq \bar{m}$,

$$e_D^*(m+1) = 1 - \frac{(M_D - (m-1))(w_C + s_C)}{r_C - s_C + (M_D - m)(w_C + s_C)} \left[\frac{1 - e_D^*(m)}{e_D^*(m)} \right] \tag{7.3}$$

And for $m > \bar{m} + 1$,

$$e_D^*(m) = 0$$

C's equilibrium strategies are given by

$$e_C^*(0) = \frac{\varepsilon_{C'}}{1 - \varepsilon_{C'}} \left[\frac{r_D - s_D}{r_D - s_D + M_C(w_D + s_D)} \right] \frac{1}{1 - e_C^*(1)} \tag{7.4}$$

For $1 \leq m \leq \bar{m}$,

$$e_C^*(m) = \left[1 + \frac{(1 - e_C^*(m+1))[r_D - s_D + (M_C - m)(w_D + s_D)]}{(M_C - (m-1))(w_D + s_D)} \right]^{-1} \tag{7.5}$$

And for $m > \bar{m}$,

$$e_C^*(m) = 0$$

Because all information sets are reached with positive probability, beliefs are simply given by Bayes' rule.

To complete the specification of the family, the range of $\bar{m}$ must be given. Use (7.1), (7.2), and (7.3) to generate a sequence of numbers, and let $\bar{M}$ be the first integer for which $e_D^*(m) > 0$, for $0 \le m \le \bar{M} + 1$, and $e_D^*(\bar{M} + 2) < 0$. Now let $\bar{N}$ be the maximum value of $\bar{n}$ such that $e_C^*(0)$ generated by (7.4), (7.5), and the initial condition $e_C^*(\bar{n} + 1) = 0$ is positive. Then the range of $\bar{m}$ is $0 \le \bar{m} \le \min\{\bar{M}, \bar{N}, M_D - 2\}$.

Proposition 7.2 is demonstrated in Appendix 7.1, and Figure 7.3 shows the regions in which sequential crisis equilibria exist. Given the formal similarities between the brinkmanship and limited-retaliation models, it is perhaps not surprising that the general patterns of escalation are also quite similar. The challenger initially believes that it is facing an irresolute defender with probability $1 - \varepsilon_{D'}$. If this probability is sufficiently high, the challenger will dispute the status quo with probability $e_C^*(0)$.

A challenge shifts the onus of escalation to the defender, which then revises its original belief about the probability of facing an irresolute challenger, $1 - \varepsilon_{C'}$, in light of a challenge actually having been made. After this reassessment, the defender is still sufficiently confident that it is facing an irresolute challenger that it will resist the challenge by escalating with probability $e_D^*(1)$. This shifts the onus of escalation back to the challenger,

Figure 7.3. The limited-retaliation sequential crisis equilibria.

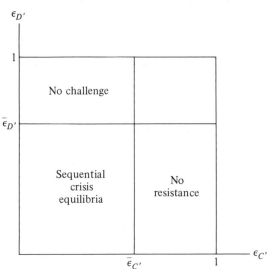

Figure 7.4. A family of limited-retaliation equilibria.

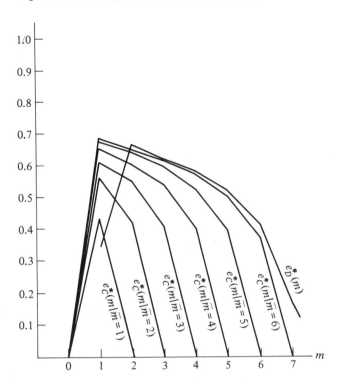

which updates its belief about the likelihood of facing a resolute defender in light of the defender's resistance. The challenger remains confident enough that it is facing an irresolute defender that it will escalate with probability $e_C^*(1)$. This shifts the burden of deciding whether or not to escalate back to the defender. The crisis continues in this way, with the onus of escalation shifting back and forth, and with each state launching limited attacks against the other, until one of the states quits.

Figure 7.4 illustrates a family of equilibria. As the confrontation continues, each state becomes increasingly confident that its adversary is resolute. After the initial exchanges, the states become less and less likely to escalate as the crisis continues.[2] The dynamics at the beginning of the crisis are more complex. The potential challenger may be more or less likely to

---

[2] As shown in Appendix 7.1, $e_C^*(m)$ is decreasing in m for $1 \le m \le \bar{m}$, and $e_D^*(m)$ is decreasing in m for $2 \le m \le \bar{m}+1$.

challenge the status quo than it is to continue to escalate if its challenge is resisted.[3] Similarly, the defender may be more or less likely to resist a challenge than it is to escalate a second time if the challenger escalates after the defender's initial resistance.[4] Nevertheless, $\beta_C^*(m)$ and $\beta_D^*(m)$ are decreasing in m as in the brinkmanship model. Because C and D are actually facing each other, but C and D become increasingly confident that they are facing D' and C', respectively, misperception becomes worse as the crisis goes on. Crisis bargaining here does not help to clarify matters, but rather tends to obscure them.

The array of punishment and the dynamics of escalation

As noted earlier, the desire to have greater flexibility by having smaller, less destructive limited options has played an important part in the evolution of American nuclear strategy since at least the early 1960s, when Secretary of Defense McNamara called for adoption of the doctrine of "flexible response" and tried to introduce more flexibility into the SIOP. But what are the consequences of having smaller, less destructive limited options for the dynamics of escalation? Because they are smaller and more limited, are they more likely to be used, thereby making war more likely? Or, conversely, is war less likely because a potential challenger, knowing that resistance is more likely, will be less likely to dispute the status quo? Asked more generally, what are the effects of making the grain of the array of punishment finer?

To investigate these effects, recall that $M_C p_C = r_D$ and $M_D p_D = r_C$, where p_C is the amount of punishment the challenger inflicts on the defender by exercising a limited option, and p_D is the amount of destruction imposed on the challenger when the defender carries out a limited attack. Accordingly, studying the consequences of decreases in p_C and p_D is akin to examining the effects of having a finer array of punishment.[5]

Having smaller, less destructive limited options makes the defender more likely to escalate throughout the crisis. More formally, a smaller p_D, which entails a larger M_D, makes the defender more likely to escalate throughout

---

[3] Formally, $e_C^*(0)$ may be greater or less than $e_C^*(1)$.

[4] That is, $e_D^*(1)$ may be greater or less than $e_D^*(2)$.

[5] Although akin, these two formulations are not completely equivalent. As illustrated in Figure 2.2, the states may initially select various levels of punishment, and a finer array of risk means that the distance between these levels will be smaller. After the initial attack, the confrontation continues, but this is left implicit in Figure 2.2. Conversely, the model of limited retaliation represents the continuing confrontation explicitly, but, in order to simplify the game, assumes that a state must inflict a single amount of punishment if it escalates. Each formulation leaves the opposite half of the problem implicit.

Table 7.1. *The expected fraction of destruction*

M	Expected fraction of D destroyed	Expected fraction of D destroyed given a crisis	Expected fraction of C destroyed	Expected fraction of C destroyed given a crisis
2	0.000000	0.000	0.000716	0.500
3	0.000179	0.105	0.000615	0.362
4	0.000265	0.122	0.000636	0.294
5	0.000312	0.125	0.000634	0.253
6	0.000308	0.116	0.000593	0.223
7	0.000341	0.118	0.000596	0.206
8	0.000363	0.118	0.000594	0.192
9	0.000361	0.113	0.000572	0.180
10	0.000378	0.114	0.000572	0.172
11	0.000374	0.111	0.000554	0.164
12	0.000389	0.111	0.000556	0.159
13	0.000400	0.111	0.000557	0.154
14	0.000397	0.109	0.000544	0.149
15	0.000407	0.109	0.000546	0.146

Note: These values are calculated for the case in which $M_C = M_D$, $\varepsilon_C = 0.01$, $\varepsilon_{D'} = 0.01$, $r_C = r_D = 10$, $w_C = w_D = 1$, and $s_C = s_D = 1$.

the crisis.[6] Similarly, if the challenger has smaller, less destructive limited options, it is also more likely to escalate throughout the crisis.[7] But the challenger is less likely to challenge the status quo.[8]

It is perhaps surprising that the dynamics of the model so closely parallel the policy debate about the effects of having smaller, less destructive limited

[6] To see this, differentiate (7.1) to obtain $\partial e_D^*(1)/\partial M_D > 0$. Differentiation of (7.2) or inspection of (A7.7) gives $\partial e_D^*(2)/\partial M_D > 0$. Solving (A7.2) for $e_D^*(3)$, noting that $\partial e_D^*(1)/\partial M_D > 0$ and $\partial e_D^*(2)/\partial M_D > 0$ imply $\partial \beta_C^*(2)/\partial M_D > 0$, and differentiating $e_D^*(3)$ show that $\partial e_D^*(3)/\partial M_D > 0$. Solving (A7.3) for $e_D^*(4)$ and differentiating give $\partial e_D^*(4)/\partial M_D > 0$. Continuing in this way yields $\partial e_D^*(m)/\partial M_D > 0$ for $m \le \bar{m} + 1$.

[7] To see that $\partial e_C^*(m)/\partial p_C < 0$ or, equivalently, that $\partial e_C^*(m)/\partial M_C > 0$, let $m = \bar{m}$ in (7.5), and differentiate to obtain $\partial e_C^*(\bar{m})/\partial M_C > 0$. Knowing $\partial e_C^*(\bar{m})/\partial M_C > 0$, differentiation of (7.5) with $m = \bar{m} - 1$ gives $\partial e_C^*(\bar{m} - 1)/\partial M_C > 0$. Continuing in this way leaves $\partial e_C^*(m)/\partial M_C > 0$ for $1 \le m \le \bar{m}$. Thus, C is more likely to escalate throughout the crisis.

[8] To see this, note that if D escalates at $\Omega_D(\bar{m} + 1)$, C will then submit immediately. Regardless of M_C, $e_C^*(\bar{m} + 1) = 0$. D, moreover, is indifferent between escalating or submitting at $\Omega_D(\bar{m} + 1)$. Applying (A7.8) at $\Omega_D(\bar{m} + 1)$ and solving for $\beta_D(\bar{m} + 1)$ give $\beta_D(\bar{m} + 1) = (r_D - s_D)/[r_D - s_D + (M_C - \bar{m})(w_D + s_D)]$. Differentiation then shows $\partial \beta_D(\bar{m} + 1)/\partial M_C < 0$. But $\beta_D(\bar{m} + 1) = (1 - \varepsilon_{C'}) \prod_{i=0}^{\bar{m}} e_C^*(i) / [\varepsilon_{C'} + (1 - \varepsilon_{C'}) \prod_{i=0}^{\bar{m}} e_C^*(i)]$. Thus, with $\partial e_C^*(m)/\partial M_C > 0$ for $1 \le m \le \bar{m}$, the only way that $\partial \beta_D(\bar{m} + 1)/\partial M_C < 0$ is for $\partial e_C^*(0)/\partial M_C < 0$. C, therefore, is less likely to challenge the status quo.

options. In the model, having these options does make escalation more likely. But they also make a challenge less likely. This immediately implies that the defender is better off if the challenger has smaller, more limited options.[9]

In brinkmanship, there is only one type of war: an unlimited nuclear exchange that completely destroys the two states. In limited retaliation, however, there are many types of war, ranging from one in which a state escapes with little or no damage to one in which a state suffers horribly high levels of destruction. What, then, are the effects of a more finely grained array of punishment on the amounts of destruction that the states will inflict on one another? Table 7.1 shows how the expected destruction of a state varies with the destructiveness of the limited options. If, for example, the array of punishment is rather coarse, so that each limited attack will destroy one-third of what an adversary values (i.e., $M_C = M_D = 3$), then the expected fraction of the challenger that will be destroyed is 0.0006 in the longest and most destructive crisis in the family of crises. The expected fraction of the defender destroyed is 0.00018.[10]

The expected damage a state will suffer in the strategy of limited retaliation generally appears to be quite small. An important reason for this is that challenges to the status quo generally seem to be unlikely. In fact, the probability of a challenge never exceeds one chance in a hundred in the equilibria summarized in the table.[11] Indeed, the maximum expected fraction of the challenger that will be destroyed, given that there has been a challenge, rises to 0.075, and the maximum expected fraction of the defender that will be destroyed, given a challenge, is 0.042. Worse, the expected fraction of the defender destroyed, given that there is a crisis, is at least 10 percent, and for the challenger it may be as high as 50 percent. Limited exchanges seem to be difficult to start, but once started, they may be very destructive.

The strategy of limited retaliation links the use or threatened use of force to states' attempts to secure their ends through an array of limited options. In

[9] Because the defender uses a mixed strategy at $\Omega_D(1)$, it must be indifferent to escalating or quitting. Accordingly, its payoff in the game is $r_D - [(1 - \varepsilon_{C'})e_C^*(0) + \varepsilon_{C'}]s_D$, which falls as the probability of a challenge rises. So anything that makes a challenge less likely leaves the defender better off.

[10] To obtain the expression for the expected percentage of C destroyed, observe that the probability that D will attack C m times is $[\prod_{i=0}^{m-1} e_C^*(i)e_D^*(i+1)](1 - e_C^*(m)e_D^*(m+1))$. Thus, the expected damage is $\sum_{m=0}^{\bar{m}+1} [(\prod_{i=0}^{m-1} e_C^*(i)e_D^*(i+1))(1 - e_C^*(m)e_D^*(m+1))mp_D]$, and this divided by r_C gives the expected fraction of C that D will destroy. A similar expression gives the expected fraction of D destroyed by C.

[11] However, (7.4) shows that for any given $e_C^*(1)$, $e_C^*(0)$ can, in principle, be very close to 1 if the probability of initially facing a resolute challenger, $\varepsilon_{C'}$, is sufficiently large.

this approach, the sanctions are imposed deliberately. The states do not have to be able to lose collective control. It is enough that events are not fully under control in the sense that no state controls the actions and reactions of another. The sanctions are also limited. Imposing a limited sanction leaves an adversary with something left to lose, and if the threat to destroy this can be made sufficiently credible, an adversary may come to terms in order to preserve what has not yet been destroyed. This chapter has examined the dynamics of limited retaliation.

The model studied here is consistent with the stylization of the nuclear revolution. Throughout the confrontation, a state can destroy its adversary by launching a general nuclear attack. Damage limitation is impossible. No state can defend itself by being physically able to protect itself. If a state is to avoid destruction, it must do so by deterring its adversary from doing what that adversary is physically capable of doing. Nevertheless, the model suggests that states still will desire smaller, less destructive limited options, as well as counterforce capabilities, but for bargaining purposes rather than damage-limitation purposes. The effect of these options on the dynamics of escalation is to make escalation more likely throughout the confrontation, but also to make a challenge to the status quo less likely.

Appendix 7.1

This appendix demonstrates Proposition 7.2. The demonstration of Proposition 7.2 is quite similar to that of Proposition 4.1. The first of three steps is to show that if a sequential crisis equilibrium exists, it must satisfy certain initial conditions. Then it will be shown that if a sequential crisis equilibrium satisfies these conditions, it must be of the form described by Proposition 7.2. Finally, $\varepsilon_{C'}$ and $\varepsilon_{D'}$ will be restricted to ensure that a sequential crisis equilibrium actually exists.

Turning to the first step, if a sequential crisis equilibrium exists, then two conditions must hold. First, C must be indifferent between escalating and submitting at $\Omega_C(m)$, and $e_C^*(m) > 0$ for $0 \leq m \leq \bar{m}$, where $\bar{m}$ is some integer. Second, $e_C^*(m) = 0$ for $m > \bar{m}$. To see this, let $\bar{m}$ be the maximum integer m such that $e_C^*(m) > 0$. Clearly, such an $\bar{m}$ exists, for in a sequential crisis equilibrium, $e_C^*(0) > 0$. By construction, $e_C^*(m) = 0$ for $m > \bar{m}$; so it remains only to show that if a sequential crisis equilibrium exists, then it satisfies the first condition. To do this, assume the contrary. That is, for some $m' \leq \bar{m}$, C strictly prefers to escalate at $\Omega_C(m')$, strictly prefers to submit, or is indifferent between them, but with $e_C^*(m') = 0$. In both of the latter cases, $e_C^*(m') = 0$, and this leads to a contradiction. To reach this contradiction, note that $e_C^*(m') = 0$ implies that the defender is sure that it is facing the resolute challenger C' at $\Omega_D(m' + 1)$: $\beta_D^*(m' + 1) = 0$. This means that

$e_D^*(m'+1)=0$. But $e_D^*(m'+1)=0$ implies that $\beta_C^*(m'+1)=0$ and then that $e_C^*(m'+1)=0$. Continuing in this way leaves $e_C^*(m)=0$ for $m \geq m'$. In particular, $e_C^*(\bar{m})=0$, because $\bar{m} \geq m'$, and this is a contradiction.

Assuming that C strictly prefers to escalate at $\Omega_C(m')$ also leads to a contradiction. Without loss of generality, let m' be the largest integer for which C strictly prefers to escalate at $\Omega_C(m')$; then,

$$\left(\frac{r_C - m'p_D}{r_C} \right)(r_C - s_C)$$
$$< \beta_C^*(m')(1 - e_D^*(m'+1))\left[\left(\frac{r_C - m'p_D}{r_C} \right)(r_C + w_C) \right]$$
$$+ [1 - \beta_C^*(m')(1 - e_D^*(m'+1))]\left[\left(\frac{r_C - (m'+1)p_D}{r_C} \right)(r_C - s_C) \right]$$

Clearly, this inequality implies that $e_D^*(m'+1) < 1$ and therefore that D's expected payoff at $\Omega_D(m'+1)$ is $[(r_D - m'p_C)/r_D](r_D - s_D)$. Now consider D's decision at $\Omega_D(m')$. If D submits, it obtains $[(r_D - (m'-1)p_C)/r_D](r_D - s_D)$. If D escalates, then D is certain to reach $\Omega_D(m'+1)$ because $e_C^*(m')=1$. Thus, the payoff to escalating at $\Omega_D(m')$ is $[(r_D - m'p_C)/r_D](r_D - s_D)$. Submission offers the larger payoff; so $e_D^*(m')=0$. But this means $\beta_C^*(m')=0$, which implies that $e_C^*(m')=0$ is C's best reply. This, however, contradicts the assumption that C strictly prefers to escalate at $\Omega_C(m')$.

In sum, if a sequential crisis equilibrium exists, then C is indifferent between escalating and submitting at $\Omega_C(m)$, and $e_C^*(m) > 0$ for $m \leq \bar{m}$, where $\bar{m}$ is some integer. If, moreover, $m > \bar{m}$, then $e_C^*(m)=0$.

The second step is to demonstrate that if a sequential crisis equilibrium exists, then its strategies are defined by the expressions reported in Proposition 7.2. Suppose that C is indifferent to escalating or submitting at $\Omega_C(m)$, and $e_C^*(m) > 0$ for $m \leq \bar{m}$; then, for $1 \leq m \leq \bar{m}$,

$$\left(\frac{r_C - mp_D}{r_C} \right)(r_C - s_C)$$
$$= \beta_C^*(m)(1 - e_D^*(m+1))\left[\left(\frac{r_C - mp_D}{r_C} \right)(r_C + w_C) \right]$$
$$+ [1 - \beta_C^*(m)(1 - e_D^*(m+1))]\left[\left(\frac{r_C - (m+1)p_D}{r_C} \right)(r_C - s_C) \right]$$
$$\tag{A7.1}$$

Recall that $M_D = r_C/p_D$, and solve for $\beta_C(m)$:

$$\beta_C^*(m) = \left(\frac{r_C - s_C}{r_C - s_C + (M_D - m)(w_C + s_C)} \right) \frac{1}{1 - e_D^*(m+1)} \tag{A7.2}$$

But Bayes' rule also implies

$$\beta_C(m) = (1 - \varepsilon_{D'}) \left[\prod_{i=1}^{m} e_D(i) \right] \left[\varepsilon_{D'} + (1 - \varepsilon_{D'}) \prod_{i=1}^{m} e_D(i) \right]^{-1} \quad \text{(A7.3)}$$

Substitute this expression into (A7.2), and solve for $\prod_{i=1}^{m} e_D^*(i)$:

$$\prod_{i=1}^{m} e_D^*(i) = (\varepsilon_{D'}/(1 - \varepsilon_{D'}))[r_C - s_C][(M_D - m)(w_C + s_C) - e_D^*(m+1)]$$

$$\times [r_C - s_C + (M_D - m)(w_C + s_C)]]^{-1} \quad \text{(A7.4)}$$

where (A7.4) holds for $1 \le m \le \bar{m}$. Reindex (A7.4) to obtain an expression for $\prod_{i=1}^{m-1} e_D^*(i)$. Divide this into (A7.4) and solve for $e_D^*(m+1)$:

$$e_D^*(m+1) = 1 - \frac{(M_D - (m-1))(w_C + s_C)}{r_C - s_C + (M_D - m)(w_C + s_C)} \left(\frac{1 - e_D^*(m)}{e_D^*(m)} \right) \quad \text{(A7.5)}$$

Equation (A7.5) links $e_D^*(2), \ldots, e_D^*(\bar{m}+1)$ recursively and is the relation reported in Proposition 7.2. (Generically, $e_D^*(\bar{m}+1) \neq 0$, but $e_D^*(M_D)$ must be zero. Thus, to avoid a contradiction, $\bar{m} + 1 < M_D$.)

Now note that because $e_C^*(\bar{m}+1) = 0$, then $\beta_D^*(\bar{m}+2) = 0$ and $e_D^*(\bar{m}+2) = 0$. Indeed, $\beta_D^*(m) = 0$ and $e_D^*(m) = 0$ for all $m > \bar{m}+1$. Thus, to complete the specification of D's strategies, $e_D^*(1)$ and an initial condition for (A7.4) must be specified. To determine $e_D^*(1)$, note that C's indifference at $\Omega_C(0)$ implies

$$r_C = (1 - \varepsilon_{D'})(1 - e_D^*(1))(r_C + w_C) + [1 - (1 - \varepsilon_{D'})(1 - e_D^*(1))]$$

$$\times \left(\frac{r_C - p_D}{r_C} \right) (r_C - s_C)$$

Solving for $e_D^*(1)$ leaves

$$e_D^*(1) = 1 - \frac{r_C - s_C + M_D s_C}{(1 - \varepsilon_{D'})[r_C - s_C + M_D(w_C + s_C)]} \quad \text{(A7.6)}$$

To find $e_D^*(2)$, set $m = 1$ in (A7.4) and solve for $e_D^*(2)$ to obtain

$$e_D^*(2) = 1 - \frac{r_C - s_C}{r_C - s_C + (M_D - 1)(w_C + s_C)} \left[1 + \frac{\varepsilon_{D'}}{1 - \varepsilon_{D'}} \left(\frac{1}{e_D^*(1)} \right) \right] \quad \text{(A7.7)}$$

Finally, substituting (A7.6) into (A7.7) gives the expression for $e_D^*(2)$ reported in Proposition 7.2.

In sum, (A7.5), (A7.6), and (A7.7) define $e_D^*(1)$ through $e_D^*(\bar{m}+1)$. Equation (A7.6) gives $e_D^*(1)$, which then gives $e_D^*(2)$ through (A7.7). This value of $e_D^*(2)$ then provides the initial condition for the recursive relation (A7.5), which specifies $e_D^*(3), \ldots, e_D^*(\bar{m}+1)$. For $m \ge \bar{m}+1$, $e_D^*(m) = 0$. These are the strategies reported in Proposition 7.2.

To determine C's strategies, recall that $e_C^*(0) = 0$ for $m > \bar{m}$. The expressions for $e_D^*(m)$ show that, generically, $1 > e_D^*(m) > 0$ for $1 \leq m \leq \bar{m} + 1$. Hence, D is indifferent between escalating and submitting at $\Omega_D(m)$ for $1 \leq m \leq \bar{m} + 1$. This implies

$$
\left(\frac{r_D - (m-1)p_C}{r_D} \right)(r_D - s_D)
$$
$$
= \beta_D^*(m)(1 - e_C^*(m))\left[\left(\frac{r_D - (m-1)p_C}{r_D} \right)(r_D + w_D) \right]
$$
$$
+ [1 - \beta_D^*(m)(1 - e_C^*(m))]\left[\left(\frac{r_D - mp_C}{r_D} \right)(r_D - s_D) \right] \qquad \text{(A7.8)}
$$

where $m \leq \bar{m} + 1$. Paralleling the argument used to derive D's strategies gives

$$
\prod_{i=0}^{m-1} e_C^*(i) = \left(\frac{\varepsilon_{C'}}{1 - \varepsilon_{C'}} \right)\left[\frac{r_D - s_D}{r_D - s_D + (M_C - (m-1))(w_D + s_D)} \right] \frac{1}{1 - e_C^*(m)} \qquad \text{(A7.9)}
$$

Reindexing, dividing, and then solving for $e_C^*(m)$, one finds

$$
e_C^*(m) = \left[1 + \frac{(1 - e_C^*(m+1))[r_D - s_D + (M_C - m)(w_D + s_D)]}{(M_C - (m-1))(w_D + s_D)} \right]^{-1} \qquad \text{(A7.10)}
$$

where $1 \leq m \leq \bar{m}$.

Equation (A7.10) links $e_C^*(1), \ldots, e_C^*(\bar{m} + 1)$ recursively. But recall that $e_C^*(\bar{m} + 1) = 0$. With this initial condition, (A7.10) determines $e_C^*(1), \ldots,$ $e_C^*(\bar{m} + 1)$. Because $e_C^*(m) = 0$ for all $m > \bar{m}$, only $e_C^*(0)$ remains to be specified. To do so, let $m = 1$ in (A7.9). Then

$$
e_C^*(0) = \left(\frac{\varepsilon_{C'}}{1 - \varepsilon_{C'}} \right)\left[\frac{r_D - s_D}{r_D - s_D + M_C(w_D + s_D)} \right] \frac{1}{1 - e_C^*(1)} \qquad \text{(A7.11)}
$$

To summarize the argument to this point, if a sequential crisis equilibrium exists, the strategies must be given by the expressions derived earlier and reported in Proposition 7.2. It remains only to ensure that a sequential crisis equilibrium actually exists. To do this, it is enough to constrain $\varepsilon_{C'}$ and $\varepsilon_{D'}$ so that the strategies of C and D are feasible.

If D's strategies are to be feasible, then $0 < e_D^*(1) \leq 1$. Imposing this restriction on (A7.6) and solving for $\varepsilon_{D'}$,

$$
\varepsilon_{D'} < \bar{\varepsilon}_{D'} = \frac{M_D w_C}{r_C - s_C + M_D(w_C + s_C)}
$$

To ensure that $e_D^*(2)$ is between 0 and 1, use (A7.6) to substitute for $e_D^*(1)$ in (A7.7) and then solve for $\varepsilon_{D'}$ subject to $1 < e_D^*(2) < 1$. This leaves

$$\varepsilon_{D'} < \bar{\bar{\varepsilon}}_{D'} = \bar{\varepsilon}_{D'} \left[\frac{(M_D - 1)(w_C + s_C)}{r_C - s_C + (M_D - 1)(w_C + s_C)} \right]$$

Note, moreover, that $\bar{\varepsilon}_{D'} < \bar{\bar{\varepsilon}}_{D'}$.

To ensure that $e_D^*(m)$ is feasible for $m > 2$, assume $\varepsilon_{D'} < \bar{\bar{\varepsilon}}_{D'}$. [If $\varepsilon_{D'} > \bar{\bar{\varepsilon}}_{D'}$, then $e_D^*(2)$ is not feasible, and so the feasibility of $e_D^*(m)$ for $m > 2$ is no longer of any interest.] Suppose further that it can be established that $e_D^*(m)$ is decreasing in m as long as $m \geq 2$. Then let $\bar{M}$ be the largest integer m for which $e_D^*(m + 1) > 0$. Generically, $e_D^*(\bar{M} + 2)$ will be less than zero and thus infeasible. If $\bar{M} = 0$, then $e_D^*(2) < 0$, and the feasibility of $e_D^*(m)$ for $m > 2$ is not of any interest. If, however, $\bar{M} > 0$, then $e_D^*(m)$ for $2 \leq m \leq \bar{M} + 1$ are feasible, for $e_D^*(2) > e_D^*(3) > \cdots > e_D^*(\bar{M} + 1) > 0 > e_D^*(\bar{M} + 2)$. In sum, if $\varepsilon_{D'} < \bar{\bar{\varepsilon}}_{D'}$ and $e_D^*(m)$ is decreasing in m, then $e_D^*(m + 1)$ are feasible for $1 < m \leq \bar{M} < M_D - 1$.

To see that $e_D^*(m)$ for $m \geq 2$ is actually decreasing in m as long as $e_D^*(m) > 0$, solve (A7.5) for $e_D^*(m + 1)$ and substitute this in $e_D^*(m) > e_D^*(m + 1)$. Then solve for $e_D^*(m)$ to obtain

$$e_D^*(m) < U_D(m) = \frac{(M_D - (m - 1))(w_C + s_C)}{r_C - s_C + (M_D - m)(w_C + s_C)}$$

This means that if $e_D^*(m) < U_D(m)$, then $e_D^*(m) > e_D^*(m + 1)$. Now calculate $\bar{e}_D^*(m)$, where $\bar{e}_D^*(m)$ is the value of $e_D^*(m)$ defined by (A7.5) and the initial condition

$$\bar{e}_D^*(2) = \frac{(M_D - 1)(w_C + s_C)}{r_C - s_C + (M_D - 1)(w_C + s_C)}$$

This gives

$$\bar{e}_D^*(m) = \frac{(M_D - (m - 1))(w_C + s_C)}{r_C - s_C + (M_D - (m - 1))(w_C + s_C)}$$

Inspection shows that $\bar{e}_D^*(m + 1) < U_D(m)$. Finally, differentiation of (A7.5) gives $\partial e_D^*(m + 1)/\partial e_D^*(m) > 0$ if, as is assumed, $r_C - s_C - (w_C + s_C) > 0$. Putting all of this together gives $e_D^*(2) \leq \bar{e}_D^*(2) < U_D(2)$, where the first inequality follows from (A7.7). Because $\partial e_D^*(m + 1)/\partial e_D^*(m) > 0$ and $e_D^*(2) \leq \bar{e}_D^*(2)$, then $e_D^*(3) \leq \bar{e}_D^*(3)$. But $\bar{e}_D^*(3) < U_D(3)$; so $e_D^*(3) \leq \bar{e}_D^*(3) < U_D(3)$. Continuing in this way yields $e_D^*(m) < U_D(m)$, and this means that $e_D^*(m)$ is decreasing in m as long as $m \geq 2$ and $e_D^*(m) > 0$. Accordingly, D's strategies are feasible if $\bar{m} \leq \bar{M}$.

In sum, if $\varepsilon_{D'} > \bar{\bar{\varepsilon}}_{D'}$, there are no sequential crisis equilibria. Equation

(A7.1) cannot be satisfied: $\varepsilon_{D'}$ is too large, and the payoff to not challenging the status quo at $\Omega_C(0)$ is always greater than the payoff to disputing the status quo. The probability that C is facing a resolute defender is too great, and there is no challenge. If $\bar{\bar{\varepsilon}}_{D'} < \varepsilon_{D'} < \bar{\varepsilon}_{D'}$, then, assuming C's strategies to be feasible, $e_D^*(1)$ is given by (A7.6), and $e_D^*(m) = 0$ for $m > 1$. If $\varepsilon_{D'} < \bar{\bar{\varepsilon}}_{D'}$, then (A7.6) defines $e_D^*(1)$, (A7.7) gives $e_D^*(2)$, and (A7.5) yields $e_D^*(3), \ldots, _D^*(\bar{m}+1)$, where $\bar{m} \le \bar{M} < M_D - 1$.

To find the restrictions on $\varepsilon_{C'}$ that will ensure that C's strategies are feasible, let $e_C^*(\bar{n}+1) = 0$ be the initial condition, and use (A7.10) and (A7.11) to determine $e_C^*(0), \ldots, e_C^*(\bar{n})$. Inspection of (A7.10) shows that $1 > e_C^*(m) > 0$ for $1 \le m \le \bar{n}$. Thus, only the feasibility of $e_C^*(0)$ is at issue. Constrain (A7.11) to be between 0 and 1, and then solve for $e_C^*(1)$:

$$e_C^*(1)_{\bar{n}} < 1 - \frac{\varepsilon_{C'}}{1 - \varepsilon_{C'}} \left(\frac{r_D - s_D}{r_D - s_D + M_C(w_D + s_D)} \right) \tag{A7.12}$$

where the subscript $\bar{n}$ on $e_C^*(1)$ indicates that $e_C^*(1)$ was obtained from the initial condition $e_C^*(\bar{n}+1) = 0$. Now assume that (A7.12) is satisfied for some $\bar{n}$. Then, starting the recursive relation (A7.10) at any $\bar{n}' < \bar{n}$ [i.e., letting $e_C^*(\bar{n}'+1) = 0$ for any $\bar{n}' < \bar{n}$] will also produce a set of feasible strategies. This follows from the observation that (A7.10) implies $\partial e_C^*(m)/ \partial e_C^*(m+1) > 0$. Then $e_C^*(\bar{n}')_{\bar{n}} > e_C^*(\bar{n}')_{\bar{n}'}$ because $e_C^*(\bar{n}'+1)_{\bar{n}} > e_C^*(\bar{n}'+1)_{\bar{n}'} = 0$. This, in turn, gives $e_C^*(\bar{n}'-1)_{\bar{n}} > e_C^*(\bar{n}'-1)_{\bar{n}'}$, and, in general, $e_C^*(m)_{\bar{n}} > e_C^*(m)_{\bar{n}'}$. Letting $m = 1$ shows that $e_C^*(1)_{\bar{n}'}$ satisfies (A7.12). Now let $\bar{N}$ be the maximum value of $\bar{n}$ for which $e_C^*(1)_{\bar{n}}$ satisfies (A7.12). Then if $\bar{m} \le \bar{N}$, all of C's strategies are feasible. Indeed, if $\bar{m} \le \min\{\bar{M}, \bar{N}, M_D - 2\}$, then both C's and D's strategies are feasible.

To ensure that at least one sequential crisis equilibrium exists, $M_D \ge 2$ and $\bar{M}$ and $\bar{N}$ must be greater than or equal to zero. Taking $\varepsilon_{D'} < \bar{\varepsilon}_{D'}$ makes $\bar{M} \ge 0$. To make sure that $\bar{N} \ge 0$, $e_C^*(1)_{\bar{n}=0}$ must satisfy (A7.12). But the definition of $\bar{n}$ implies $e_C^*(\bar{n}+1) = 0$. So if $\bar{n} = 0$, $e_C^*(1) = 0$ must satisfy (A7.12). Letting $e_C^*(1)_{\bar{n}} = 0$ and solving (A7.12) for $\varepsilon_{C'}$ will give

$$\varepsilon_{C'} < \bar{\varepsilon}_{C'} = \frac{r_D - s_D + M_C(w_D + s_D)}{2(r_D - s_D) + M_C(w_D + s_D)}$$

Thus, if $\varepsilon_{D'} < \bar{\varepsilon}_{D'}$ and $\varepsilon_{C'} < \bar{\varepsilon}_{C'}$, a family of sequential crisis equilibria exists, the members of which are indexed by $\bar{m}$, where $0 \le \bar{m} \le \min\{\bar{M}, \bar{N}, M_D - 2\}$. ∎

Although the demonstration of Proposition 7.2 is now complete, it will be useful to show that $e_C^*(m)$ is also decreasing in m for $1 \le m \le \bar{m}$. Use (A7.10) to substitute for $e_C^*(m)$ in $e_C^*(m) - e_C^*(m+1) > 0$, and solve for $e_C^*(m+1)$. The result is

$$e_C^*(m+1) < U_C(m) = \frac{(M_C - (m-1))(w_D + s_D)}{r_D - s_D + (M_C - m)(w_D + s_D)}$$

That is, as long as $e_C^*(m) > 0$, $e_C^*(m+1) > 0$, and $U_C(m) > 0$, then $e_C^*(m) > e_C^*(m+1)$ if and only if $e_C^*(m+1) < U_C(m)$. Note, moreover, that because $r_D - s_D$ is assumed to be greater than $w_D + s_D$, then as long as $U_C(m) > 0$, $U_C(m)$ is decreasing in m. This means that if $e_C^*(\bar{k}+1) < U_C(\bar{k})$ for some $\bar{k}$, then $e_C^*(\bar{k}) < U_C(\bar{k}-1)$. This can be seen by assuming the contrary. With $e_C^*(\bar{k}) \geq U_C(\bar{k}-1)$, $e_C^*(\bar{k}+1) \geq e_C^*(\bar{k})$. This and the fact that $U_C(m)$ is decreasing imply $e_C^*(\bar{k}+1) \geq e_C^*(\bar{k}) \geq U_C(\bar{k}-1) > U_C(\bar{k})$. This contradicts the assumption that $e_C^*(\bar{k}+1) < U_C(\bar{k})$. Thus, $e_C^*(\bar{k}) < U_C(\bar{k}-1)$. Generalizing, $e_C^*(m+1) < U_C(m)$ for $m \leq \bar{k}$. This then gives $e_C^*(m) > e_C^*(m+1)$ for $1 \leq m \leq \bar{k}$. That is, $e_C^*(m)$ is decreasing from $e_C^*(1)$ to $e_C^*(\bar{k}+1)$. To show that $e_C^*(m)$ is decreasing in m for $1 \leq m \leq \bar{m}+1$, it will suffice to show that $e_C^*(\bar{m}+1) < U_C(\bar{m})$. But the definition of $\bar{m}$ implies $e_C^*(\bar{m}+1) = 0$. It need only be shown now that $U_C(\bar{m}) > 0$. The definition of $U_C(m)$ shows that as long as $\bar{m} \leq M_C$, then $U_C(\bar{m}) > 0$. But $\bar{m}$ cannot exceed M_C, for the definition of M_C means that there are no information sets $\Omega_C(\bar{m})$ for which $\bar{m} > M_C$. Hence, $e_C^*(m)$ is decreasing in m from $e_C^*(1)$ to $e_C^*(\bar{m}+1)$.

CHAPTER 8

An appraisal

The nuclear revolution undercut the classical logic of war. The stylized relation that appeared to link the use or threatened use of force to states' attempts to secure their interests before the nuclear revolution no longer seems to apply. Explaining how that relation has changed and the consequences of that change is the task of nuclear deterrence theory. By tracing the search for credibility, the preceding chapters have tried to present a general and unifying perspective on the ways that nuclear deterrence theory has tried to understand and explain this relation. This perspective seeks to provide a context in which questions about the relation between force and states' political objectives in the nuclear age can be asked more precisely and related more carefully and clearly to other aspects of this relation. This chapter summarizes the previous discussion and offers an appraisal of it.

The review begins with the nuclear revolution, the challenge it posed, and the general approach that nuclear deterrence theory has taken toward linking force to political objectives after the nuclear revolution. There follows a technical summary and critique of the models and the findings based on them. Finally, this appraisal takes a step back from the models to discuss the problem of evidence, or rather the lack thereof, and the inherent difficulty in assessing or evaluating nuclear deterrence theory empirically.

The stylized classical logic of war assumed that punitive and defensive capabilities were conflated. The same military forces that a state could use to limit the costs that an adversary could impose on it could also be used to impose costs on its adversary, especially by taking its territory. The conflation of these capabilities meant that greater military strength was generally the key to greater security in the classical logic, for that conflation implied that the stronger a state's military forces, the stronger both its punitive and defensive capabilities. That was likely to enhance a state's deterrent capacity and improve its ability to secure its political ends in two ways. First, the greater a state's punitive capability, the more an adversary would have to pay if the state actually used that capability against its adversary. Second, the greater a state's defensive capability, the more willing that state might be to use its punitive capability, because its better

174

defensive capability would make it less vulnerable to its adversary's retaliation. In the classical logic, great wars fought over profound conflicts of interest were contests of relative strength.

The series of developments culminating in the technological condition of mutually assured destruction separated the ability to punish from the ability to limit the punishment one might have to suffer. This undercut the classical logic. The stylized conflation of these capabilities on which this logic was based was no longer tenable. After the nuclear revolution, coercing an adversary into doing a state's bidding still required the state to be able to put its adversary in a situation whose continuation would appear to be more costly than would complying with the state's demands. To do that, the state had to be able to impose a sufficient amount of punishment on its adversary and be able to make the threat to do so sufficiently credible. The first requirement certainly seemed to be satisfied in a condition of mutually assured destruction. But could the second condition be satisfied when each state could be destroyed by its adversary's retaliatory second strike? That was the credibility problem posed by the nuclear revolution.

Nuclear deterrence theory has tried to solve the credibility problem with limited options that link the use or threatened use of force to states' efforts to further their interests. These options span the gap between doing too much by launching an unlimited, society-destroying nuclear attack, as in the doctrine of massive retaliation, and doing too little by acquiescing to an adversary.

There are, however, two approaches to solving the credibility problem in this way. What distinguishes these approaches is the way that the distance between doing too much and doing too little is measured. If one measures this distance in terms of the autonomous risk of an unlimited nuclear attack that exercising an option will generate, then the set of limited options forms an array of risk. The strategy in this approach is based on Schelling's "threats that leave something to chance." In brinkmanship, states take steps that create a risk that they will lose collective control of events. This risk is the primary source of coercive pressure. If, however, one measures the gap between doing too much and doing too little in terms of the level of damage or punishment that exercising a limited option will inflict, the set of limited options spanning this gap constitutes an array of punishment. In the strategy of limited retaliation, states use this array to exert coercive pressure on each other. Each inflicts a limited amount of punishment to make the threat of future punishment more credible, and in this way each tries to convince its adversary that the cost of continuing the confrontation would exceed the cost of ending it.

These two approaches try to link the use or threatened use of force to states' political objectives in the same general way. But at a somewhat lower level of generality they are primarily concerned with different issues. The defining concern of brinkmanship is to explain how a sanction that would never be imposed deliberately might nevertheless still be used to exert coercive pressure. Given this concern, all the rest follows, such as the need for events not to be fully under control in the sense that there must be some chance that the states can lose collective control. The central concern of the strategy of limited retaliation is different. The emphasis here moves away from an unlimited sanction to study the dynamics of a confrontation based on sanctions that will inflict limited amounts of punishment and will be imposed deliberately. The challenge is to see if there is a coherent strategy in which adversaries will try to exert coercive pressure on each other by deliberately using their power to hurt and will do this when each is completely vulnerable to the other. The key to the credibility problem in this approach is that limited options, because they are limited, leave an adversary with something more to lose, and the adversary, if sufficiently afraid of losing what is left, may quit the confrontation rather than retaliate. The coherence of the strategy of limited retaliation does not depend on there being any risk of losing collective control. It is enough that events are not fully under control only in the second sense, in that no state can control the actions and reactions of the other.

Although these two variants focus on different concerns at this somewhat lower level of generality, it is important to emphasize one property they share: the central role of risk in both strategies. A brinkmanship crisis in which states pursue their ends through the strategy that leaves something to chance has been described as a "competition in risk taking" (Schelling 1966, pp. 94–106, 166–8; Jervis 1984, p. 130). As emphasized throughout, brinkmanship does require a special kind of risk: There must be some autonomous risk of a general nuclear exchange. But the more general risk that the confrontation will end in a situation that neither state prefers to the status quo is common to both the strategy that leaves something to chance and the strategy of limited retaliation. A brinkmanship crisis may end in a general nuclear exchange, and a crisis in which the states rely on the strategy of limited relation may end only after they have imposed such grave punishment on each other that even the state that prevails would have preferred the status quo ante to prevailing at such a high cost. In both strategies there is a danger of undesired and in this sense unintended or inadvertent consequences. It is the states' willingness to run these risks in the hope of securing more preferred ends that drives escalation. The risk of undesired and unintended consequences and inadvertent escalation is at the heart of both approaches.

The problem of crisis stability and first-strike advantages examines the likelihood that a crisis will escalate to an unlimited nuclear exchange when there is at least one situation in which a state will deliberately launch a first strike. The concerns underlying this problem fall between those motivating brinkmanship and the strategy of limited retaliation. Accordingly, an examination of crisis stability and first-strike advantages in some ways connected those two strategies. The sanction in the problem of crisis stability is unlimited; once a state imposes it, the state can do no more to its adversary. Fear of future punishment no longer constrains its adversary, and a state can anticipate having to bear the full weight of its adversary's retaliation. All of this is just the same as in brinkmanship. What is not the same, but, in effect, amounts to an attempt to relax the demanding assumption that there is no situation in which states would launch a deliberate first strike, is that the sanction need not be imposed autonomously when there are first-strike advantages. The states do not have to be able to lose collective control, for the unlimited sanction may be imposed deliberately. If the prospects of war are sufficiently high, and it is better to strike first rather than second if there is to be a war, then attacking will become the best of a set of dreadful alternatives. The fact that states may impose the sanction deliberately is more in keeping with the strategy of limited retaliation. Because of these shared features, an analysis of the problem of crisis stability links brinkmanship and the strategy of limited retaliation.

The models of brinkmanship, crisis stability, and limited retaliation help to elaborate the two approaches that nuclear deterrence theory has taken to linking force or the threat of it to states' attempts to secure their ends. But many different models would be consistent with the broad outlines of the approaches based on the arrays of risk and punishment. A more detailed critique of the specific models studied in the preceding chapters should help to identify some of the strengths and weaknesses of those models and perhaps suggest better, more appropriate models.

The critique begins with a brief summary of some of the specific results. The brinkmanship models examined earlier support the intuitive notion that the more severe the conflict of interest underlying the crisis, the more dangerous and less stable the crisis. But the models also call into question other intuitive conclusions. The general problem here seems to be that these conclusions have failed to take into account the interactions between strategies and beliefs that the models have helped to illuminate. The image of a brinkmanship crisis as a contest of resolve appears quite problematic, for many of the inferences this image suggests do not hold. In the models, the state with the greatest resolve may not prevail. A state may be more, not less, likely to escalate the greater the resolve of its adversary. A state's expected payoff may decrease if its resolve increases. In fact, the states' strategies depend on a combination of payoffs that cannot be reduced to an expression involving only the states' levels of resolve. Whether or not these particular findings weather future empirical work or the analysis of better formal models, these findings do suggest that even very intuitive claims about the dynamics of crises based on simple images or analogies like brinkmanship are suspect.

The potential challenger's stake in the status quo has also played an unexpected role in brinkmanship bargaining. It might at first seem that crises would be less likely if a potential challenger had a larger stake in the status quo, because a challenge would mean putting something of more value at risk and would therefore seem less likely. It was found that the challenger's having a greater stake in the status quo generally did make a crisis less likely, but not necessarily because the challenger was less likely to dispute the status quo; the defender might, instead, be less likely to resist a challenge.

It was seen that the situation actually facing a state could be distinguished from the situation a state believed itself to be facing. Indeed, given the simple ways that incomplete information was modeled, there was a natural measure of the degree of a state's misperception. If, for example, a state was actually facing a resolute adversary, then the probability measuring the strength of that state's belief that it was facing an irresolute adversary was also a measure of the state's misperception. That measure made it possible to examine the effects of changes in the level of misperception on the dynamics of escalation. The results were inconclusive. In some circumstances, greater misperceptions made escalation more likely and crises less stable, whereas in other circumstances, increased misperception made escalation less likely and crises more stable.

Finally, the brinkmanship models have formally illustrated the problem of selection bias that may be encountered in historical work focusing solely on a sample of crises. For example, severe conflicts of interest will be relatively infrequent in any sample of crises. That might be taken to indicate that there are few severe conflicts of interest in the international system. That, however, would be a mistake, for the models also showed that situations in which there is a severe conflict of interest tend not to become crises. Thus, situations with severe underlying conflicts of interests tend not to appear in samples composed entirely of crises. A second example of the potential effects of the selection bias inherent in studying only crises is that such a study would suggest that the primary effect of making the grain of the array of risk or punishment finer would be to make escalation more likely. But such a conclusion would miss the effect that the finer grain also makes a challenge less likely, for this effect will not be present in a sample composed only of crises. Failing to take this bias into account may lead to distorted conclusions.

The investigation of the strategy of limited retaliation showed that even after the nuclear revolution, smaller, less destructive limited options and counterforce capabilities still may have roles to play. Although defense is impossible, states still may desire these options and capabilities. But they do not do so for the purpose of being physically able to limit damage to themselves, for in the stylization of the nuclear age that cannot be done. Rather, states desire these options and capabilities for bargaining purposes. Clearly, the model of limited retaliation is much too simple to be anything more than suggestive. But it does indicate that the desire for smaller, less destructive limited options, as well as counterforce capabilities, is not logically inconsistent with the nuclear revolution.

The limited-retaliation model has also captured remarkably well the debate in American nuclear strategy about the effects of smaller and less destructive limited options on the dynamics of escalation. Those options, it was argued in the debate, would reduce stability by making escalation less costly and therefore more likely. Conversely, it was also argued that those options would enhance deterrence precisely because they were more likely to be used. A potential challenger, recognizing that a challenge was more likely to be resisted, would be less likely to mount one. The model's equilibria reflect these dynamics well. Having less destructive options does make escalation more likely, but it also makes a challenge less likely. On balance, the defender is better off the smaller and less destructive the limited options.

Several patterns are common to the model of brinkmanship and the model of limited retaliation. Escalation generally becomes less and less likely the longer the confrontation lasts. As the crisis continues, each state becomes increasingly confident that it is facing a resolute adversary. If that adversary is actually resolute, then misperception will have increased during the crisis. Indeed, the models indicate that even in crises that do not end disastrously, crisis bargaining may not reduce misperceptions and may actually exacerbate them. Changes in the grain of the arrays of risk and punishment affect the dynamics of brinkmanship and limited retaliation similarly. The finer the grain, the more likely the defender is to escalate throughout the crisis. As long as the defender's resolve is not too high, the challenger is also more likely to escalate the finer the array, but the less likely the challenger is to dispute the status quo. Conversely, the coarser the grain, the less likely the challenger and defender are to escalate, but the more likely the challenger is to dispute the status quo.

This apparent similarity, however, must be interpreted carefully. The game trees of the brinkmanship and limited-retaliation models are much alike. Moves alternate back and forth between the two states, and each state must always choose one of the three options: quitting, escalating, or launching a general nuclear attack. Moreover, the lack of complete information is modeled in the same way in the games. Much of the structural similarity between the models is due to the need to have models that are sufficiently simple that they are tractable. Therefore, it may be that the similarity in the dynamics of brinkmanship and limited retaliation is more a reflection of the structural similarity of these simple models than a reflection of the fundamental similarity of the two approaches. Richer, more elaborate models will help to decide this.

After bringing beliefs into the analysis, a reconsideration of the conventional logic of crisis stability in that light has shown that that logic focused too narrowly on the size of any first-strike advantages. Stability results from a more subtle interaction of several factors. Four conditions ensure that a crisis will be completely stable even though there are advantages to striking first. The first condition is that there is no autonomous risk of an unlimited attack. The states always retain collective control of this. Second, a state can attempt to quit a crisis, and if its adversary has not already attacked, a state's attempt to end the crisis by submitting will succeed. There will be no general nuclear exchange. Third, neither superpower will launch a first strike unless it believes that the probability that war is inevitable is greater than $\frac{1}{2}$. Finally, the states fully understand their situation. Because these conditions are sufficient to ensure stability, their specification also serves to identify the potential sources of instability.

The assumption that there is no autonomous risk can be relaxed. Doing so relates the probability of a deliberate first strike to the threshold of inevitability needed to justify an unlimited attack, the number of nuclear superpowers, and the degree of risk of losing collective control. Stability decreases as the threshold falls, as the number of nuclear superpowers rises, or as the risk of losing collective control increases. In the end, this analysis provides a firmer foundation for the conclusion of the conventional logic of crisis stability that if the threshold of inevitability needed to justify attacking is close to 1, then it is difficult to cross, and crises are relatively stable.

To help point the way toward better models, it may be useful to identify some of the specific weaknesses of the brinkmanship and limited-retaliation models. The first is that the strategy space is too simple. The set of alternatives from which the states must choose when deciding what to do is too limited. If a state decides, for example, to escalate, it can do so in only one way. In the brinkmanship models it must raise the risk of disaster by a fixed amount, and in the limited-retaliation model it must inflict a fixed increment of punishment. A natural extension of these models would be to permit the states to escalate by chosing from different levels of risk or damage.

The quitting structure of the models is also quite artificial. The games end as soon as a state fails to escalate. There is no passing. In the confrontation at the brink, a state is assumed to have quit if it does not take another step toward the brink. A state cannot simply stand its ground and force its adversary to continue to bear the burden of escalation. There is a technical advantage to the prohibition against passing. The states cannot be very far off the equilibrium path anywhere in the game tree. This greatly simplifies the analysis by avoiding many of the difficult questions about what conjectures a state might reasonably hold when it is off the equilibrium path.[1]

As advantageous as this simple quitting structure may be for some technical reasons, it is troubling for other technical reasons, as well as for some substantive reasons. Technically, the way that a game ends may profoundly affect the character of the sequential equilibrium strategies. In solving the games, many strategies can be disregarded because they are not sequentially rational in that they rely on an inherently incredible threat at the end of the game. For example, the strategy of always standing firm in the complete-information model of brinkmanship could not be part of a sequential equilibrium because it would require a state to generate an autonomous risk of 1 at the end of the game. Because of the influence of the way the game ends on the nature of the equilibria, poor assumptions made about the quitting structure may distort the insights provided by the models. More substantively, deterrence theory often has been criticized for paying too little attention to the situation on the ground (Maxwell 1968; Freedman 1989, p. 221). Once a confrontation has become a contest of manipulating the risk of a general nuclear exchange or of inflicting limited amounts of punishment, deterrence theory has generally been indifferent "to the course of the war on the ground" (Freedman 1989, p. 221). Which state is more likely to prevail on the battlefield is of little, if any, import. The quitting structure of the models also leaves them open to this criticism. Suppose a state is close to achieving it ends on the battlefield. In this situation, this state might simply want to let the battle run its course and not otherwise generate additional risks of disaster. In effect, this state wants to pass and not take another step toward the brink, although, of course, this state cannot prevent its adversary from taking additional steps. But as just noted, the states cannot pass in the brinkmanship and limited-retaliation models. In this way, these models also pay too little attention to the situation on the ground.

---

[1] The general problem of what conjectures are reasonable to have when one is off the equilibrium path has been an important concern in recent work in game theory. See, for example, Kreps and Wilson (1982b), Rubinstein (1985), Grossman and Perry (1986), Banks and Sobel (1987), Kreps and Ramey (1987), and Cho (1987); see also the introduction to this problem in the Appendix following Chapter 8.

In the models, the onus of escalation shifts back and forth until one of the states submits or until the states are destroyed. This alternating bidding structure is rather artificial. A more natural formulation would allow the states to act at any time regardless of whether or not their adversaries had just acted. Alas, if a state can also choose among several alternatives at any moment in such a formulation, then a game of this type is also likely to be much more difficult to analyze.

Uncertainty and the lack of complete information are also modeled quite simply. There are only two possible types of adversaries: one resolute and the other irresolute. One advantage of this simple formulation is that it provides a natural measure of misperception and a means of examining the effects of changes in the degree of misperception on the dynamics of escalation. In a less restrictive treatment of uncertainty, however, there would be more than two types of potential adversaries, and a state would be assumed to have an initial probability distribution over these types. Unfortunately, one consequence of this less confining formulation may be the loss of a well-defined measure of misperception. It is not clear how one would order the possible probability distributions, which might differ in many ways, along a single dimension of greater or lesser misperception. Without such an ordering, however, the meaning of a general increase in misperception would not be well defined, and that would make it difficult to study the consequences of changes in the level of misperception.

Another aspect of the simplicity with which uncertainty is modeled is the assumption that the probabilities representing the initial level of uncertainty are common knowledge. Each state, for example, knows that the probability that the challenger is resolute is $\varepsilon_{C'}$, that the other states know that it knows that the probability that the challenger is resolute is $\varepsilon_{C'}$, that it knows that the other states know that it knows that the probability that the challenger is resolute is $\varepsilon_{C'}$, and so on. Although this is a standard modeling technique in game theory, it is nevertheless a demanding consistency requirement.[2]

This strong consistency requirement does, however, provide an interesting counterpoise to the way that the conventional logic of crisis stability treats beliefs. In that logic, beliefs were completely exogenous. No formal restrictions were placed on them. The common-knowledge assumption is at the other extreme. It imposes very demanding consistency requirements. Interestingly, these two extremes support the same conclusion: If first-strike advantages are small, so that the threshold needed to justify attacking is close to 1, then crises are relatively stable.

A final criticism begins with the brinkmanship model and ends by

---

[2] See Myerson (1985) for a discussion of this.

suggesting a motive for integrating the brinkmanship and limited-retaliation models. Schelling's threat that leaves something to chance solved the credibility problem in principle by assuming that there was some chance of loss of collective control that would lead directly to a general nuclear exchange. That solution in principle, however, is difficult to interpret or apply in practice. The models, for example, indicate that a finer array of limited options reduces the probability that a potential challenger will dispute the status quo. But what military forces, operations, and actions actually raise the kind of autonomous risk on which brinkmanship is predicated? What changes in real forces would affect the array of risk? The answer to this question is clearer for the array of punishment, for the military forces that correspond to the theoretical notion of a limited option are much clearer. These are forces and operations that are capable of destroying things of intrinsic value to an adversary. This greater clarity gives one a better sense of what it means to have smaller and less destructive limited options. The ambiguity surrounding the actual forces, operations, and capabilities that correspond to the theoretical concept of a limited option in the array of risk makes it difficult to relate the analysis of the brinkmanship models to anything beyond these models. This is a significant weakness in this approach.

The approach based on the strategy that leaves something to chance would be stronger if it more explicitly described how states actually take a step toward the brink. How do states use real forces to generate a risk that the states will lose collective control over whether or not there will be a general nuclear war? For example, did the U.S. anti-submarine-warfare activities against Soviet submarines during the Cuban missile crisis create this kind of risk? Or did the American attempts to force Soviet submarines to the surface, like the assassination of the archduke in Hinsley's interpretation (1963, p. 296) of the July 1914 crisis, create the more general kind of risk of further escalation that characterizes both the strategy that leaves something to chance and the strategy of limited retaliation?[3]

The need to specify more explicitly how a state actually generates an autonomous risk that the crisis will go out of collective control and escalate to a general nuclear exchange is one reason for combining the brinkmanship and limited-retaliation models. The limited-retaliation model makes very demanding assumptions about command and control. These might be relaxed by assuming, instead, that as a state imposes more and more punishment, it also begins to destroy its adversary's command and control capabilities. That destruction would then be the source of the risk that the states would lose collective control that brinkmanship needs in

[3] See Sagan (1985, pp. 112–18) for a discussion of the navy's antisubmarine efforts during the missile crisis.

order to be logically coherent. Taking that to be the source of the autonomous risk in effect, amounts to merging the arrays of risk and punishment.

The preceding critique has focused narrowly on the technical aspects of the
models. It would certainly be better to have models that would answer the
criticisms just outlined. The brinkmanship and limited-retaliation models
are, at most, a first step toward formalization of the relation between force
or the threat of it and states' efforts to secure their ends after the nuclear
revolution. But simple and basic as these models are, they do make
predictions about, for example, the effects of changes in the states' levels of
resolve, the relative stability of crises depending on the severity of the
underlying conflict of interest, the distribution of types of brinkmanship
crises, the consequences of having smaller, less destructive limited options,
and, more generally, the effects of changing the grain of the arrays of risk
and punishment on the dynamics of escalation. But how much confidence
can one place in these predictions? This question raises a larger issue, one
that has to do not just with the models examined here, but with nuclear
deterrence theory more broadly: the problem of evidence and the inherent
difficulty of assessing and evaluating nuclear deterrence theory empirically.

This difficulty arises in part because the most important predictions of
nuclear deterrence theory concern nuclear crises. But the superpowers have
little experience with nuclear crises, and no one wants any more. This lack
of evidence is one of the more important reasons for wanting to have a
theory of nuclear deterrence, for one of the functions of theory is to extend
understanding beyond the limits of direct empirical experience. But this
lack of evidence also makes it difficult to evaluate nuclear deterrence theory
empirically in the domain about which one cares most. Ironically, one of
the greatest obstacles to evaluating nuclear deterrence theory is also one of
the strongest reasons for wanting it.

One way to attempt to surmount this obstacle is to try to expand the set
of potential points of contact between the empirical realm and the two
approaches that nuclear deterrence theory has taken to linking force and
states' political ends. These approaches need to be elaborated in such a way
that there will be more places at which empirical evidence can be brought to
bear to help assess these approaches and the models based on them. One
means of doing this may be to try to represent the nuclear revolution in the
game's payoffs, rather than in the game form (i.e., in the structure of the
tree). For example, the stylization of the nuclear revolution, which is that
defense is impossible, has been built into the structure of the brinkmanship
and limited-retaliation models. Throughout the confrontation, each state
always has the ability to launch a massive nuclear attack and destroy its
adversary. It would be better to have models that would be structurally

consistent with both the stylization of the nuclear revolution and the classical logic of war. Which stylization would actually obtain would then be determined by the particular values of the payoffs. The preemption game in Figure 5.1 illustrates this. The structure of the game, that is, the game form, can be fixed, and the game can be parameterized to be consistent with both the stylization of the nuclear revolution and the classical logic of war, depending on the particular payoffs. To make the game consistent with the former, the payoffs can be defined so that there is no advantage to striking first or, perhaps somewhat more loosely, so that the only fate worse than striking first is being struck first. That is, the payoffs should satisfy $L > F > f > S > W$. The game can also be made to conform to the classical logic of war by assuming, for example, that the payoff to a successful first strike is greater than the payoff to submitting (i.e., $F > L$). Thus, the nuclear revolution can be parameterized by selecting different values for the payoffs, while the underlying structure of the game remains the same. One can therefore trace the effects of the nuclear revolution on the game's equilibria and on the dynamics of escalation by varying the game's payoffs. Expanding the scope of the analysis by parameterizing the nuclear revolution would mean that historical cases from before the nuclear revolution could be brought to bear to evaluate and refine the models. And if, in the course of that analysis, the models seemed to accord well with the cases antedating the nuclear revolution, then one might have more confidence in their ability to explain nuclear crises.

Although expanding the scope of the models to make them more empirically accessible may help, evaluating them will remain difficult. One reason for this is that so many of the models' primitives, such as states' beliefs and payoffs, are extremely difficult, if not impossible, to measure. It is, however, important to emphasize that this difficulty is not limited to formal models. The formalizations may make what has to be measured clearer. But the measurement problem confronts any analysis, whether formal or not, that appeals to underlying notions like beliefs and payoffs.

It remains to be seen to what extent future work can overcome the difficulties in assessing nuclear deterrence theory empirically. In these circumstances, how ought one to view discussions of nuclear deterrence theory? The models and analysis presented in the preceding chapters are, at best, sources of insight into the dynamics of nuclear confrontation. Like any insights not buttressed by strong empirical support, the insights suggested by this analysis must be used carefully and cautiously. Seen as sources of insight, there is a parallel between formal modeling efforts like this one and historical case studies. Both, if done well, can offer insights into how things are related, how they fit together. Indeed, formal modeling efforts and case studies are quite complementary. Models often try to refine and extend the insights derived from case studies by formalizing them. Albeit at the risk of distorting the analysis in undesirable ways by making it conform to the requirements of the analytic tools, formalizations, by abstracting away from the details of the case, attempt to bring the essence of the issues into sharper focus. Formalizations, if successful, make it possible to see connections linking these issues that formerly were obscure. These new insights may then raise new questions or suggest new avenues of inquiry for further empirical work that in turn may give rise to new models. This is the process of deepening insight to which this book has tried to contribute by bringing the essence of some issues in nuclear deterrence theory into sharper focus and by illuminating the relations among these issues.

Some introductory notes on game theory

The mathematical analysis in the preceding chapters, for the most part, involves nothing more than algebra. The analysis does, however, appeal to a game-theoretic vocabulary and set of concepts that may be unfamiliar. This Appendix introduces those concepts and vocabulary in order to give readers with little or no background in game theory a better sense of the tools used to analyze deterrence theory and some of the strengths and weaknesses of those tools.[1]

The extensive form

The brinkmanship and limited-retaliation models are examples of games in extensive form. A *game in extensive form* is composed of two parts.[2] The first is the *game form* or *game tree*. The second is the players' *payoffs*. The game form or tree is an abstract summary of the situation facing the players. The tree tells the order of play, the set of alternatives from which each player must choose when it plays, and what each player knows when it must choose. The tree defines who moves after whom, what each player can do, and what each player knows about what the other players have done when it must decide what to do.

Two very simple trees are illustrated in Figure A1. In both Figure A1(a) and A1(b) the order of play is the same. Player *I* moves first, and then player *II* moves. When *I* moves, the trees show that it can choose between two alternatives: It can choose up, *U*, or down, *D*. Similarly, *II* has only two alternatives: top, *T*, and bottom, *B*. The trees also define what *II* knows when it must decide between *T* and *B*. In Figure A1(a), *II* is assumed to know what *I* did, perhaps because *II* could watch *I*. In Figure A1(b), however, *II* does not know what *I* did. This is the meaning of the dashed line connecting *II*'s two decision nodes in Figure A1(b). Of course, *II* may have beliefs about whether it is at its upper or lower decision node, and more will be said later about beliefs and their formation. At this point, it is important

---

[1] For an excellent though somewhat more technical introduction to game theory than the one presented here, see Tirole (1988, pp. 423–59).

[2] For a formal definition, see Luce and Raiffa (1957), Owen (1982), Selten (1975), or Kreps and Wilson (1982b).

to note that only the tree in Figure A1(b) is intended as a model of a situation in which *II* must decide what to do without knowing what *I* has done. There is simply not enough information.

If a player is unable to distinguish between some of its decision nodes, then these indistinguishable nodes constitute an *information set*. In Figure A1(b), *II* has one information set because its two decision nodes are indistinguishable. But in Figure A1(a), *II* can distinguish between its two decision nodes because it knows what *I* did when it has to decide what to do. *II*, therefore, has two information sets in this tree, each composed of a single node. In both Figure A1(a) and A1(b), *I* has a single information set consisting of a single decision node.

If, as in Figure A1(a), every information set consists of a single decision node or *singleton*, so that a player at any information set knows exactly what alternatives the other players have previously played, then the game has *perfect information*. Chess is a game of perfect information. Whenever a player must decide what to do in chess, it is completely certain of what all of the preceding moves have been. That is not the case in the tree in Figure A1(b), where *II* does not know what *I* has done.

The *terminal nodes* of a tree are the points at which a path through the tree ends. In Figure A1(a) and A1(b), for example, there are four terminal nodes, each of which follows one of the four branches that *II*'s decision can take. The terminal nodes correspond to the possible *outcomes* of the game.

The game tree abstractly defines the situation in which the players must act. Each path through the tree leads to a terminal node that is associated

Figure A1. Some simple game trees.

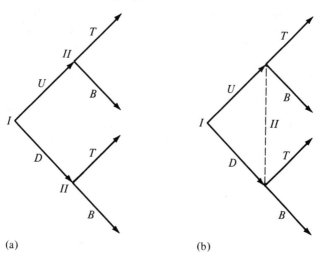

(a)   (b)

with some possible outcome. But to have any hope of analyzing what will be done in this situation, more than the structure of the situation must be described; the players' preferences over the possible outcomes must also be defined. This is the second part needed to complete the specification of the game. That is, each player associates with each possible outcome a *payoff* or *utility* that reflects its preferences over the set of possible outcomes.[3]

Three examples will make this description more concrete. The first is the game of chicken. There are two players: *I* and *II*. Each player has two alternatives: It can stand firm, *F*, or submit, *S*. The decision whether to stand firm or submit is made in ignorance of what the other player is doing. The game tree in Figure A2(a) illustrates this situation. The tree begins with *I* having to decide between *F* and *S*. *II* must then decide between *F* and *S*. The tree also models the assumption that neither player knows what the other player is doing when it must decide what to do. *I* clearly cannot determine what *II* has done when *I* is making its decision, because the information set at which this decision is made precedes the information set at which *II* makes its decision. Similarly, *II* does not know what *I* is doing because both of *II*'s decision nodes are in the same information set, and, by definition, a player cannot distinguish among the nodes in any one of its information sets. *II* cannot tell if it is at its upper node, in which case *I* is standing firm, or if it is at its lower node, in which case *I* is submitting. In the tree, both players make informationally isolated decisions; each player must decide what to do without knowing what the other player is doing. One natural interpretation of this informational isolation is that the tree is a model of a situation in which decisions are made simultaneously. That is, in the actual situation for which Figure A2(a) is a model, *I* and *II* make their decisions to stand firm or submit simultaneously. Simultaneity, in turn, implies that no player can know what the other is doing when it must decide what to do. In this way, simultaneity makes for informationally isolated decisions, and that is what is modeled in the tree in Figure A2(a).

To complete the specification of the game of chicken, the players' payoffs or preferences over the possible outcomes of the game must be specified. If one player stands firm and the other submits, then the player who stands firm wins, and the other loses. If both stand firm, there is a disaster that is worse than losing. If both submit, a compromise results that is better than losing, but not as good as prevailing. Picking numbers to represent these payoffs, suppose that if one player stands firm and the other submits, then the player who stands firm receives 1, whereas the player who submits loses

---

[3] Usually, utilities are assumed to be von Neumann–Morgenstern utilities. That is, the utility of an uncertain event is the expected utility of the possible events. For example, the utility of a lottery that will give utility u_1 with probability ρ and utility u_2 with probability $1 - \rho$ is $\rho u_1 + (1 - \rho)u_2$.

1. If both players stand firm, both lose 5. If both submit, then each obtains the compromise payoff of zero. Thus, the payoffs at the end of the branch along which *I* plays *F* and *II* plays *S* are (1, −1), where the first element in the pair of payoffs is *I*'s payoff, and the second is *II*'s. The complete specification of the game is given in Figure A2(b).

The second example is the game of matching pennies. In this game, two players act simultaneously, and each reveals one side of a penny. If both players show heads or tails, player *I* wins and collects a penny from *II*. If one player shows heads and the other tails, then *II* wins and takes a penny from *I*. The extensive form of this game is depicted in Figure A3. *I* begins by making an informationally isolated decision between heads, *H*, and tails, *T*, after which *II* makes an informationally isolated decision between *H* and *T*. If *I* and *II* play the same face, the payoffs are (1, −1) and if they make different choices, the payoffs are (−1, 1).

Finally, consider a more complicated game that is a much-simplified version of poker. In this game, one card is dealt to player *I*, and another card is dealt to *II*. Each player can see only the card dealt to it. Then, knowing its card, but not its opponent's, *I* must decide whether to bid a dollar, *B*, or fold, *F*. If *I* folds, it loses its ante of one dollar to *II*. If *I* bids, *II* must either bid a dollar or fold. If *II* folds, *I* collects *II*'s ante of a dollar. If *II* bids, then both players expose their cards. If both cards are of the same color, the players divide the pot, which leaves a net gain of zero. If the colors differ, then black beats red, and the player holding the black card collects the pot of four dollars for a net gain of two dollars.

Figure A2. Chicken in extensive form.

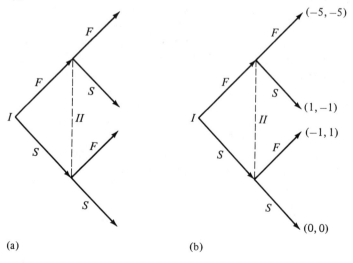

(a)   (b)

Figure A4 shows the extensive form of this simple poker game. A player called "Nature" or N makes the first move. Assuming there to be a player called Nature is simply a modeling device used to introduce random or probabilistic elements into the game. For example, four combinations of colored cards could be dealt in the game, (B, B), (B, R), (R, B), (R, R), where the first element of the pair corresponds to the color of I's card, and the second element is the color of II's card. To represent this in the game, Nature begins the game by playing one of the four alternatives, where each alternative corresponds to one possible deal. With a very large deck, the probability of dealing one of these combinations will be $\frac{1}{4}$, and so Nature will play each of these alternatives with probability $\frac{1}{4}$.

After N plays, I must decide whether to bid or fold. When making this decision, I knows the color of its card, but not the color of its opponent's card. Accordingly, I cannot distinguish between a deal of (B, B) and (B, R) or between a deal of (R, B) and (R, R). This means that I has two information sets, with the nodes representing the deals (B, B) and (B, R) in one information set, and the nodes representing the deals (R, B) and (R, R) in the other. At these information sets, I has two alternatives: bidding, B, or folding, F. If it folds, the game ends, and the payoffs are $(-1, 1)$. If I bids, II must then decide whether to bid or fold. II, like I, knows only the color of its card and consequently cannot distinguish between the deals of (B, B) and (R, B) or between the deals of (B, R) and (R, R). II, therefore, also has two information sets, as shown in Figure A4. If II folds, the payoffs are $(1, -1)$. If II bids, the players expose their cards and obtain the payoffs described earlier and illustrated in Figure A4.

Figure A3. Matching pennies.

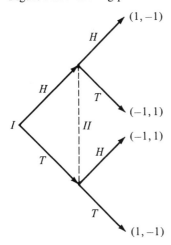

Strategies and the normal form

Now that a game has been described, one can begin to discuss ways of analyzing it. The first step is to define what is meant by a player's *behavioral strategy*. A player's behavioral strategy is simply a complete plan for how this player will play the game. This strategy tells what this player will do in each contingency that might arise in the game. More formally, a player's behavioral strategy is a rule that specifies which alternative this player will select at each of its information sets. If, as in the games of chicken or matching pennies, a player has a single information set, then a player's behavioral strategy merely tells what this player will do at this one information set. In matching pennies, a strategy for *I* is to play *H*. A second strategy for *I* would be to play *T*. In the simple poker game in Figure A4, each player has two information sets. Accordingly, a player's behavioral strategy must specify what the player will do at both of its information sets. A behavioral strategy for *I* is "fold if *I*'s card is red, and bid if the card is black." The instruction "fold if *I*'s card is red" cannot be a behavioral strategy for *I*, for it is not a complete plan for playing the game; it does not specify what *I* is to do if it is dealt a black.

Figure A4. The extensive form of the simple poker game.

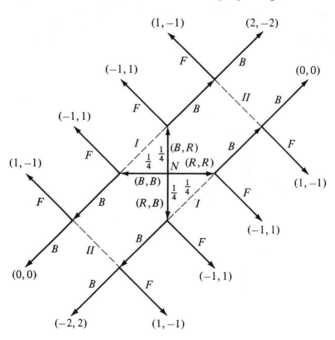

It will be useful to distinguish between pure behavioral strategies and mixed behavioral strategies. In a *pure strategy*, the rule defining a player's strategy specifies that the player is certain to choose a single alternative at each of its information sets. In a *mixed strategy*, a player is allowed to randomize over the alternatives from which it must choose. That is, the rule defining a player's mixed behavioral strategy specifies a probability distribution over the set of alternatives at each of this player's information sets. This distribution gives the probability that any of the alternatives available at a given information set will be played. In matching pennies, for example, I has two pure strategies. It can play H for sure, or it can play T for sure. A mixed behavioral strategy for I in this game would be to show heads with probability $\frac{1}{2}$ and tails with probability $\frac{1}{2}$. A second mixed behavioral strategy would be to play H with probability $\frac{2}{3}$ and T with probability $\frac{1}{3}$. In the simple poker game, a pure behavioral strategy for I would be to "bid regardless of the color of I's card." A mixed behavioral strategy would be to "bid with probability $\frac{3}{4}$ and fold with probability $\frac{1}{4}$ if I's card is black, and bid with probability $\frac{3}{8}$ and fold with probability $\frac{5}{8}$ if I's card is red."

The use of pure behavioral strategies makes it possible to define the *normal form* of a game, which is more compact and sometimes more useful in analyzing the game than the extensive form. Suppose that there are M players in some extensive-form game. Let s_i be some pure behavioral strategy for player i. That is, s_i is a rule that tells which alternative i is certain to play at each of its information sets. Now consider the m-tuple $(s_1, s_2, \ldots, s_M)$, where each s_i in this m-tuple is a complete plan for how player i will play the game. This means that $(s_1, s_2, \ldots, s_M)$ describes what will be done at every information set in the game. Accordingly, one can imagine giving the plan $(s_1, s_2, \ldots, s_M)$ to a referee and then having the referee play out the game according to the players' strategies. If, for example, the first information set in the tree belonged to player i, then the referee would consult s_i in $(s_1, s_2, \ldots, s_M)$ to see which alternative i would choose at that information set. The referee would then follow the branch in the tree corresponding to that alternative and go down the tree to the next information set. If that set belonged to k, the referee would consult s_k to see what s_k would have k do at that information set. In that way, the referee could follow the plan defined by $(s_1, s_2, \ldots, s_M)$ and eventually reach a terminal node that would mark the end of the game. Put another way, the plan $(s_1, s_2, \ldots, s_M)$ defines a path through the tree, or, if Nature is making random moves in the tree, the plan defines the probability of reaching each possible terminal node or outcome of the game. Now recall that each player attaches some utility to every possible outcome of the game. If, therefore, a plan like $(s_1, s_2, \ldots, s_M)$ defines the probabilities of reaching the possible outcomes, then each player can attach an expected utility to the plan. That is, each player knows what its expected utility will be if the game is played according to the plan $(s_1, s_2, \ldots, s_M)$. Let $U_i(s_1, s_2, \ldots, s_M)$ be the utility player i receives if the game is played according to $(s_1, s_2, \ldots, s_M)$. Now, the game can be described by the set of all possible plans (i.e., the set of all possible m-tuples of pure behavioral strategies, and the utility functions that specify the utility the players receive if the game is played according to a specific plan). This description is the normal form of the game.

To make this description of the normal form more concrete, the extensive-form representations of the games of chicken, matching pennies, and poker will be translated into their normal forms. In chicken and matching pennies, each player has two pure behavioral strategies. This means that there are four different plans for playing the game. One way to keep track of these plans is with a matrix, where each row corresponds to one of player I's strategies, and each column corresponds to one of II's strategies. Each cell in the matrix then corresponds to a different combination of I's and II's strategies or, in other words, to a different complete plan for playing the game. The utility each player receives if the game is played according to a particular plan is placed in the cell associated with that plan. The normal form for chicken is shown in Figure A5(a), and that for matching pennies in Figure A5(b).

To translate the simple poker game into its normal form, note that I has four pure strategies. One strategy is to bid if a black card is dealt and to fold if a red card is dealt. Let $\{(B, b), (R, f)\}$ denote this strategy, where the first element in a parenthetical pair stands for the color of the card that may be dealt, and the second element tells what to do if this color is actually drawn; so (B, b) means bid, b, if a black card, B, is dealt. Then the other three strategies are $\{(B, b), (R, b)\}$, $\{(B, f), (R, b)\}$, and $\{(B, f), (R, f)\}$. Player II also has the same four strategies. It can bid or fold depending on whether it has a red or black card. Because each player has four strategies, there are sixteen different combinations of strategies (i.e., sixteen different complete plans for

Figure A5. The normal forms of chicken and matching pennies.

(a)   (b)

playing the game). As before, one can keep track of these different combinations in a matrix, where each row corresponds to one of I's strategies, and each column corresponds to one of II's strategies. This is done in Figure A6.

As an example of how the payoffs are calculated, consider the cell associated with I's strategy of bidding if it has a black card and folding if it has a red card, which is denoted $\{(B,b),(R,f)\}$, and with II's strategy of folding with a black card and bidding with a red card, which is given by $\{(B,f),(R,b)\}$. This corresponds to the cell at the intersection of the second row and the third column, where the payoffs are $(\frac{3}{4}, -\frac{1}{4})$. To derive these payoffs, suppose that Nature deals a red card to I and a red to II; then play follows the branch (R, R) in the extensive form in Figure A4. Given that I is holding a red card, its strategy is to fold. The game ends with payoffs $(-1, 1)$. Now suppose that Nature deals a black card to I and a red card to II. Play then proceeds down the (B, R) branch. I's strategy is to bid. Because II is holding a red card, it also bids. Because black beats red, the payoffs are $(2, -2)$. If Nature had dealt two black cards, I would have bid, but II would have folded, leaving the players with $(1, -1)$. Finally, a deal of red to I and black to II has I folding immediately, to give the payoffs $(-1, 1)$. Because Nature will deal each of these combinations with probability $\frac{1}{4}$, the expected

Figure A6. The simple poker game in normal form.

		II		
	$\{(B,b),(R,b)\}$	$\{(B,b),(R,f)\}$	$\{(B,f),(R,b)\}$	$\{(B,f),(R,f)\}$
$\{(B,b),(R,b)\}$	$0,0$	$0,0$	$1,-1$	$1,-1$
$\{(B,b),(R,f)\}$	$0,0$	$-\frac{1}{4},\frac{1}{4}$	$\frac{3}{4},-\frac{1}{4}$	$0,0$
$\{(B,f),(R,b)\}$	$-\frac{3}{4},\frac{3}{4}$	$0,0$	$-\frac{1}{4},\frac{1}{4}$	$0,0$
$\{(B,f),(R,f)\}$	$-1,1$	$-1,1$	$-1,1$	$-1,1$

(I labels the rows.)

payoff to I from this combination of strategies is $(\frac{1}{4})(-1) + (\frac{1}{4})(2) + (\frac{1}{4})(1) + (\frac{1}{4})(-1) = \frac{3}{4}$. Similarly, II's expected payoff is $(\frac{1}{4})(1) + (\frac{1}{4})(-2) + (\frac{1}{4})(-1) + (\frac{1}{4})(1) = -\frac{1}{4}$. The payoffs for the other cells are calculated in the same way.

Best replies and Nash equilibria

The notion of a player's *best reply* or *best response* is crucial to defining a game's Nash equilibria. Continuing to work with the normal form, suppose that there are M players. Viewing the game from player i's perspective, the plans of the other players, which are denoted by $s_{-i} = (s_1, s_2, \ldots, s_{i-1}, s_{i+1}, \ldots, s_M)$, give almost a complete plan for playing the game. It tells how every player other than i will play. Then, a best reply for i to s_{-i} is a strategy that gives i its highest payoff given that the other players are playing according to s_{-i}. If, for example, II's pure strategy is to stand firm in the game of chicken in Figure A5(a), then I's best reply is to submit. This strategy leaves I with -1, whereas standing firm would give -5. Sometimes a player has more than one best response. If I's strategy in the simple game of poker in Figure A6 is always to bid, that is, to play $\{(B, b), (R, b)\}$, then II has two best replies. Always bidding or bidding only with a black card, that is, $\{(B, b), (B, b)\}$ or $\{(B, b), (R, f)\}$, will yield II its highest payoff of zero given that I is following the strategy of always bidding. (This can be seen easily by looking across the row associated with I's strategy of always bidding. In this row, the highest payoff II can attain is zero, and any column or strategy that gives II this payoff is a best reply.) In sum, a player's best reply to a combination of the other players' strategies is a strategy that will maximize this player's payoff given that the other players are following this combination of strategies.

A *Nash equilibrium* of a game is a complete plan for playing the game such that each player's strategy is a best reply to the other players' strategies. That is, the combination $(s_1^*, s_2^*, \ldots, s_M^*)$ is a Nash equilibrium if s_i^* is a best reply to s_{-i}^* for every player i. A reason for calling a combination of strategies that has this property an equilibrium is that no player has an incentive to change what it is doing by following some other strategy. Player i has no incentive to deviate from s_i^* given that the other players are following s_{-i}^*, because s_i^* is a best response to s_{-i}^*, and, by definition, a player's best reply to a combination of strategies maximizes its payoff given that the other players follow this combination of strategies. If, however, a combination of strategies, say $(s_1', s_2', \ldots, s_M')$, did not satisfy the Nash property that every player's strategy is a best reply to the other players' strategies, then there would be at least one player, say k, such that s_k' would not be a best reply to s_{-k}'. Thus, k could increase its payoff by deviating from s_k' by actually playing a best reply to s_{-k}'. In brief, no player has an incentive to deviate from its strategy if and only if the strategies form a Nash equilibrium.

The game of chicken in Figure A5(a) has three Nash equilibria. In the first, I stands firm, and II submits. This combination of strategies corresponds to the cell in the upper-right corner. Clearly, I has no incentive to deviate from F by playing S, for I's payoff to playing S, given that II is playing S, would drop from 1 to 0. Similarly, II has no incentive to deviate from S given that I is playing F, for if it played F, its payoff would fall from -1 to -5. In the second equilibrium, II stands firm, and I submits. This is the combination at the lower left. As in the previous case, no state has an incentive to deviate from its strategy.

The third equilibrium involves mixed strategies. Suppose that each player will stand firm with probability 0.2 and submit with probability 0.8; then each player's strategy is a best response to the other's, and therefore this combination is a Nash equilibrium. To see that I's strategy is a best reply to II's, calculate I's expected payoff to standing firm: This is I's payoff if both I and II stand firm times the probability that II will stand firm plus the payoff if I stands firm and II submits times the probability that II will submit. This is $0.2(-5) + 0.8(1) = -0.2$. Similarly, I's payoff to submitting is $0.2(-1) + 0.8(0) = -0.2$. This shows that if II stands firm with probability 0.2 and submits with probability 0.8, then the payoffs to I of standing firm and of submitting are the same. Thus, I is indifferent to its pure strategies of standing firm or submitting. Indeed, I is indifferent among its mixed strategies as well, for if I stands firm with probability ρ and submits with probability $1 - \rho$, then its expected payoff will be ρ times the expected payoff of standing firm, which is -0.2, plus $1 - \rho$ times the expected payoff of submitting, which is also -0.2. This leaves $\rho(-0.2) + (1 - \rho)(-0.2) = -0.2$, regardless of the value of ρ. In sum, I is indifferent among all of its strategies, both pure and mixed. Consequently, all of I's strategies are best replies to II's strategy of standing firm with probability 0.2 and submitting with probability 0.8. In particular, I's strategy of standing firm with probability 0.2 and submitting with probability 0.8 is a best response to II's strategy.

Just as II's strategy of standing firm with probability 0.2 left I different among all of its strategies, I's strategy of standing firm with probability 0.2 leaves II indifferent to all of its strategies. All of II's strategies are best responses to I's strategy. Thus, each player's strategy is a best reply to the other's; so the combination of strategies forms a Nash equilibrium.

In general, a finite game, that is, a game that has finite numbers of players and pure strategies, has at least one Nash equilibrium.[4] But there may

---

[4] See Ordeshook (1986, pp. 120–37) and Tirole (1988, pp. 444–5) for a proof of the existence of at least one Nash equilibrium in a finite game.

not be an equilibrium in pure strategies; a Nash equilibrium may exist only
in mixed strategies. The matching-pennies game illustrates this. No
combination of pure strategies forms a Nash equilibrium. For example, in
the combination in which *I* plays *H* and *II* plays *T*, then, given *II*'s strategy
of *T*, *I*'s best reply is to deviate from *H* by playing *T*. Although there are no
pure-strategy equilibria, there is a mixed-strategy equilibrium in which
each player plays *H* with probability $\frac{1}{2}$. If *II* follows this strategy, then *I* will
be indifferent between *H* and *T* and all mixed strategies. All of *I*'s strategies
are best replies, and, in particular, the strategy of playing *H* with
probability $\frac{1}{2}$ is a best response. But if *I* follows this strategy, then *II* is
indifferent among all of its strategies. So *II*'s playing *H* with probability $\frac{1}{2}$ is
a best reply. Thus, this combination of strategies is a Nash equilibrium.

The mixed strategies illustrate an important fact that is useful in finding the equilibria of the brinkmanship and limited-retaliation models in
Chapters 3 through 7. If a player is mixing over two strategies in equilibrium, then both of these strategies must be best replies and consequently
provide the same payoff. That is, if a player *i* plays a pure strategy s_i^1
with probability $p > 0$ and another pure strategy s_i^2 with probability
$q > 0$, then both s_i^1 and s_i^2 must be best responses, and the utility of playing s_i^1 must equal the utility of playing s_i^2. If these strategies did not yield
the same utility, then one would be preferred to the other. That is, the
utility of playing one of the strategies, say s_i^1, would be greater than the
utility of playing s_i^2. This would mean that the player could increase its
payoff by deviating from the mixed strategy in which it plays s_i^1 with
probability p and s_i^2 with probability q by choosing a strategy in which it
would play s_i^1 with probability $p + q$ and s_i^2 with probability zero. But, by
definition, no state can improve its payoff in equilibrium by deviating from
its equilibrium strategy. So it must be that s_i^1 and s_i^2 yield the same payoff.
Similarly, these strategies must also be best replies, for if they were not, then
the player would also be able to increase its payoff by not playing either of
them, but playing instead a best reply with probability $p + q$.

The mathematical appeal of mixed strategies is clear. Without them,
many games would have no equilibrium. Allowing mixed-strategy
equilibria assures that an equilibrium exists. But the empirical meanings
and interpretations of mixed strategies and mixed-strategy equilibria are
fraught with difficulties.[5] To illustrate some of these, consider the more
general game of chicken in Figure A7, where the numerical payoffs in
Figure A5(a) have been replaced by variables. The payoff to standing firm if
the other player submits is *w*, the payoff to submitting if the other player

---

[5] For further discussion of this and some attempts to justify mixed equilibria, see Luce and
Raiffa (1957, pp. 74–6), Harsanyi (1973), and Harsanyi and Selten (1988, pp. 14–15).

stands firm is s, the payoff to the compromise outcome that obtains if both players submit is c, and the payoff to the disaster that occurs if both stand firm is d. The game will be one of chicken as long as the payoffs satisfy the following relation: The payoff to prevailing is greater than the payoff to compromising, which is greater than the payoff to submitting, which is better than the payoff to disaster: $w > c > s > d$ for both players I and II.

Now consider the mixed equilibrium in which I stands firm with probability ϕ_I and II stands firm with probability ϕ_{II}. To calculate ϕ_I, note that II's expected payoff to standing firm is the payoff to its standing firm and I's standing firm, d_{II}, times the probability that I will stand firm, ϕ_I, plus II's payoff if it stands firm and I submits, w_{II}, times the probability that I will quit, $1-\phi_I$. This is $d_{II}\phi_I + w_{II}(1-\phi_I)$. Similarly, II's expected payoff to submitting is $s_{II}\phi_I + c_{II}(1-\phi_I)$. But now recall that because II uses a mixed strategy in equilibrium, II must be indifferent between standing firm and submitting. (If it strictly preferred one of these alternatives, then it could improve its payoff by deviating from its mixed strategy to the preferred pure strategy.) II's indifference implies that the expected payoff to standing firm equals the payoff to submitting: $d_{II}\phi_I + w_{II}(1-\phi_I) = s_{II}\phi_I + c_{II}(1-\phi_I)$. Solving for the probability that I will stand firm gives $\phi_I = (w_{II}-c_{II})/[(w_{II}-c_{II})+(s_{II}-d_{II})]$. Similarly, the chances that II will stand firm are $\phi_{II} = (w_I - c_I)/[(w_I - c_I)+(s_I - d_I)]$.

The mixed equilibrium has some intuitively appealing properties. One would expect a compromise to be more likely the higher the payoff to compromise, the greater the cost of disaster, and the smaller the payoff to prevailing. The mixed equilibrium conforms to these expectations. The chance of a compromise outcome is the probability that both I and II will

Figure A7. A more general game of chicken.

		II Stand firm	*II* Submit
I	Stand firm	d_I, d_{II}	w_I, s_{II}
	Submit	s_I, w_{II}	c_I, c_{II}

Figure A8. The massive-retaliation game.

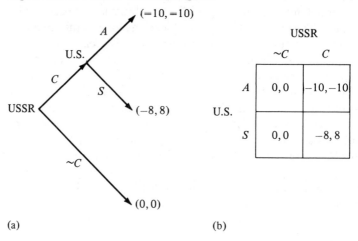

(a)   (b)

submit: $(1 - \phi_I)(1 - \phi_{II})$. This probability increases as the payoff to compromise rises or as the payoffs to disaster and prevailing fall.[6]

But much about this mixed equilibrium is not especially appealing intuitively. Note that the probability that I will stand firm, ϕ_I, does not depend on I's payoffs, but on II's. Thus, if I's payoff to prevailing increases, I's strategy does not change. Rather, II becomes more likely to stand firm; ϕ_{II} rises as w_I increases. The mathematical reason for this is that in a mixed equilibrium, I's strategy must keep II indifferent between standing firm and submitting. If, therefore, II's payoffs do not change, as they do not when only I's payoff to prevailing rises, then I's strategy cannot change, for otherwise II would no longer be indifferent. Instead, II's strategy must change in order to keep I indifferent. A higher payoff to prevailing tends to raise I's expected payoff to standing firm. This, however, can be offset and I's indifference restored if II becomes more likely to stand firm, for that will make the prospect of disaster more likely if I stands firm and thus will tend to lower I's expected payoff to standing firm.[7]

Although the mathematical reasons for these interactions are clear, what, if any, empirical interpretation to attach to them is not so clear, and the interpretations offered in Chapters 3 through 7 must be treated cautiously. One approach to building confidence in any finding is to see if it holds in a wide variety of models. This is very much in keeping with the most important objective of this volume, which is to articulate a general analytic

---

[6] $\partial(1 - \phi_I)(1 - \phi_{II})/\partial c > 0$; $\partial(1 - \phi_I)(1 - \phi_{II})/\partial d < 0$; $\partial(1 - \phi_I)(1 - \phi_{II})/\partial w < 0$.

[7] This argument does not apply to games with more than two players. In those games, a player's mixed strategy may depend on its payoffs.

perspective on nuclear deterrence theory that will help point the way to richer and better models.

Returning to the extensive form, a Nash equilibrium is a combination of behavioral strategies in which each player's behavioral strategy is a best reply to the other players' behavioral strategies. This, however, raises a question. Does it matter whether one analyzes a game in terms of mixed behavioral strategies, in which a player may randomize over the alternatives at each of its information sets, or in terms of mixed strategies, in which a player randomizes over complete plans? If the game is one of *perfect recall*, as the games in this volume are, then these two formulations are equivalent, and the adjective "behavioral" will generally not be used.[8]

Subgame perfection

The game in Figure A8(a) is a simple formulation of the doctrine of massive retaliation when both the United States and the Soviet Union have secure second-strike forces. The Soviet Union begins the game by deciding whether or not to challenge the status quo. If there is no challenge, the status quo continues, and the game ends with payoffs $(0,0)$. If the Soviet Union challenges the status quo, the United States must decide what to do. It can either carry out a massive nuclear attack or submit by acquiescing to the Soviet challenge. If the United States attacks, the Soviet Union is assumed to retaliate in kind. The game ends in a general nuclear exchange, with payoffs of $(-10, -10)$. If the United States submits, then the United States suffers a loss, and the Soviets gain. The payoffs to this are taken to be $(-8, 8)$.

The normal form of this game is illustrated in Figure A8(b). The game has two Nash equilibria in pure strategies. In the first, the United States plays A, which is a threat to launch a massive nuclear attack if the Soviet Union challenges the status quo, and the Soviet Union accepts the status quo by playing $\sim C$. There is no challenge in this equilibrium. In the second pure-strategy equilibrium, the Soviet Union challenges the status quo by playing C, and the United States acquiesces with S.

[8] A game is one of perfect recall if no player ever forgets what it previously knew and did. If one thinks of bridge as a two-player game in which each player is playing two hands, then bridge is a game in which there is not perfect recall. When a player is playing one hand, it cannot "remember" its other hand, which it knew when it was bidding that hand. More formally, a game has perfect recall if for any two decision nodes x and y that are in the same information set belonging to a player k, if x' is a decision node preceding x that is in one of k's information sets, then there must also be a node y' that precedes y and is in the same information set as x', and the paths leading from x' to x and from y' to y must follow the same alternatives at x' and y'. For a discussion of perfect recall and of the equivalence of these two formulations, see Luce and Raiffa (1957, pp. 159–62) or Selten (1975).

Although both equilibria are Nash (i.e., each state's strategy is a best response to the other's strategy), the first seems implausible as a solution to the game. The American strategy of A seems inherently incredible. If, in the tree in Figure A8(a), the United States must actually follow through on its threat by playing A, its payoff will be -10. But if the United States submits, it will receive -8. Assuming that the United States will act to maximize its payoff whenever it must actually act, then it will play S rather than A. Accordingly, an equilibrium based on the Soviet Union's believing that the United States will play A would seem to be an unreasonable solution for the game.[9]

Much work in game theory has been devoted to refining the notion of an equilibrium by imposing additional restrictions on combinations of strategies beyond the Nash criterion that each strategy be a best reply to the other strategies. These restrictions are intended to exclude unreasonable equilibria like the one just examined from the set of acceptable solutions to the game. One of the simplest restrictions is to demand that a solution be subgame perfect.

Before defining subgame perfection, a subgame must be described. A *subgame* is piece of a game tree that is itself a well-defined game. To find a game's subgames, start with the game's extensive form. Then pick any node in the tree and examine that node and all of the nodes in the tree that come after it. This set of nodes is informationally isolated from the rest of the tree if no information set contains some members of this set of nodes and some nodes in the rest of the tree. If this set of nodes is informationally isolated, then this set of nodes forms a well-defined game beginning at the original node and constitutes a subgame of the original game.

Consider, for example, the American decision node in the massive-retaliation game in Figure A8(a). This decision node and its successors, of which there are none, are informationally isolated. No information set connects the American node with the rest of the tree. A well-defined, albeit very simple, game begins at the American decision node. Accordingly, a subgame begins at this node. The tree in Figure A9 provides another example. A subgame begins at each of I's decision nodes. For the same reasons outlined for the massive-retaliation game, a subgame begins at the two nodes where I must choose between T and B. A subgame begins at I's first decision node because every game is a subgame of itself. This follows,

---

[9] It might at first seem that the United States would have an incentive to deviate from its strategy of playing A and thus that the combination of strategies $(A, \sim C)$ could not be a Nash equilibrium. But if the Soviet Union does play $\sim C$, then the American decision node in the tree is never reached. Regardless of what the United States would do if this node were reached, the United States will receive zero because the Soviet Union does not challenge the status quo. Every American strategy is a best reply to the Soviet strategy of not challenging the status quo. Thus, there is no incentive for the United States to deviate from A if the Soviet Union plays $\sim C$.

Figure A9. Some examples of subgames.

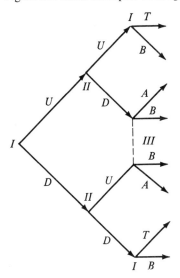

rather vacuously, from the definition of a subgame, for the first decision node (along with all the nodes that follow it) is informationally isolated from the rest of the tree, because there is no rest of the tree.

But a subgame does not begin at either of *II*'s decision nodes. *II*'s upper node and its successors are informationally linked to the rest of the tree, because one of these nodes, *III*'s upper node, is in an information set containing nodes in the rest of the tree, namely, *III*'s lower node. Thus, a well-defined game does not begin at *II*'s upper node, and so a subgame does not begin there. For similar reasons, a subgame does not begin at *II*'s lower node or at either of *III*'s decision nodes.

Given this description of a subgame, a *subgame perfect equilibrium* can be defined. A combination of strategies forms a subgame perfect equilibrium if the strategies form a Nash equilibrium in every subgame of the original game. In effect, requiring an equilibrium to be subgame perfect means that no player can threaten to play a strategy that is inherently incredible in the sense that this player has an incentive to deviate from this strategy in some subgame. A player cannot threaten to do something in a subgame when doing something else in that subgame would make the player better off. The strategy embodying such a threat would not be Nash in this subgame and so could not be part of a subgame perfect equilibrium. In this way, focusing on subgame perfect equilibria eliminates some unreasonable equilibria.[10]

---

[10] Because every game is a subgame of itself, and a subgame perfect equilibrium is Nash in every subgame, a subgame perfect equilibrium is also a Nash equilibrium. This means that the set of subgame perfect equilibria is a subset of the set of Nash equilibria.

To show that looking for subgame perfect equilibria eliminates the unreasonable equilibrium in the massive-retaliation game, first note that there are two subgames of this game. The first is the game itself, and the second is the subgame beginning at the American decision node. Now consider the strategy $(A, \sim C)$, in which the United States would attack if the Soviet Union challenged the status quo, but the Soviet Union does not dispute the status quo. As shown earlier, this set of strategies is a Nash equilibrium in the original game and therefore is also Nash in the first subgame. But this combination of strategies is not Nash in the subgame beginning at the American node. In this very simple subgame, the United States has an incentive to deviate from A. Playing A will give -10, and playing S will bring -8; the United States' best reply is to submit. Because the combination of strategies $(A, \sim C)$ is not Nash in all subgames, it is not a subgame perfect equilibrium. Thus, looking for subgame perfect equilibria rather than simply Nash equilibria will exclude the unreasonable equilibrium in the massive-retaliation game.

The other equilibrium of the massive-retaliation game, (S, C) is, however, subgame perfect. As demonstrated previously, this combination is Nash in the first subgame of the massive-retaliation game. It is also Nash in the second subgame. In the subgame beginning at the American node, the United States has no incentive to deviate from its strategy of S.

In sum, analyzing a game in terms of subgame perfect equilibria rather than solely in terms of Nash equilibria helps to eliminate some unreasonable Nash equilibria that seem to be based on inherently incredible threats.

Sequential equilibria

Requiring solutions of a game to be subgame perfect excludes some implausible equilibria. But subgame perfection is limited by the fact that many games cannot be cut into very many subgames, because the informational complexity of the games means that few sections of the game tree are informationally isolated from the rest of the tree. In such games, even subgame perfect equilibria may depend on what seem to be inherently incredible threats.

Consider the game in Figure A10. The Soviet Union has three alternatives at the beginning of the game. If it does not challenge the status quo, $\sim C$, the game ends with the status quo payoffs $(0, 0)$. The Soviet Union may also pursue a limited strategy, L, or an unlimited strategy, U. If the Soviet Union pursues a limited strategy and the United States then submits, the payoffs will be $(-4, 4)$. If, however, the Soviet Union is pursuing an unlimited strategy and the United States acquiesces, then the United States will pay a higher cost. Here the payoffs are $(-8, 8)$. Whether the Soviet Union pursues a limited or unlimited strategy, the United States can launch a massive nuclear attack, A, which will end the game with $(-10, -10)$. Finally, when the United States must decide whether to attack or submit, it does not know whether the Soviet strategy is limited or unlimited. This means, formally, that both of the American decision nodes are in the same information set.

The combination of strategies $(A, \sim C)$ in which the Soviet Union does not challenge the status quo and the United States attacks if there is a challenge is a Nash equilibrium. Given the Soviet strategy of $\sim C$, the American payoff is zero regardless of what it does. Every American strategy is a best response, and, in particular, A is a best reply. Given the American strategy of A, the best the Soviet Union can do is not challenge the status quo: $\sim C$ is the Soviet Union's best reply. Because each player's strategy is a best response to the other's strategy, $(A, \sim C)$ is a Nash equilibrium.

This combination of strategies is also subgame perfect. To see this, note that the game in Figure A10 has only one subgame, which is the game itself. A subgame does not begin at either American decision node, because the part of the tree beginning at either of these nodes is not informationally isolated from the rest of the tree. The United States' information set links the part of the tree beginning at one of the American decision nodes with the rest of the tree. Because $(A, \sim C)$ is Nash in all of the game's subgames,

Figure A10. A game with only one subgame.

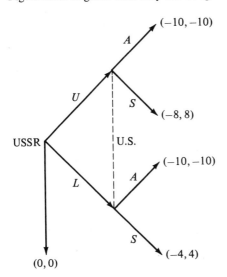

which in this case amounts to being Nash only in the game itself, $(A, \sim C)$ is subgame perfect.

Although this combination of strategies is subgame perfect, the equilibrium does not seem reasonable. The American strategy of playing A seems incredible. Just as it seemed implausible that the United States would attack in the massive-retaliation game in Figure A8(a), because if it actually had to act it would always do better by submitting, it also seems unreasonable for the United States to attack in the game in Figure A10. Whether the United States is at its upper or lower node, submitting always offers a higher payoff than attacking. Attacking at the upper node in the information set would bring -10, and submitting would bring -8. Attacking at the lower node would also yield -10, but acquiescing would be even less costly, giving -4. Accordingly, an equilibrium based on a Soviet assumption that the United States will play A would seem to be an unreasonable solution for the game.

Sequential equilibria may in part be seen as an attempt to exclude equilibria like $(A, \sim C)$ by extending the basic idea underlying subgame perfection.[11] Subgame perfection requires that each player behave reasonably in all subgames in the sense that no player can have an incentive to deviate from its equilibrium strategy in any subgame. Clearly, the United States in Figure A10 has an incentive to deviate from its strategy of A if it ever actually has to act. But because a well-defined subgame does not start at this information set, the criterion of acting reasonably in all subgames cannot rule out this American strategy. Suppose, however, one could define a player's payoffs beginning at any information set, not just from a single node at the start of a subgame. Then, just as subgame perfection requires that no player have an incentive to deviate from its strategy in any subgame, one might require that no player have an incentive to deviate from its strategy at any information set given the other players' strategies. This requirement would then rule out an equilibrium like $(A, \sim C)$ in the game in Figure A10, for the United States would always have an incentive to deviate from A. In effect, a sequential equilibrium first specifies a way of calculating a player's payoffs not just within a subgame but starting at any one of its information sets. Then a sequential equilibrium demands that no player have any incentive to deviate from its equilibrium strategy at any of its information sets.

To make this description of a sequential equilibrium meaningful, a way of calculating a player's payoffs starting from any information set must be defined. Suppose a player wanted to calculate the expected payoff of following a specific strategy starting from one of its information sets and

[11] See Kreps and Wilson (1982b) and Kreps and Ramey (1987) for a discussion of sequential equilibria.

given the other players' strategies. If the player knew where it was in this information set, then calculating this strategy's expected payoff would be easy. The player could simply trace the path through the tree starting from this node and specified by this player's strategy and the other players' strategies. Consider, for example, the problem confronting I in the simple poker game in Figure A4 if it wants to determine the expected payoff to bidding given that it has drawn a red card and that II's strategy is to bid if it has a black card and to fold if it has a red card. I knows that it has a red card, but does not know if it is at the upper-right node or the lower-left node in the information set associated with Nature dealing I a red card. If, however, I knows that it is at the upper-right node, that is to say that Nature has actually followed the branch (R, R), then I can easily calculate the expected payoff of bidding, given II's strategy. If I bids, II's strategy is to fold, because II is holding a red card. I's expected payoff is 1. Similarly, if I knows that it is at the lower-left node [i.e., Nature has dealt (R, B)], then I's expected payoff to bidding, given II's strategy (which, if holding a black card, is to bid), is -2. The problem in calculating the expected payoff of following a particular strategy at a specific information set is that a player does not know where it is in this information set. In the simple poker game, I does not know whether it is at its upper-right node or lower-left node. But suppose that a player has some beliefs about where it is in an information set. That is, a player attaches some probability to being at a specific node given that this player is somewhere in this information set. Then the expected value of following a specific strategy at this information set is the sum over all of the nodes in this information set of the probability of being at any given node times the expected utility of following this strategy starting from this node. I may, for example, believe, after drawing a red card, that the probability that it is at its upper-right node in the simple poker game is $\frac{1}{4}$. Thus, the expected payoff to bidding at this information set is the probability of being at the upper-right node times the expected payoff of bidding at this node, which is 1, plus the probability of being at the lower-left node times the utility of bidding there. This is $(\frac{1}{4})(1) + (\frac{3}{4})(-2) = -\frac{1}{2}$. In sum, once a player's beliefs about where it is in an information set are specified, then this player's expected payoff to following some strategy, given the other players' strategies, can be calculated.

To generalize this way of calculating the expected payoff at a player's information set, let i be some player in an arbitrary game. Player i is assumed to have a *system of beliefs*, which is denoted by μ_i. For each of i's information sets, μ_i specifies the probability with which i believes that it is at a particular node given that the play of the game has reached the information set containing this node. More formally, μ_i specifies the probability of being at each node conditional on being in the information set containing this node. In the simple poker game, a system of beliefs for I would define the probability that I would be at the upper-right node and the lower-left node given that I was at the information set associated with its holding a red card. I might, for example, believe, as before, that these probabilities were $\frac{1}{4}$ and $\frac{3}{4}$, respectively. I's system of beliefs, μ_I, would also have to specify what I would believe should it find itself holding a black card. Recalling that each player is assumed to have a system of beliefs, let μ denote the set of all the players' belief systems. In the simple poker game, $\mu = \{\mu_I, \mu_{II}\}$. Accordingly, μ specifies for each node in the game the probability that the player who owns this node attaches to being at this node given that the play of the game has reached the information set containing this node. Now let (μ, π) be an *assessment* of a game, where μ is a system of beliefs and π is a combination of the players' strategies that provides a complete plan for playing the game. An assessment contains enough information to permit the calculation of a player's expected utility to following a particular strategy at any one of its information sets. With π, one can calculate any player's expected payoff to following this strategy starting from a specific node in this information set. Then, with μ specifying the relative likelihood of being at a particular node in this information set, one can calculate the expected payoff to following this strategy at this information set, as was done earlier in the poker-game example.

A *sequential equilibrium* can now be defined as a special type of assessment. More specifically, an assessment (μ, π) is a sequential equilibrium if it satisfies two conditions. The first is that the assessment must be *sequentially rational*. This means that no player has an incentive to deviate from its strategy at any one of its informations sets given its beliefs and the other players' strategies. This is merely the extension of the basic idea underlying subgame perfection.

To clarify what it means to be sequentially rational, consider the following assessment. I's strategy is to bid if dealt a black card and to fold with a red card. II's strategy is always to bid: $\pi = (\pi_I, \pi_{II}) = (\{(B, b), (R, f)\}, \{(B, b), (R, b)\})$. Suppose further that I believes that if it is holding a red card, the chance that II's card is black is $\frac{1}{2}$, and therefore the probability that II's card is red is also $\frac{1}{2}$. Or, equivalently, given that play has reached the information set belonging to I at which I holds a red card, then the probability of actually being at the lower-left node in this information set is $\frac{1}{2}$. Similarly, I also believes that if it has been dealt a black card, then the probability that II has been dealt a red card is $\frac{1}{2}$, and the chance that it has a black card is also $\frac{1}{2}$. II's beliefs are simpler. Regardless of what its card is, II is certain that I has a red card. Momentarily setting aside the question of whether or not these beliefs are reasonable, the assessment composed of this system of beliefs and strategies is sequentially rational.

To be sequentially rational, no player can have any incentive to deviate from its strategy given its beliefs and the other players' strategies. *II* clearly has no reason to change its strategy given its beliefs. Believing that *I* is certain to be holding a red card, bidding brings 2 if *II*'s card is black, and 0 if *II*'s card is red. Folding always brings -1. Given *II*'s beliefs, bidding is its best reply. *I* also has no incentive to alter its strategy given its beliefs and *II*'s strategy. Given that *II* will always bid, *I*'s payoff to bidding if it has a black card is 0 if *II* actually has a black card, and 2 if *II*'s card is red. *I* believes that the probability that *II*'s card is black is $\frac{1}{2}$; so *I*'s expected payoff to bidding is $(0)(\frac{1}{2}) + (2)(\frac{1}{2}) = 1$. If, however, *I* deviates by folding with a black card, its payoff will be -1. If, instead, *I* tries a mixed strategy of bidding with probability p, then this strategy's payoff is the probability of bidding times the expected payoff to bidding plus the probability of not bidding times the payoff to that. So a mixed strategy yields $p(1) + (1-p)(-1) = 2p - 1$, which is also less than or equal to 1. Thus, *I* cannot improve its payoff by deviating; bidding with a black card is *I*'s best reply given its beliefs. A similar argument shows that folding with a red card is *I*'s best response given its beliefs and *II*'s strategy. No player has any incentive to deviate from its strategy given its beliefs and the other player's strategy; so this assessment is sequentially rational.

Sequential rationality is one of two conditions an assessment must satisfy in order to be a sequential equilibrium. The second condition has to do with the system of beliefs. Just as some Nash equilibria were excluded because the strategies seemed unreasonable, some belief systems seem unreasonable and will be excluded. Indeed, although the assessment just described is sequentially rational, the beliefs underlying it do not seem sensible. When *II* bids, it is, according to its system of beliefs, certain that *I*'s card is red. But *II* will bid only if *I* has already bid, and *I*, according to its strategy, will bid only if it has a black card. Given *I*'s strategy, *II* should believe that *I* is holding a black card if and when *II* has to decide whether or not to bid. *II*'s beliefs are incompatible with *I*'s strategy.

The second condition an assessment must satisfy if it is to be a sequential equilibrium is that the belief system must be "reasonable" in the sense that it is *consistent*.[12] Requiring beliefs to be consistent entails a number of subtleties and difficulties.[13] Fortunately, the games analyzed in the

[12] The questions what constitute "reasonable" beliefs and, more generally, how to "refine" Nash equilibria in order to eliminate the unreasonable ones have motivated an immense amount of recent work in game theory. For further discussion of this, see Kreps and Wilson (1982b), Rubinstein (1985), Grossman and Perry (1986), Banks and Sobel (1987), Kreps and Ramey (1987), and Cho (1987).

[13] See Kreps and Wilson (1982b) and Kreps and Ramey (1987) for the formal definition of a consistent assessment and some of its subtleties.

preceding chapters are sufficiently simple that these difficulties and subtleties do not arise. The only important consistency criterion for the models examined in the preceding chapters is that the system of beliefs satisfy Bayes' rule where this rule can be applied. An assessment like this that is sequentially rational and satisfies Bayes' rule where this rule applies is a *perfect Bayesian equilibrium*.[14] Bayes' rule is a means of revising a prior probability in light of some new information or evidence. In the present context, Bayes' rule provides a way of updating a prior probability of reaching a given decision node in light of play having actually reached the information set containing this node. It provides a way, for example, for *I*, after being dealt a red card, to revise the belief it held before the deal that red cards would be dealt to both it and *II*.

Bayesian updating of beliefs is crucial to understanding the dynamics of the models analyzed in this volume. But before discussing Bayesian updating in a game-theoretic context where strategic interactions must be taken into account, it will be useful to discuss Bayesian updating in a simpler context in which there is only one player and no strategic interaction. Suppose that an urn can be filled with either of two possible mixtures. The urn may contain seventy-five green marbles and twenty-five blue ones, or it may hold twenty-five green marbles and seventy-five blue ones. The player believes that the two mixtures are equally likely. (This probability might be a subjective estimate; it could be based on a statistical analysis of some previously obtained data, or, if guessing the contents of this urn was a rather dull parlor game, then this probability might be due to the way that the mixture was chosen, say by flipping a coin.) Now the player is allowed to draw two marbles. Both are green. Given this new evidence, how should the player update the probability that the mixture is 75 percent green? Bayes' rule provides a means of doing this.

The key to Bayes' rule is to observe that there are two ways of thinking about the probability that two events, say X and Y, will happen. Let $P(X \cap Y)$ denote the probability that both X and Y will occur. In the urn example, X is the event "two green marbles are drawn," and Y is the event "the mixture is 75 percent green." One way to think about the probability that both X and Y will happen is that this is the same as the probability that X will happen, given that Y will occur, times the probability that Y will happen. The probability that X will happen given that Y will occur is the *conditional probability of X given Y* and is denoted by $P(X \mid Y)$. In the example, $P(X \mid Y)$ is the probability of drawing two green marbles given that the mixture is 75 percent green. This is the probability that the first draw

---

[14] This is the weakest notion of a perfect Bayesian equilibrium. Stronger ones are obtained by making assumptions about what "reasonable" beliefs are where Bayes' rule cannot be applied.

will be green, which is $\frac{75}{100}$, times the probability that the second marble will be green, which, because there are only ninety-nine marbles left and seventy-four are green, is $\frac{74}{99}$. The probability of drawing two greens is therefore $(\frac{75}{100})(\frac{74}{99}) = 0.561$. Letting $P(Y)$ be the initial or *prior probability* of Y, which in this example is the initial probability of a mostly green mixture or $\frac{1}{2}$, then the probability of both X and Y is equal to the chance of X happening, given Y, times the probability of Y occurring, or $P(X \cap Y) = P(X \mid Y)P(Y) = (0.561)(\frac{1}{2}) = 0.280$.

But there is another way to think about the chances that both X and Y will happen. This is also the probability that Y will occur, given X, times the probability that X will happen, or $P(X \cap Y) = P(Y \mid X)P(X)$. The conditional probability $P(Y \mid X)$ is, in the example, the probability that the mixture is 75 percent green given that both the drawn marbles are green. This, moreover, is the updated probability that the player is trying to calculate.

To find an expression for this updated probability, bring together the two ways of thinking about the chances that both X and Y will occur, to obtain $P(Y \mid X)P(X) = P(X \cap Y) = P(X \mid Y)P(Y)$. Solving this for the updated probability that the player is trying to calculate, $P(Y \mid X)$, gives Bayes' rule for updating probabilities: $P(Y \mid X) = P(X \cap Y)/P(X) = P(X \mid Y)P(Y)/P(X)$. That is, the probability of Y, given X, is the probability of X and Y divided by the prior probability of X. Or, in the urn example, the probability of a 75 percent green mixture, given that two greens have been drawn, is the probability of a mostly green mixture and a draw of two greens divided by the prior probability of drawing two greens. These probabilities are readily calculated. The former, as calculated earlier, is the probability of two greens, given a mostly green mixture, times the prior probability of a mostly green mixture, or $(0.561)(\frac{1}{2}) = 0.280$. The prior probability of drawing two greens, $P(X)$, is the probability of two greens, given a mostly green mixture, times the probability of a mostly green mixture plus the probability of drawing two greens from a mostly blue mixture times the probability of a mostly blue mixture. This is $(\frac{75}{100})(\frac{74}{99})(\frac{1}{2}) + (\frac{25}{100})(\frac{24}{99})(\frac{1}{2}) = 0.311$. Thus, the Bayesian update of the chance that the mixture is mostly green after two green marbles have been drawn is $0.280/0.311 = 0.902$. After drawing two green marbles, the prior probability that the mixture was mostly green, which was $\frac{1}{2}$, has been updated to 0.902.

Returning now to a game-theoretic context, consider I's beliefs in the sequentially rational assessment described earlier for the simple poker game. They are consistent with Bayes' rule, as they must be in a sequential equilibrium or in a perfect Bayesian equilibrium. The prior probability of being at any one of I's decision nodes is $\frac{1}{4}$. That is, before the deal, I's estimate or prior probability of being at a specific decision node, say the node associated with Nature's dealing (R, R), is $\frac{1}{4}$. But after the deal, I knows that it is holding a red card and can then revise its beliefs to incorporate this new information. According to Bayes' rule, the probability of being at (R, R), given that play has reached I's information set associated with I's holding a red card, is the prior probability of being at (R, R), which is $\frac{1}{4}$, divided by the probability that the play of the game will reach this information set. This latter probability is simply the sum of the probabilities of reaching all of the individual nodes in this information set or, in this case, the probability of reaching (R, R) plus the probability of reaching (R, B), which is $\frac{1}{2}$. Bayes' rule assigns a probability of $(\frac{1}{4})/(\frac{1}{4} + \frac{1}{4}) = \frac{1}{2}$ to being at (R, R), given that I knows it is holding a red card. This is precisely what I's belief system in the sequentially rational assessment says that I believes about II's card, given that I is holding a red card. I's beliefs are consistent with Bayes' rule.

Now consider II's beliefs. When bidding, II believes that I is certain to be holding a red card. As noted earlier, this belief seems unreasonable, given I's strategy, because II will have an opportunity to bid only if I bids, and I will bid only if its card is black. Indeed, the only thing that it seems reasonable for II to believe about I's card, given I's strategy, is that I's card is black. Requiring beliefs to be consistent with Bayes' rule simply formalizes this reasoning, and this shows that II's beliefs do not conform to Bayes' rule. The sequentially rational assessment described earlier is therefore not a sequential equilibrium.

To see that II's beliefs are incompatible with Bayes' rule, suppose that II holds a black card, and I bids. II, therefore, is somewhere in its lower information set in Figure A4. But where does II believe it is? What, for example, is the probability that it is at the upper-left node? Or, equivalently, what is the probability that Nature has dealt (B, B) and I has bid? The first step in calculating this probability is to find the prior probability of reaching this node (i.e., the probability of reaching this node as calculated before the game begins). This is the probability that Nature will deal (B, B) times the probability that I will bid with this deal. Nature will deal (B, B) with probability $\frac{1}{4}$, and I, according to its strategy, will always bid when dealt a black card. The prior probability of reaching II's upper-left decision node in its lower information set is $\frac{1}{4}$. Similarly, the probability of reaching the lower-right node in this information set is the probability that Nature will deal (R, B) and that I will bid. This is $(\frac{1}{4})(0) = 0$. The updated probability of being at II's upper-left node, given that I has actually bid, or, in other words, that play has actually reached the information set containing this decision node, is then obtained by dividing the prior probability of reaching this node by the probability of reaching this information set. This latter probability is $\frac{1}{4} + 0$; so the updated probability is $(\frac{1}{4})/(\frac{1}{4}) = 1$. That is, II, according to Bayes' rule, is certain that it is at its upper-left decision node.

Similarly, II believes that the probability that I is holding a red card when II is actually bidding is $0/(\frac{1}{4}+0)=0$, not 1 as in the sequentially rational assessment. Beliefs in this assessment are not in accord with Bayes' rule, and this means that the assessment cannot be a sequential equilibrium.

To state the requirement that beliefs satisfy Bayes' rule somewhat more generally, let y be some decision node, and let h be the information set containing y. Then, for any assessment (μ, π), the probability of reaching y can be calculated. Let $P(y|(\mu, \pi))$ denote this probability. Similarly, the probability of reaching h can be calculated. It is $P(h|(\mu, \pi)) = \sum_{x \in h} P(x|(\mu, \pi))$, where x is a node in h, and the summation is taken over all of the nodes in h. Then, if $P(h|(\mu, \pi)) > 0$, Bayes' rule says that the probability of being at y, given that play has actually reached h, is $P(y|(\mu, \pi))/P(h|(\mu, \pi))$.

Clearly, Bayes' rule cannot be applied if the probability of reaching an information set is zero [i.e., if $P(h|(\mu, \pi)) = 0$], for trying to use the rule in this case would entail dividing by zero. However, as long as $P(h|(\mu, \pi)) > 0$, Bayes' rule can be used, and the only consistency criterion required of beliefs in the models in this volume is that beliefs satisfy Bayes' rule at information sets where this rule can be applied.[15]

Games of incomplete information

The final issue to be discussed is the problem of incomplete information.[16] Players in a situation may have incomplete information about the other

---

[15] What distinguishes a sequential equilibrium from the weakest notion of a perfect Bayesian equilibrium, which is the one employed here, is that a sequential equilibrium places weak consistency restrictions on beliefs at information sets that are reached with probability zero. To describe a consistent assessment and to specify more formally what conditions consistent beliefs must satisfy at information sets that are reached with zero probability, let π^1 be a completely mixed set of strategies for playing the game. A set of strategies is completely mixed if each participant plays every alternative at each of its information sets with a positive probability. That is, no alternative is played with zero probability in π^1. Because every alternative is played with positive probability, every information set h is reached with positive probability. Accordingly, Bayes' rule can be applied at every information set in the game. Let $\mu^1(y)$ be the probability of being at y given that play has reached the information set containing y, which will be denoted by $h(y)$. Then, by Bayes' rule, $\mu^1(y) = P(y|\pi^1)/P(h(y)|\pi^1)$. In brief, Bayes' rule can always be used to define a system of beliefs μ^1 when π^1 is completely mixed. An assessment (μ, π) is consistent if and only if there exists a sequence of completely mixed assessments that converges to (μ, π). Symbolically, there must exist a sequence of $\{(\mu^i, \pi^i)\}_{i=1}^{\infty}$, where the π^i are completely mixed and are such that $\lim_{i \to \infty}(\mu^i, \pi^i) = (\mu, \pi)$. For a detailed discussion of consistency and some of the subtleties associated with it, see Kreps and Wilson (1982b) and Kreps and Ramey (1987).

[16] Harsanyi (1967–8) originated this approach.

players. A player may be uncertain of the other players' payoffs or of the set of alternatives from which the other players can choose. In crises, for example, states often are said to be unsure of the resolve of their adversaries. That is, a state lacks complete information about its adversary's willingness to run risks or about what the adversary sees as being at stake in the crisis. Games of incomplete information are used to model situations in which players are uncertain about some aspects of the situations confronting them. An important feature about these games is that players can try to learn about the other players by observing what they do. Of course, an adversary, understanding this, also may have an incentive to try to misrepresent its type, to try, for example, to appear to be more resolute than it actually is. Games of incomplete information are used to study these competing influences and their effects on the players' strategies.

An example may be the best way to illustrate how games of incomplete information are set up and analyzed. The example is a variant of the simple model of massive retaliation used earlier in the discussion of subgame perfection. In this variant, the Soviet Union is uncertain of the cost to the United States of acquiescing to a Soviet challenge. Suppose, that is, that when the United States is relatively invulnerable to Soviet retaliation, the United States attempts to prevent a Soviet challenge by threatening to retaliate massively to a Soviet provocation. In the game, the status quo payoffs are $(0, 0)$, and the respective payoffs to the United States and the Soviet Union will be $(-5, -10)$ if there is a Soviet challenge and a massive American nuclear attack in response. (The payoff of -5 reflects an assumed relative American invulnerability.) The Soviet Union will also receive 5 if the United States acquiesces to a Soviet challenge. The Soviet Union, however, lacks complete information about the United States. In particular, the Soviet Union is unsure if the United States attaches a high value to what is at stake, so that submission will bring a large loss of -7, or if the United States puts a low value on what is at stake, so that submission will bring only a small loss of -3.

Figure A11(a) shows the tree and payoffs if the cost to giving in is high, and Figure A11(b) depicts the tree and payoffs if the cost is low. The problem would be easy to analyze if the Soviet Union were sure of the American payoff to acquiescing. If the cost to giving in were known to be high, the Soviet Union would be in the game in Figure A11(a), where the unique subgame perfect equilibrium is for the Soviet Union not to challenge and for the United States to attack if challenged. Similarly, if the cost of American acquiescence were known to be low, the game in Figure A11(b) would be the relevant one. Here the unique subgame perfect equilibrium has the Soviet Union challenging the status quo and the United States submitting.

The difficulty is, of course, that the Soviet Union is uncertain whether the cost to the United States of submitting is high or low. To model this lack of complete information, the two games in Figure A11 are combined into a single, larger game. Suppose that the Soviet Union believes that the probability that the United States attaches a high cost to submitting is ρ, and the probability of a low cost is $1 - \rho$. Then the games in Figure A11 may be combined to form the game in Figure A12. This game begins with Nature making a random move. This is the modeling device used to create the Soviet Union's uncertainty about the American cost of submission. If Nature takes the upper branch, which it will do with probability ρ, then the rest of the tree beginning at the Soviet decision node is the same as the tree in Figure A11(a). (The prime on "U.S." indicates that along this path through the tree, the United States attaches a high cost to submitting and will play accordingly.) Thus, if the Soviet Union were certain that it was at the upper node in its information set in the game in Figure A12, this game would be played in exactly the same way as the game in Figure A11(a). Similarly, if Nature takes the lower branch, which it will do with probability $1 - \rho$, then the rest of the game starting from the Soviet Union's lower decision node corresponds to the tree in Figure A11(b). If the Soviet Union were certain that it was at this lower node, then the game in Figure A12 would be played just like the game in Figure A11(b). The Soviet Union, however, does not know if it is at its upper or lower node, for they are in the same information set. Rather, the Soviet Union forms beliefs about where it is in its information set. Following Bayes' rule, the Soviet Union believes

Figure A11. Massive retaliation with high and low stakes.

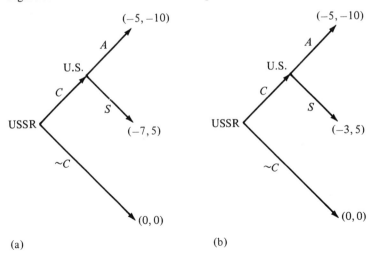

(a)   (b)

that it is at its upper node with probability ρ and at its lower node with probability $1 - \rho$. In effect, the Soviet Union begins the game believing that the probability that the United States attaches a high cost to submitting is ρ and that the probability that the United States attaches a low cost is $1 - \rho$. In this way, the larger game in Figure A12 models the Soviet Union's lack of complete information and beliefs about the American payoffs. This game can then be solved for its sequential equilibria, and the equilibrium strategies in this larger game will incorporate the Soviet Union's uncertainty about the American payoffs.

A second example of an incomplete-information game will illustrate the interaction between beliefs and strategies. In this game, which is depicted in Figure A13(a), a potential challenger, C, begins by deciding whether or not to challenge the status quo. If it decides not to mount a challenge, the game ends with continuation of the status quo. If the potential challenger disputes the status quo, the defender, D, can either resist, R, or submit, S. If the defender submits, the game ends. If it resists, then the challenger must decide whether to attack, A, or back down, S.

Figure A12. Massive retaliation with incomplete information.

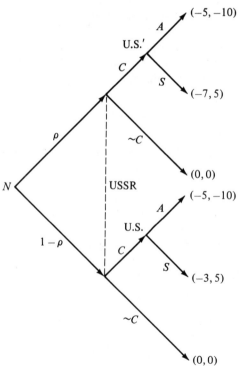

The status quo payoffs are (0, 0), where the first element of this pair is the challenger's payoff. If the defender submits, the challenger receives 10, and the defender loses 10. If the defender resists and the challenger backs down, the challenger loses 10, and the defender gains 10. If the challenger attacks, the defender's payoff to the ensuing war is -15. The defender is, however, uncertain of the challenger's payoff to fighting. There are two possibilities. (There could, of course, be more possibilities, but that would make the resulting game difficult to analyze.) The challenger's payoff to attacking may be sufficiently low, say -15, that it will prefer backing down to attacking if D resists the challenge. These are the payoffs in Figure A13(a). Or the challenger's payoff to fighting may be high enough, say -5, that it will rather attack than submit if resisted. Figure A13(b) shows these payoffs, where C' denotes the more determined challenger.

As in the massive-retaliation example, the situation would be easy to analyze if the defender were certain of the challenger's payoffs. If, as in Figure A13(a), the challenger's payoff to attacking is so low that it will

Figure A13. Escalation with different payoffs to fighting.

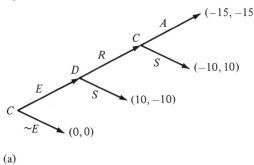

(a)

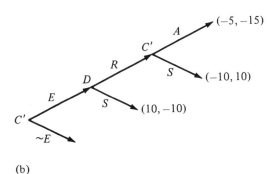

(b)

prefer backing down to attacking, then the defender should resist, for the challenger will then submit. Indeed, foreseeing that it will eventually back down, the potential challenger will not even dispute the status quo. The unique subgame perfect equilibrium of the game in Figure A13(a) has the potential challenger accepting the status quo, the defender resisting if challenged, and the challenger backing down. (Remember that an equilibrium describes what will be done at every information set even if in equilibrium some of these information sets are not reached.)

If the defender is certain that the challenger prefers attacking to backing down, then resistance will bring −5, whereas submitting will cost only 10. In this case, *D* will not resist, and the potential challenger will actually challenge the status quo. The unique subgame perfect equilibrium for the game in Figure A13(b) is for the challenger to mount a challenge, the defender to submit, and the challenger to fight should the defender resist.

But the defender is uncertain of the challenger's payoffs. Suppose the prior probability of facing a challenger that prefers fighting is ρ, and the probability of confronting a challenger that would rather quit is $1 - \rho$. The game in Figure A14 represents this situation. Once again, incomplete information is modeled by having Nature begin the game with a random move that leaves *D* uncertain about the type of its adversary.

Note, however, that what the defender believes about the challenger

Figure A14. Escalation with incomplete information.

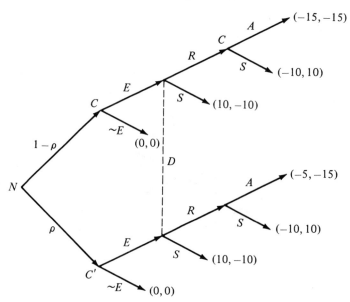

depends both on the defender's prior belief and on what the challenger does. This was not an issue in the previous example of an incomplete-information game, because the Soviet Union moved before the United States. Thus, the Soviet Union, which was the state that lacked complete information about its adversary in that example, could not update its beliefs about the United States' payoffs based on what the United States had actually done. This new information was not yet available. In the current example, however, the uncertain state, D, decides what to do after the other state has moved. Accordingly, the defender can update its prior belief about the challenger's willingness to fight in light of the challenger's decision whether or not to challenge the status quo.

To illustrate the interdependence between the challenger's strategy and the defender's updated beliefs, suppose initially that both C and C' are certain to escalate. Intuitively, if C and C' will behave identically, there is nothing to be learned from seeing what the challenger actually does. The updated probability of facing a particular type of challenger will not differ from the prior probability of facing that type of challenger. That is what Bayes' rule shows. The probability of facing the determined challenger C' if D has actually been challenged, according to Bayes' rule, is the prior probability of reaching the lower decision node in D's information set divided by the probability that play will actually reach this information set. The prior probability of reaching the lower decision node is the prior probability of facing the more determined challenger C', which is the probability that Nature will follow the lower branch times the probability that C' will mount a challenge. Given that the more determined challenger's strategy is always to mount a challenge, the prior probability of reaching D's lower node is $\rho \cdot 1 = \rho$. The probability of actually reaching D's information set, that is, the probability that the potential challenger will really challenge the status quo, is the probability that Nature will take the upper branch, which is $1 - \rho$, times the probability that C will challenge the status quo plus the probability that Nature will follow the lower branch, which is ρ, times the probability that C' will challenge the status quo. This is $\rho \cdot 1 + (1 - \rho) \cdot 1 = 1$. So the probability of facing C', given the potential challengers' strategies and the fact that the status quo has actually been challenged, is ρ. If both types of challengers will behave in the same way, the challenger's actual behavior reveals nothing about it, and the Bayesian update of the probability of facing a specific type of challenger is unchanged from the prior probability.

But suppose that the two types of challengers will behave differently. Then, observing what has actually happened may say something about the type of the challenger. To illustrate this, assume that the determined challenger still will be certain to dispute the status quo, but the probability that the less determined challenger will dispute the status quo is 0.1. If, given these strategies, the defender is challenged, it would seem that the chance that the challenger is more determined rather than less is quite high. The updated probability of facing C' rather than C is high. Bayes' rule again formalizes this. The updated probability of facing C' if there has been a challenge is the prior probability of facing C', which is still ρ, divided by the probability of there being a challenge or, equivalently, of play actually reaching D's information set. This latter probability is, as before, the prior probability of facing C' times the probability that C' will dispute the status quo plus the prior probability of facing C times the probability that it will challenge the status quo. The updated probability of facing C', given the potential challengers' strategies and the fact that there has been a challenge, is $\rho/[\rho \cdot 1 + (1-\rho)(0.1)]$, which is much greater than ρ. (If, for example, $\rho = 0.25$, then the updated probability is $(0.25)/[(0.25)+(1-0.25)(0.1)] = 0.77$.)

In this case, the defender has used what has actually happened in the game to revise its beliefs about the type of its adversary. This is a common feature of games of incomplete information. Of course, the challenger realizes that the defender is trying to ascertain the challenger's type by watching what it does. This may create an incentive for the challenger to behave differently than it otherwise would in order to misrepresent its type. C, for example, may want to try to convince the defender that it is facing C' and thus should not resist a challenge. These are some of the issues that games of incomplete information and their sequential equilibria help to illuminate.

In both examples of incomplete-information games there was one-sided incomplete information. Only the Soviet Union was uncertain about some aspects of the United States; the United States was completely certain of the relevant aspects of the Soviet Union. Similarly, only the defender was uncertain of some aspects of the situation in the second example. Nevertheless, the same approach to modeling incomplete information may be extended to the case in which every player is uncertain about some aspects of the other players. Incomplete information can, in general, be modeled by creating a game in which Nature will behave probabilistically, so that each player will begin this game with beliefs that reflect its uncertainty or lack of complete information about the other players. The equilibrium strategies in this often very large and complicated game will then reflect the players' incomplete information and the players' attempts to resolve and exploit this uncertainty.

References

Axelrod, Robert (1981). "The Emergence of Cooperation Among Egoists." *American Political Science Review*, 75, 306–18.

Axelrod, Robert (1984). *The Evolution of Cooperation.* New York: Basic Books.

Ball, Desmond (1980). *Politics and Force Levels.* Berkeley: University of California Press.

Ball, Desmond (1981). *Can Nuclear War Be Controlled?* London: International Institute for Strategic Studies.

Ball, Desmond (1982–3). "U.S. Strategic Forces: How Would They Be Used?" *International Security*, 7, 31–60.

Ball, Desmond (1985–6). "Nuclear War at Sea." *International Security*, 10, 3–31.

Banks, Jeffrey, and Joel Sobel (1987). "Equilibrium Selection in Signalling Games." *Econometrica*, 55, 647–61.

Betts, Richard K. (1987). *Nuclear Blackmail and Nuclear Balance.* Washington, D.C.: Brookings Institution.

Blair, Bruce G. (1985). *Strategic Command and Control.* Washington, D.C.: Brookings Institution.

Bracken, Paul (1983). *The Command and Control of Nuclear Forces.* New Haven: Yale University Press.

Brams, Steven J. (1985) *Superpower Games.* New Haven: Yale University Press.

Brams, Steven J., and D. Marc Kilgour (1985). "Optimal Deterrence." *Social Philosophy and Policy*, 3, 118–35.

Brams, Steven J., and D. Marc Kilgour (1987). "Threat Escalation and Crisis Stability." *American Political Science Review*, 81, 833–50.

Brams, Steven J., and D. Marc Kilgour (1988). *Game Theory and National Security.* New York: Basil Blackwell.

Brodie, Bernard (1959). *Strategy in the Missile Age.* Princeton University Press.

Brodie, Bernard (1966). *Escalation and the Nuclear Option.* Princeton University Press.

Carter, Ashton B. (1987). "Sources of Error and Uncertainty." In Ashton B. Carter, John D. Steinbruner, and Charles A. Zracket (eds.), *Managing Nuclear Operations*, pp. 611–39. Washington, D.C.: Brookings Institution.

Cho, In-Koo (1987). "A Refinement of Sequential Equilibrium." *Econometrica*, 55, 1367–89.

Clausewitz, Carl von (1976). *On War*, edited and translated by Michael Howard and Peter Paret. Princeton University Press.

Davis, Lynn Etheridge (1976). *Limited Nuclear Options: Deterrence and the New American Doctrine.* London: International Institute for Strategic Studies.

Ellsberg, Daniel (1959). "The Theory and Practice of Blackmail." In Oran Young (ed.), *Bargaining: Formal Theories of Negotiations* (1975), pp. 343–63. Urbana: University of Illinois Press.

Enthoven, Alain C., and Wayne K. Smith (1971). *How Much Is Enough?* New York: Harper & Row.

Freedman, Lawrence (1986). "The First Two Generations of Nuclear Strategists." In Peter Paret (ed.), *Makers of Modern Strategy*, pp. 735–78. Princeton University Press.

Freedman, Lawrence (1989). *The Evolution of Nuclear Strategy*, 2d ed. London: Macmillan.

Gaddis, John Lewis (1981). *Strategies of Containment*. Oxford University Press.

Grossman, Sanford, and Motty Perry (1986). "Sequential Bargaining Under Asymmetric Information." *Journal of Economic Theory*, 39, 120–54.

Halperin, Morton H. (1963). *Limited War in the Nuclear Age*. New York: Wiley.

Harsanyi, John C. (1967–8). "Games with Incomplete Information Played by 'Bayesian' Players." Parts I–III. *Management Science*, 14, 159–82, 320–34, 486–502.

Harsanyi, John C. (1973). "Games with Randomly Distributed Payoffs: A New Rationale for Mixed-Strategy Equilibrium Points." *International Journal of Game Theory*, 2, 1–23.

Harsanyi, John C., and Reinhard Selten (1988). *A Theory of Equilibrium Selection in Games*. Cambridge, Mass.: Massachusetts Institute of Technology Press.

Hinsley, F. H. (1963). *Power and the Pursuit of Peace*. Cambridge University Press.

Jervis, Robert (1972). "Bargaining and Bargaining Tactics." In J. Roland Pennock and John W. Chapman (eds.), *Coercion*, pp. 272–88. Chicago: Aldine-Atherton.

Jervis, Robert (1976). *Perception and Misperception in International Politics*. Princeton University Press.

Jervis, Robert (1978). "Cooperation Under the Security Dilemma." *World Politics*, 30, 167–214.

Jervis, Robert (1979). "Deterrence Theory Revisited." *World Politics*, 31, 289–323.

Jervis, Robert (1979–80). "Why Nuclear Superiority Doesn't Matter." *Political Science Quarterly*, 94, 617–33.

Jervis, Robert (1982–3). "Deterrence and Perception." *International Security*, 7, 3–30.

Jervis, Robert (1984). *The Illogic of American Nuclear Strategy*. Ithaca, N.Y.: Cornell University Press.

Jervis, Robert (1986). "The Nuclear Revolution and the Common Defense." *Political Science Quarterly*, 101, 689–703.

Jervis, Robert, Richard Ned Lebow, and Janet Gross Stein (1985). *Psychology and Deterrence*. Baltimore: Johns Hopkins University Press.

Kahan, Jerome H. (1975). *Security in the Nuclear Age*, Washington, D.C.: Brookings Institution.

Kahn, Herman (1962). "Some Comments on Controlled Nuclear War." In Klaus Knorr and Thorton Read (eds.), *Limited Strategic War*, pp. 32–66. Princeton University Press.

Kahn, Herman (1965). *On Escalation: Metaphors and Scenarios.* New York: Praeger.

Kaplan, Morton A. (1962). "Limited Retaliation as a Bargaining Process." In Klaus Knorr and Thorton Read (eds.), *Limited Strategic War*, pp. 142–62. Princeton University Press.

Kaufmann, William W. (1956). "The Requirements of Deterrence." In William W. Kaufmann (ed.), *Military Policy and National Security*, pp. 12–38. Princeton University Press.

Knorr, Klaus (1962). "Limited Strategic War." In Klaus Knorr and Thorton Read (eds.), *Limited Strategic War*, pp. 3–37. Princeton University Press.

Kohn, Richard H., and Joseph P. Harahan (eds.) (1988). "U.S. Strategic Air Power, 1948–1962: Excerpts from an Interview with Generals Curtis E. LeMay, Leon W. Johnson, David A. Burchinal, and Jack J. Catton." *International Security*, 27, 78–95.

Kreps, David M., Paul Milgrom, John Roberts, and Robert Wilson (1982). "Rational Cooperation in the Finitely Repeated Prisoners' Dilemma." *Journal of Economic Theory*, 27, 245–52.

Kreps, David M., and Garey Ramey (1987). "Structural Consistency, Consistency, and Sequential Rationality." *Econometrica*, 55, 1331–48.

Kreps, David M., and Robert Wilson (1982a). "Reputation and Imperfect Information." *Journal of Economic Theory*, 27, 253–79.

Kreps, David M., and Robert Wilson (1982b). "Sequential Equilibria." *Econometrica*, 50, 862–87.

Langlois, Jean-Pierre P. (1988). "Rational Deterrence and Crisis Stability." Unpublished manuscript, Department of Mathematics, San Francisco State University.

Lebow, Richard Ned (1981). *Between Peace and War.* Baltimore: Johns Hopkins University Press.

Litwak, Robert S. (1984). *Detente and the Nixon Doctrine.* Cambridge University Press.

Luce, R. Duncan, and Howard Raiffa (1957). *Games and Decisions.* New York: Wiley.

McNamara, Robert S. (1962). "Defense Arrangements of the North Atlantic Community." Address given at the University of Michigan, Ann Arbor, June 16, 1962. *Department of State Bulletin*, 47(July 9, 1962), 67.

Maxwell, Stephen (1968). *Rationality in Deterrence.* London: International Institute for Strategic Studies.

Milgrom, Paul, and John Roberts (1982). "Predation, Reputation, and Entry Deterrence." *Journal of Economic Theory*, 27, 280–312.

Myerson, Roger B. (1985). "Bayesian Equilibrium and Incentive Compatibility: An Introduction." In Leonid Hurwicz, David Schmeidler, and Hugo Sonnenschine (eds.), *Social Goals and Social Organization*, pp. 229–59. Cambridge University Press.

Nalebuff, Barry (1986). "Brinkmanship and Nuclear Deterrence: The Neutrality of Escalation." *Conflict Management and Peace Science*, 9, 19–30.

Nixon, Richard (1971). *United States Foreign Policy for the 1970's: Building for Peace.* Report to Congress (February 25, 1971), 170.

O'Neill, Barry (1986). "International Escalation and the Dollar Auction." *Journal of Conflict Resolutions,* 30, 33–50.

O'Neill, Barry (1987). "A Measure of Crisis Instability with an Application to Space-Based Antimissile Systems." *Journal of Conflict Resolution,* 31, 631–72.

Ordeshook, Peter C. (1986). *Game Theory and Political Theory.* Cambridge University Press.

Owen, Guillermo (1982). *Game Theory.* New York; Academic Press.

Powell, Robert (1985). "The Theoretical Foundations of Strategic Nuclear Deterrence." *Political Science Quarterly,* 100, 75–96.

Powell, Robert (1987). "Crisis Bargaining, Escalation, and MAD." *American Political Science Review,* 81, 717–35.

Powell, Robert (1988). "Nuclear Brinkmanship with Two-Sided Incomplete Information." *American Political Science Review,* 82, 155–78.

Powell, Robert (1989a). "Crisis Stability in the Nuclear Age." *American Political Science Review,* 83, 61–76.

Powell, Robert (1989b). "Nuclear Deterrence Theory and the Strategy of Limited Retaliation." *American Political Science Review,* 83, 503–19.

Powell, Robert (1989c). "The Dynamics of Longer Brinkmanship Crises." In Peter C. Ordeshook (ed.), *Models of Strategic Choice in Politics,* pp. 151–75. Ann Arbor: University of Michigan Press.

Quester, George (1966). *Deterrence Before Hiroshima.* New York: Wiley.

Reston, James (1954). *New York Times,* January 17, 1954.

Rosenberg, David Alan (1983). "The Origins of Overkill." *International Security,* 7, 3–71.

Rubinstein, Ariel (1982). "Perfect Equilibrium in a Bargaining Model." *Econometrica,* 50, 97–109.

Rubinstein, Ariel (1985). "Choice of Conjectures in a Bargaining Game with Incomplete Information." In Alvin E. Roth (ed.), *Game Theoretic Models of Bargaining,* pp. 99–114. Cambridge University Press.

Sagan, Scott D. (1985). "Nuclear Alerts and Crisis Management." *International Security,* 9, 99–139.

Sagan, Scott D. (1989a). "Accidents at the Brink: Nuclear Operations and Crisis Stability." Unpublished manuscript, Department of Political Science, Stanford University.

Sagan, Scott D. (1989b). *Moving Targets: Nuclear Strategy and American Security.* Princeton University Press.

Schelling, Thomas C. (1960). *The Strategy of Conflict.* Cambridge, Mass.: Harvard University Press.

Schelling, Thomas C. (1962a). "Comment." In Klaus Knorr and Thorton Read (eds.), *Limited Strategic War,* pp. 241–58. Princeton University Press.

Schelling, Thomas C. (1962b). "Nuclear Strategy in Europe." *World Politics,* 14, 421–32.

Schelling, Thomas C. (1965). *Controlled Response and Strategic Warfare*. London: International Institute for Strategic Studies.

Schelling, Thomas C. (1966). *Arms and Influence*. New Haven: Yale University Press.

Schilling, Warner R. (1981). "U.S. Strategic Concepts in the 1970s." *International Security*, 6, 49–79.

Selten, Reinhard (1975). "Reexamination of the Perfect Concept for Equilibrium Points in Extensive Games." *International Journal of Game Theory*, 4, 25–55.

Shubik, Martin (1971). "The Dollar Auction Game: A Paradox in Noncooperative Behavior and Escalation." *Journal of Conflict Resolution*, 15, 545–7.

Slocombe, Walter (1981). "The Countervailing Strategy." *International Security*, 5, 18–27.

Snyder, Glenn H. (1961). *Deterrence and Defense*. Princeton University Press.

Snyder, Glenn H. (1971). "'Prisoner's Dilemma' and 'Chicken' Models in International Politics." *International Studies Quarterly*, 15, 66–103.

Snyder, Glenn H. (1972). "Crisis Bargaining." In Charles Hermann (ed.), *International Crises*, pp. 217–56. New York: Free Press.

Snyder, Glenn H., and Paul Diesing (1977). *Conflict Among Nations*. Princeton University Press.

Steinbruner, John D. (1974). *The Cybernetic Theory of Decision*. Princeton University Press.

Tirole, Jean (1988). *The Theory of Industrial Organization*. Cambridge, Mass.: Massachusetts Institute of Technology Press.

Trachtenberg, Marc (1985). "The Influence of Nuclear Weapons in the Cuban Missile Crisis." *International Security*, 10, 137–63.

Trachtenberg, Marc (1989). "The Coming of the First World War: A Reassessment." Unpublished manuscript, Department of History, University of Pennsylvania.

Wagner, R. Harrison (1982). "Deterrence and Bargaining." *Journal of Conflict Resolution*, 26, 329–58.

Waltz, Kenneth N. (1959). *Man, the State and War*. New York: Columbia University Press.

Waltz, Kenneth N. (1979). *Theory of International Politics*. Reading, Mass.: Addison-Wesley.

Wells, Samuel F., Jr. (1981). "The Origins of Massive Retaliation." *Political Science Quarterly*, 96, 31–52.

Zagare, Frank C. (1985). "Toward a Reconciliation of Game Theory and the Theory of Mutual Deterrence." *International Studies Quarterly*, 29, 155–70.

Zagare, Frank C. (1987). *The Dynamics of Deterrence*. University of Chicago Press.

Index

array of punishment, 18, 24, 31, 32, 175–6
  grain of, effects of changes in, 148–9,
    164–6, 167, 179
array of risk, 16–17, 31, 32, 33–4, 175–6
  grain of, effects of changes in, 98–102,
    103, 178, 179
assessment, 208
auction
  brinkmanship as, 154–5
  strategy of limited retaliation as, 154–5
  strategy that leaves something to chance
    as, 154–5
autonomous risk
  in crisis stability, problem of, 131–2,
    144–7
  and events not being fully under control,
    18, 19–23, 110–11, 124–5, 131–2, 144–7
  modeled as random move, 39, 45
  source of, beyond threatener's control,
    22–3
  strategy that leaves something to chance
    dependence on, 21–3
  see also array of risk
Axelrod, Robert, 88n

Ball, Desmond, 14n, 23n, 157
Banks, Jeffrey, 181n, 209n
Bayes' rule, 210–11
behavioral strategy, *see* strategies,
  behavioral
beliefs
  Bayesian updating of, 210–13
  conventional logic of crisis stability and
    exogeneity of, 121–3, 132–3, 182
  crisis bargaining and endogeneity of, 121
  endogeneity of, in formal models of
    crisis stability, 121–3, 132–3
  and strategies, interaction between, 60–1,
    65–6, 69–70, 94–5, 97–8, 102, 121–3,
    177, 216–20
  see also sequential equilibrium, belief
    systems in
best reply, 196
best response, *see* best reply
Betts, Richard, 13n, 127
Blair, Bruce, 23n

bluffing, 53, 59–60
Bracken, Paul, 23n, 124
Brams, Steven, 35, 129
brinkmanship (*see also* strategy that leaves
  something to chance)
  as analogy for strategy that leaves
    something to chance, 4, 34, 69–71,
    102–3, 177–8
  as an auction, 154–5
  chicken model of, 35–7
  complete-information model: description
    of, 38–40; sequential equilibria of,
    41–5
  defining concern of, 4, 103, 110–13, 176
  description of analogy, 34–5
  essential elements of, 37–8, 45–6
  incomplete-information models of: and
    array of risk, effects of changes in
    grain of, 85–6, 98–102, 103, 178, 179;
    and crisis stability, 57–9, 62–5, 95–7,
    177; crisis stability, effects of
    incomplete information on, 97–8;
    crisis stability, effects of
    misperception on, 56, 62–5, 69, 85,
    102–3, 178; description of, 45–9, 86–9;
    distribution of crises, 66–8, 69, 178;
    irresolute challenger more likely,
    66–8, 69; length of crisis defined, 93;
    rationality of irrational in, 88; and
    resolve, 56, 59–61, 69, 85, 94–5, 102–3,
    177–8; and sequential equilibria
    derivation of, 75–84, 103–9;
    sequential equilibria description of,
    49–56, 71–5, 89–93; severe conflicts of
    interest unlikely in, 66–8, 69;
    simplifying assumption making for
    shorter crises in, 70–1, 85–6, 93; as
    source of insight, 185–6; and status
    quo, 56, 65–6, 69, 85, 95–7, 102–3,
    178; strategies, interaction with beliefs
    in, 60–1, 65–6, 69–70, 94–5, 97–8, 102,
    177; tit for tat strategy in, 88;
    weaknesses of, 180–4
  integrated with strategy of limited
    retaliation, 182–4
  no first-strike advantages in, 4, 110, 177

226